# Thinkers of the Jungle

# Thinkers of the Jungle

Gerd Schuster, Willie Smits, Jay Ullal

h.f.ullmann

# Thinkers of the Jungle

In the animal kingdom, the orangutans range amongst our closest relatives. Genetically, they are about 97 percent identical with us; they are highly intelligent, thoughtful, and inventive. They possess culture and a sense of beauty, and they take after us in facial expression, gestures, and in many other respects. The red apes, which are left only on Borneo and Sumatra, are far more "humane" than human beings and it seems they are therefore too good for this world. They are incredibly strong, yet they do not defend themselves against poachers or the logger gangs of the oil palm companies— and they are slaughtered without mercy. An unusual portrait of the being named orangutan, which extends far beyond the limits of mere zoology because it is supported by the unique personal experiences of Dr Willie Smits—the leading world expert on orangutans—who provides a mass of documentation to unsparingly disclose the reasons for the slaughter of our shaggy cousins, and who shows where hope still exists.

# Preface by Dayak chief Sina Sinam

*Sina Sinam always remembers the tragedy. As his house (top left in picture at first bend) is right by the Rungan River, he lives at the border between the cleared areas and the area of his tribe, where a little forest still remains. Opposite his house lies Kaja Island, formed by a split in the Rungan, where BOS prepares many orangutans for their final release into the wild.*

It is more than 120 years since the first white Dutchmen penetrated through to our tribal territory, including our village, Ragan Tate, which lies in the province of Central Kalimantan on the River Kahayan. We fought against the foreigners, sank their ships and refused to trade with them. Although the colonial power forbade many of our old customs, for example head-hunting, and the white officials stared mockingly at our one-foot-long ear-lobes, we tried to remain true to our traditional way of life. My grandfather, the great Sina Sinam Buhu, was thrown into prison in 1913 for head-hunting. At that time we thought we had problems. We had no inkling of what the future would bring.

In 1958, when we founded the village of Sungai Gohong, the first ketintings, motorized canoes, came up the rivers, carrying chainsaws. These made it very easy to deforest a ladang. A ladang is an area of forest around five acres in size, which we would clear to grow rice and other crops. After two years we would move on and clear another ladang. When we returned eight or ten years later, the soil had rested.

In 1969 many loggers came. They gave us work, and we learned how to use chainsaws. Everywhere there was still good virgin forest, which rained down blessings upon us: resins, rattan, fruit, and many, many wild pigs. The rivers were clean, swarmed with fish, and floods were infrequent even in the rainy season. The suffocating yellow smoke which shrouds our villages and our whole world for months on end was then unknown.

That changed in 1997. Many people from other Indonesian islands arrived and destroyed our forests like ants devour a piece of moldy wood. They started fires, and biting smoke covered our settlements. Many children and old people died.

We had not recovered from the disaster when troops of timber thieves, animal traders, gold hunters, and other adventurers appeared. They poisoned our rivers, and stole our animals. where once the Mahluk halus, our gods, the little spirits and the voices of our ancestors lived, the forest disappeared to be replaced suddenly by plantations of alien trees stretching to the horizon. We had to trek for many weeks before we could find a patch of forest in which to look for our traditional medicinal plants.

We could not go on living like this. So the Dayak started cutting off heads as our forefathers had done before us. While the crooked merchants avoided our area after that, the fires continued to burn.

Today we're almost finished. The forest in which our people lived since time immemorial has disappeared. There are no more wild animals, the Kapuas and other rivers are constantly bursting their banks, flooding our villages, while diseases are killing our children. It is getting harder and harder to find food.

The Borneo Orangutan Foundation (BOS) gives us work in sapling nurseries, on fishponds and in their efforts to save the numerous homeless orangutans wandering around aimlessly in the palm oil plantations. Three of my children are employed by the BOS. The work helps us very much, and the BOS now protects some of our islands. We used to hunt orangutans and cut off their heads to use for our rituals, but now we realize that the orangutans and we are fellow-sufferers. We too will not survive without the rainforest. We still hope that our gods will help us. Maybe they can get our voice heard in other parts of the world.

## Little Bali's tale of woe
A taste of orangutan reality
16

## Queen Victoria's abhorrence and the lack of interest of the explorers
The discovery of the orangutan
26

## Who is this, the "Forest Man"?
Description of a little-known cousin of the jungle
32

## Medication against migraine and malaria
The "green pharmacy" of the ape field botanist
56

## Seven years of training, five years of mother's milk and eternal ape-love
The sheltered childhood of the orangutans
74

## Brains, genius, or common sense
What is inside an ape's head?
94

## Alma and the tin-opener, Unyil's "rope trick" and Uce's love for symbols
Encounters with orangutan intelligence
106

## Ape culture
Could this be possible?
120

## From bushmeat to a 50,000-dollar export article
The history of a genocide
140

## The oil which nobody knows
The palm oil boom and the end of the last rainforests
160

## Nightmare and ape apocalypse

A journey to the logger front in Kalimantan                                      178

## "Nobody is doing anything!"

The mournful search for animal-welfare activists who give real support to orangutans   188

## Grand words and nothing behind them

How UNEP helps orangutans                                                        196

## From Meranti proliferator to orangutan protector

Willie Smits' journey to the apes                                                204

## Human beings as climbing teachers and jungle trainers for orangutans

An almost impossible task                                                        214

## Mawas, the last refuge for the orangutans

Why ape protection is also protection for human beings                           234

## So similar and yet so different

The species and subspecies of the orangutan—from *Pongo abelii* to *Pongo pygmaeus pygmaeus*   244

## The *Pongo pygmaeus* polaroids

How ape female Uce got photos for her "family album"                             256

## Psychograph of a primate

Experiences with a thousand orangutans                                           262

## The fairy tale of Samboja Lestari

A dream comes true                                                               300

*Left: An imposing male. This pasha, a dominant chief of a territory, looks into the camera, calm and self-assured.*
*Above: Route-planning. Whilst a mother thinks about the best way through the thicket, her baby passes the time by sucking its thumb.*

12

*Above: An 'old' baby. He is already five years old, but still enjoys the 24-hour service and fresh milk as and when he sees fit. The long period of maternal care for their children (around seven years) is the reason that the red apes have the lowest reproductive rate of all mammals.*
*Right: Group-photo with lady. Orangutan babies are literally 'clingy'. Here seven little rascals are holding on to a Dayak nurse. The urge to grip is instinctive: had the hunters not shot their mothers, the little ones would have had close physical contact to them for many years.*

*Left: Tête-à-tête at dizzying heights. An orangutan attempts to gain the favor of a female with kisses and a sweet present.*
*Above: Calls in the rainforest. A young orangutan female calls a message to her fellow apes through the thick leaves.*

# Little Bali's tale of woe

## A taste of orangutan reality

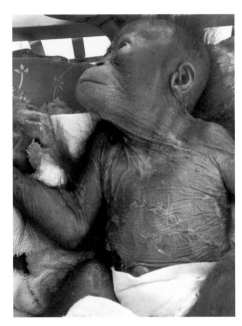

*A sorrowful image. Bali as he arrives in the BOS Nyaru Menteng rescue and rehabilitation center in Central Kalimantan (Borneo). His body is riddled with gunshots and so dehydrated that his peeling skin looks burnt. The little orangutan would have died if BOS had not taken him into care just in time.*

The tiny brown ape on the huge, bright-blue covered operating table is fighting for his life, his breath rattling. This minute bundle of fur is miserably skinny and alarmingly wrinkled, his breathing shallow and hectic. Again and again cold shivers ripple over the small body, which is shaven on the chest, back and upper arms, and whose long slim feet with their prehensile thumb-toes are reaching up as if begging for help, and locked in cramps as they are, seem to be just clinging around the branch of an invisible tree.

Several strips of white tape, which appear exaggeratedly broad on the baby's body, are covering nose and mouth mask-fashion and keep a transparent piece of plastic tube in position. One strip is leading from the left side of the mouth up between the eyes to the forehead. The right hand is bandaged, and even more plastic strips are keeping an infusion canula in place on the vein of the left arm. From the left side of the chest, a catheter protrudes like a serpent.

Bali—this is the name of the orangutan baby—has just survived an emergency operation of almost two hours and is still in a state of deep unconsciousness. A team of five doctors—thorax specialists and anesthetists—and a whole cluster of veterinary surgeons have removed a pellet from the bronchial tubes of his left lung. An attempt to remove a further lead pellet from the right armpit had to be aborted after extensive searching. The lobe of the lung, which was punctured during the operation, was sewn up, as was the 7 cm (3 inches) incision on the left side of the body.

Bali's experience had been one of luck—luck during the worst kind of ill fate that could possibly befall a little orangutan. At the age of just three months he lost his mother—for orangutan children not only their provider, protector, climbing teacher, all-round instructor, and source of hot, doting apes' love, but most of all: their one-and-only, the center of their universe.

If Bali's mother had not been shot, he would have spent seven or more years in the most intimate togetherness on the whole planet with her. At least during their first year, orangutan children remain in uninterrupted physical contact with their mother, they are carried around by her for at least three years, are nursed for up to five years, sleep for years snuggled up to her in their nest, and sometimes even climb through the branches with her hand-in-hand. As a rule, their mother is occupied solely with them for several years.

*A few weeks later. Bali receives medical care around the clock. He has to gain strength so that he can survive the necessary operation. Some of his fur has re-grown; however the small primate is still very weak from his gunshot injuries.*

*A year later. A normal ape-child has developed out of the heap of misery, and is currently tasting a plant of the genus* Mastixia *in the climbing school of Nyaru Menteng. The psychological wounds will take a long time to heal though.*

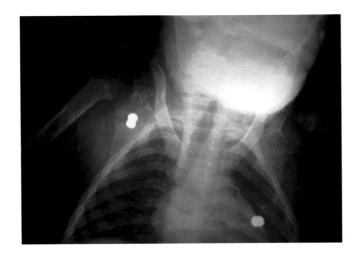

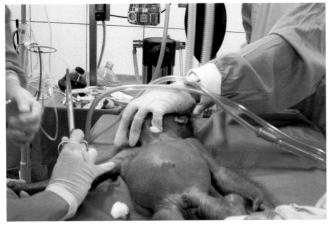

*Only the x-ray images show how badly Bali was wounded. Two of the six airgun pellets that hit him are lodged especially deep in his body: The lead pellet in the right of the picture is only a few centimeters away from his heart; the pellet on the left is in his armpit. Bali is in need of urgent surgery in the Jakarta veterinary hospital.*

But at least Bali has survived—for the time being, that is—because he was taken away from his "owner", the man who had gunned down his mother. And this was just in time because Bali would soon have succumbed to his various infections and to traumatic fevers. In the person of Danish animal welfare activist Lone Dröscher-Nielsen, however, he has found a sacrificial guardian, and in the rescue and rehabilitation centre of the Borneo Orangutan Survival Foundation (BOS) in Nyaru Menteng, which is run by the former stewardess, he has met with ideal conditions—a well-rehearsed team and a tried-and-tested infrastructure, an experienced veterinary medical division, and also the commitment, the expertise and the means to help him.

The staff of the Primates' Orphanage near Palangkaraya, capital of the Central Kalimantan Province in Borneo, delight in every rescue of an ape baby, but at the same time there is also sadness: each little ape confiscated or handed over to them is also an indication of the unabated speed with which the destruction of the natural habitat of this red primate is continuing. And for each little orangutan taken into their care, two or three less lucky baby apes have to die—and of course their mothers, too.

And this is how little Bali's story started: on 16 January 2003, a BOS-team left Nyaru Menteng and set out for Buntut Bali. They had got wind that two orangutans were being illegally kept in a village at the Katangan River (according to the "Wildordonantie" a criminal offence since 1924)—a day's journey away by SUV and motorboat.

The information proved to be correct. One of the ape infants, aged between one-and-a-half and two years and extremely wild, was crouching in a rotten cage in front of a shack. "Inside the house," Lone Dröscher-Nielsen reports on the BOS web page, "a three-month old baby stares at us with eyes stupefied with horror. One of his legs is wrapped with a dirty cloth. His little body is covered in wounds from which pus is dripping. His hands are so swollen that they have the appearance of boxing gloves. His skin looks like crinkled paper. This one is also wild and half insane from fright."

One of the helpers carefully removes the filthy cloth from Bali's leg—a "terribly swollen" and badly inflamed wound is revealed.

The owner of the house lacks any kind of sensitivity for animal suffering. Unmoved, he reports having shot the mother of the little ape five days before because she wanted to "steal" jackfruit from a tree near his hut. (The brownish-green fruit of the jackfruit tree in the shape of pears or drums, a member of the mulberry family, can reach a growth of up to 1 m (3 ft 3 in), a thickness of 50 cm (20 inches) and can weigh up to 25 kg (55 pounds); it contains up to 500 large kernels encased in yellow pulp. Both mother animals probably only approached the tree, despite the close distance to humans, because they were starving.)

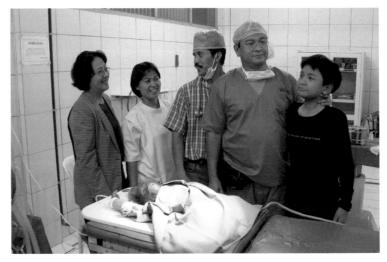

*Operation successful—patient lives. The large team of vets and doctors stand proudly around the push-bed.*

*Bali takes a little longer than his peers who have not undergone a long illness and major operation, but with time the rascal learns the secrets of the rainforest.*

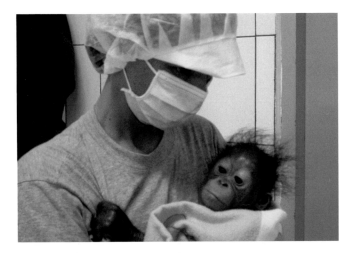

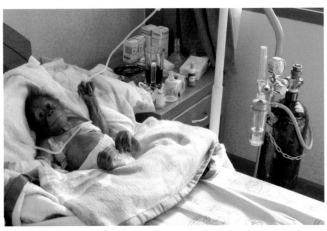

*A new life begins. A very sedated Bali awakes from the general anaesthetic in the arms of Lone Dröscher-Nielsen. The director of the BOS Nyaru Menteng station cares lovingly for the sick little ape, who has to remain on the drip for a long time after the operation.*

Just one day later, he had gunned down the mother of the older child. Both grown-up animals were then consumed by his family but he had spared the babies because he had hoped to get rid of them to a hawker of orangutans for 50,000–100.000 rupiah per animal—which converts to 5–10 dollars.

The BOS-Team named the two liberated animals after their place of discovery: the tiny ape was named Bali, and his elder fellow-sufferer Buntut.

The degree of Bali's injuries only became apparent after several X-rays were taken in Palangkaraya. Six air-rifle pellets were stuck in his body—two in his arm, not too deeply underneath the skin, which made them comparatively easy to remove, one deeply inside his badly inflamed right hand, another inside his right shoulder. The fifth pellet was in a position left of the heart, and so close that it made an emergency operation absolutely essential, because the worst was to be assumed: a migration of the pellet inside the body, resulting in an acute, life-threatening situation.

Finally, the last pellet had blasted the tibial plateau from the left knee so that the lower leg was dangling in the joint without any support, resembling a half-severed leg of a toy animal. The entire limb was swollen twice the normal size and must have caused dreadful pain. Bali's arms and hands were covered in numerous festering abscesses and the skin of his tummy was hanging down in shreds.

His mother's destiny was even worse: according to Willie Smits, Indonesian poachers frequently make use of large-caliber air rifles. First of all, to incapacitate the female ape, they aim for her eyes. After that, they pump the blind and completely helpless animal with lead bullets while trying not to hit the valuable baby. This does not always work, as Bali's case shows…

How Bali's mother might have fared is shown in a report of the Indonesian press agency Antara of 6 November 2006: after being given a tip-off, members of the animal-welfare group "Sumatra Orangutan Conservation Program" (SOCP) confiscated a fatally wounded male orangutan in a village 40 kilometers (25 miles) outside Bukit Tigapuluh National Park near the town of Jambi. According to SOCP, 62 air-rifle bullets were found in the body of the tortured animal, many of which had entered the cranium and the lungs. Both eyes were destroyed.

Little Bali has had more luck; he survived his torture and his operation on 12 February 2003, at least physically. Long gone are the days

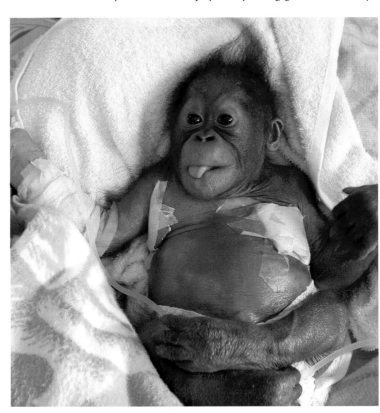

*Not arrogance, but anaesthetic hangover. Bali is not, as he appears, sticking out his tongue at the keepers and vets. His muscle coordination is still affected by the after-effects of the anaesthetic, so his gesture is unintentional.*

A good year after the operation Bali is carried into the jungle in a traditional woven child-carrier by his keeper for a climbing lesson. The babysitter from the Dayak tribe, who were once head-hunters, lives just a short walk from the BOS center Nyaru Menteng.

*Picnic in the jungle. Bali, still a bit bewildered, is gaining strength with a snack during a break in his climbing lesson.*

when—drop-by-drop—milk had to be trickled into his mouth with the aid of a syringe, long gone also the time when he weighed only 2,750 g (six pounds). He was clinically healthy in the spring of 2005. Even his knee, which had once been such a source of worry for Lone Dröscher-Nielsen, had mended without an operation; the pellet had grown into the newly formed bone-tissue.

However, the little orangutan, then three and a half years old, weighing 15 kg (33 pounds) and already quite strong (a problem), showed hardly any interest in climbing and appeared perplexed in several life-situations. Just as at the age of five months, his big and perfectly round and calmly serious baby's eyes were regarding the world with a blankly baffled and yet, in orangutan manner, amazingly composed look.

During mealtimes, he also behaved like a baby so that fruit remains were spread all over his face. If one laughed about it, again this look of deepest perplexity and absolute lack of understanding of the world entered Bali's eyes, and then he tried to distribute sticky-with-juice kisses. Lone Dröscher-Nielsen left him in the "toddlers' school". "He

is not yet prepared for anything else," she said. "And we are wondering whether this will ever be the case."

But then, somehow, Bali managed to overcome his traumatic experience. In the spring of 2006, three years after the end of his torture, he discovered his pleasure in climbing and did away with his baby's ways. According to Lone Dröscher-Nielsen, he even became a "bandito" who experienced thievish joy when pulling the hair of those Indonesian nurses who were not to his liking. He did not even shy away from pulling them from their hammocks by their hair. One of his favorite practical jokes was climbing into the crown of thin trees with two or three more of his kind and swinging about there for so long that the trees would bend under the apes' weight and finally start to break, and then crash down along with the tree.

There might be a chance for him to master life back in the rainforest.

There are people who have a problem with the fact that so much fuss is made about animals and so much effort is expended on them, while at the same time people starve or die of diseases for which no medication is available. For such people, animals are creatures to be treated indiscriminately as second class and to serve those infinitely higher-ranging humans as farm animals, domestic animals, animals to be slaughtered, zoo animals, cavalry horses, pit ponies, mine-detection dogs or experimental guinea pigs.

Such people as a rule deny that amongst animals there are some which are particularly close to us. They do not want to believe that Bali's genes are 97 percent identical with our own (scientists dispute the exact figure) and that science has put Bali and his kind together with human beings and other apes, chimpanzees, bonobos, and gorillas into the same category, the superfamily of hominoids.

Although the scholars disagree on the exact phylogenetic classification of humans and apes, the close relationship is not only apparent when looking at the "ape reflex" of the human newly born infant who can instinctively latch onto something just like a newly born ape latches itself onto his mother's fur: the close kinship also becomes

As Bali recovers from his operation and psychological trauma, he begins to explore more and more of his surroundings. He still has to learn that the rung on which he is sucking is made of pest-resistant ironwood and does not contain tasty termites like rotting soft wood. The creepy-crawlies are an important source of protein for the apes.

evident in the facial expression and behavior of the orangutans or in their intelligence, their thoughtfulness and unselfishness (see "Psychograph of a Primate", page 262), their culture, their sense of beauty, and a multitude of other features.

It is not for nothing that those scientists who are most familiar with our shaggy relatives acknowledge only slight differences. The English expert in primate research calls orangutans our "cousins" and "fellow-apes". According to Dutch anthropologist Carel van Schaik, "We, too, are only ape." Someone with a great deal of experience with apes, Willie Smits from the Netherlands, a tropical forest ecologist and head of BOS, has been carrying out research into the depth of the "souls" of these kings of the jungle and knows some 1,300 orangutans personally. Therefore, he feels increasingly uncomfortable when they are called "animals" and are all lumped together with grapevine snails and bats. For him, orangutans are "emotionally equal fellow-creatures" and "our soul mates".

For someone who is only "familiar" with orangutans from books, from the zoo or from animal films on TV, this may sound rather too lyrical or slightly quixotic. But anyone who sees (as I have done) Uce, a female ape, slap happily regarding her own Polaroid portrait photos shot by *Stern* photographer Jay Ullal, eyeing herself up in a slightly vain and coquettish manner, kissing the pictures full of delight, showing them to her baby, Matahari (also beaming), and "with her sleeve" wiping off the traces of wetness her kisses have left on the surface of those plastic squares, is able to understand what Smits means. More of this later (see page 256).

*Grimace of joy. In high spirits, Bali pokes his tongue out at the photographer. He is happy in the branches. It is a good thing that he does not know how lucky he has been. Lack of funds means BOS can no longer afford the amount of care that was given to Bali. All in all Bali's therapy cost 10,000 dollars.*

25

# Queen Victoria's abhorrence and the lack of interest of the explorers

## The discovery of the orangutan

*Queen Victoria was a young woman—in the picture the monarch had been reigning over the empire for decades—when she saw her first orangutan. She described the female Jenny as frightful.*

What kind of animals are these which are so similar to us— and if not necessarily outwardly then at least genetically and behavior-wise—and apparently emotionally, too?

There was a time when orangutans moved hand over hand throughout all the forests of South Asia. Quite probably, they spread all the way to the south of China, and their populations appeared in a far more compact way than today. Fossils about a million years old suggest a type of giant orangutan in Indonesia in times long past. Bone finds from Borneo and Sumatra, whose age is estimated at around 40,000 years, show that the ancestors of the red apes were then still about a third larger than those of our times.

However, although millions of orangutans must have inhabited the rainforests it appears incomprehensible why they were completely unknown in the West for a long time. If one believes Kathy MacKinnon, the wife of John MacKinnon, these primates were first seen by a white person in the 17th century. In Grzimek's Encyclopedia of Mammals, she writes that a physician named Bontius had "discovered" them. There were, however, "doubts whether his observations referred to a great ape or to a feeble-minded native girl".

The mistake reported here is surprising as young Indonesian women are—even if they are very ill—rarely hairy beings like apes.

In 1712, however, to quote Kathy MacKinnon, the English captain Daniel Beckman had without the trace of a doubt observed the apes during a visit to the south of Borneo, and he noted this later in his memoirs. In 1776, the first orangutans were carried off to Europe

*Photo of an orangutan in Rostock Zoo in the late 1930s, one of the first primates from Borneo to be seen in Germany. Very few zoologists knew the basic needs of the animal or how to treat the 'red import' properly.*

Wild orangutans are elusive in the rainforest, and, being silent creatures by nature, are hard to find. In order to monitor the population, one has to count their sleeping nests—a cumbersome and inaccurate method. This photo shows the nest of a member of the territory that is easy to see even for untrained eyes.

27

*In 1838, Charles Darwin encountered one of the first orangutans that had been displaced to London, one and a half years after his return from his journey on the* Beagle. *In his diary he notes the 'intelligence' of the animal.*

*Bleak cages. In the early 20th century the interests of the animals in zoos did not play a role. As is shown here in the Woodland Park Zoo in Seattle, the focus was on hygiene and good visibility of the apes on display.*

as shaggy curiosities for the scientific collection of the Dutch prince, Willem V.

Other sovereigns did not want to be left out, and in the 19th century, scientists, among them figures like the English zoologist and evolution pioneer Alfred Russell Wallace, shot a multitude of animals as trophies for museums. Edoardo Beccari really excelled in this. The Italian scientist sent skeletons, skins and organs of almost one hundred orangutans home from Borneo. Now, thousands of the red apes were captured and brought to Europe, where they dropped dead like flies.

One of the first orangutans to reach London (in 1837) was a female named Jenny, who was exhibited in the zoo there. One year before her death—she died of the pulmonary tuberculosis she contracted in her clammy exile—young Charles Darwin paid her a visit. This took place in the spring of 1838. Darwin had returned on 2 October 1836 from his circumnavigation in the *Beagle* and was to publish his epochal paper, *On the Origin of Species by Means of Natural Selection or Preservation of Favoured Races in the Struggle for Life* in 1859, and in 1868 his treatise on *The Descent of Man*. To this day, his books are vilified as "monkey theories" by opponents of evolution.

After he had seen Jenny, Darwin wrote in his diary: "Let man visit the ourang-outan in domestication … see his intelligence … Man in his arrogance thinks himself a great work … More humble, and I believe true, to consider him created from animals."

A descendant of Jenny I who, for simplicity's sake, had been given the same name, was presented to Queen Victoria, and the young monarch observed the ape with the horror-stricken fascination so typical of Victorians of that time. Later, she described Jenny II as "frightful, and painfully and disagreeably human".

Although zoos and animal shows were full of orangutans, it is hard to understand that no one was interested in exploring the life of apes in their native rainforest. People stared at animals of which nothing was known except their country of origin, and when they died (which happened every two or three years) they were simply

exchanged for new ones. After Darwin's visit to Jenny I in London Zoo, more than 130 years passed before scientists set out to study the red apes on Borneo and Sumatra.

One of the first was John MacKinnon. As a young Oxford student, he traveled to Borneo during the summer vacation of 1968, with a small university grant at his disposal. He saw 72 orangutans and filmed them with a Bolex camera. Equipped with a more ample grant, he returned a short time afterwards and observed the animals on Borneo for a year and on Sumatra for another year. Shortly afterwards, researchers such as the Dutchman Herman Rijksen and the Canadian Biruté Galdikas, who later became famous, arrived in Indonesia. In an interview with the Sumatra Orangutan Conservation Programme (SOCP) in 2005, MacKinnon explained that he was sure there must still have been "hundreds of thousands" of orangutans in the sixties.

In 1970, the red ape was an unknown entity. Around 35 years of research later, there are several dozen scientific papers on all possible aspects of life of the orangutan. The knowledge about our shaggy relatives, however, is still very fragmentary. Numerous snapshots by more or less good scientists exist but what we do not have is a complete overall picture.

Many studies suffer from the failing that they were carried out with captured animals or with animals that were released ("re-introduced") after captivity. Quite often, orangutans which are still in captivity or had once lived imprisoned on the one hand, and free-living kings of the jungle on the other, are poles apart—emotionally, physiologically, and psychologically. The differences may not be quite so great as between a German shepherd dog and a wild wolf; they are large enough, however, to be able to distort research results.

It is only in very rare cases that scientists rely on zoo apes for reasons of convenience. It is rather despair which makes them do this, as there is hardly an animal species which is harder to observe in the wild than our fellow-ape from Borneo and Sumatra. The largest tree-dwelling animals of this earth sit peacefully and quietly—as a rule alone or with a baby—at a height of 20 or 30 meters

The heat, the swamp, the insects, the difficult terrain, and the elusive nature of the biggest tree-dwelling apes make it exceedingly difficult to establish their population and distribution. The large picture shows what a particularly good, already opened-up path in the jungle looks like. BOS-staffer Odom (at left in small photo), a Dayak, is the world's best 'nest-counter'—says Zurich primatologist Professor Carel van Schaik.

*In the early 20th century stuffed 'trophies' of tropical animals were very popular— including orangutans. Shown is a 'specimen' of a female red ape. Countless animals were shot for such dust-collectors, often by famous 'naturalists', who believed this bloodbath to be a contribution to science.*

(70–100 feet) in the branches of a jungle giant and blend in with twigs and foliage. Whole legions of Ph.D. students collecting data for their dissertations must have been blissfully ignorant, fighting their way through the jungle deep beneath the objects of their research without noticing them, because orangutans have nothing of the restlessness and the screeching behavior, e.g. of chimpanzees, which makes their detection so much easier.

Moreover, even in the lowland rainforest it is extremely strenuous to search for orangutans and to follow them. It is as hot and sultry as in the sauna, and tropical rainstorms, leeches, thorn-covered rattan twines, all kinds of trip hazards and numbers of other difficulties, to say nothing of snakes and other venomous creatures, torment the researcher. Moreover, this job is far more energy consuming in flooded peat or swampy rainforests.

This is why so many population statistics sold to the public as "counts" were and are compiled almost without any face-to-face contact with orangutans. The adding-up of the sleeping-nests of the apes is nothing but a makeshift. This, however, is quite problematic because, to start with, some of the red giants build up to two nests per day from bent or broken twigs—a provisional one for the midday siesta and a solid one for their night rest—and secondly these sleeping places can serve in the branches for several months.

Another aggravating fact is that the nests may last in one tree species—such as the Bangkirai, whose heavy wood is appreciated in DIY stores as building material for terraces and outdoor showers, for one year whereas in another species, the wood might already be eaten away by fungi after a few weeks. The type of branch material used also influences the life span of the tree beds. The attempt to assess the number of orangutans living in a certain area from the number of ape bunks glued to jungle giants at dizzy heights is reminiscent of alchemy. It is in any case a science of its own, and by no means an exact science.

"It is," says Willie Smits, "not only the number of existing orangutans which is the decisive factor for the count result," but "the obser-vation ability of the particular person counting the apes." For example, BOS-staff member Odom, a member of the former head-hunter tribe of the Dayak, observed considerably more apes (and their nests) than all the other primate scouts.

This also explains the extreme seesawing behavior of the population figures, which were subject to far greater fluctuations than the prices of even the most volatile technology stocks on the Nasdaq. In 1965, the World Wide Fund for Nature (WWF) scared its members with the message that worldwide only about 5,000 orangutans existed. In 1984, Grzimek's Encyclopedia of Mammals mentions 150,000 survivors. In 1996, WWF had corrected their figures back to 100,000 but the Orangutan Foundation International (OFI) sounded the alarm again in 2003: only about 15,000 animals were still alive.

One year later, the second PHVA study provided the first fairly reliable stocktaking. The paper owes its name and existence to the "Population and Habitat Viability Assessment Workshop", a conference of leading primatologists which took place on the initiative of the BOS in Jakarta at the beginning of 2004. They came to a count of about 62,000—some 55,000 on Borneo and approximately 7,000 on Sumatra.

According to the estimates, this pathetic remainder represents about one percent of the orangutan population during their heyday. However, it is still shrinking by about ten percent a year.

In the trees shown here a dozen orangutan nests are hidden. To be able to identify them, one needs not only tenacity and endurance but also years of experience and the eyes of an eagle. Prize question: how many of the twelve nests can you see?

# Who is this, the "Forest Man"?

## Description of a little-known cousin of the jungle

*Our long-haired friend from the jungle is very eager to learn. Not only did he copy the eating and drinking habits of humans, he also mimicked their upright walk.*

After I have conveyed all the necessary "warning hints" I can finally turn to something more gripping, the description of our mysterious relative who is seriously threatened by extinction and whose name is composed of the Malay words for person *(orang)* and forest *(hutan)* and is supposed to mean "person of the forest".

It is only in the West, however, that the orangutan is called by this name. At home, his name is "mawas" or "maia", "kahiyu" and a dozen other local names. The National Primate Research Center of the University of Wisconsin in Madison (with reference to a work by Herman Rijksen) even points out that the term "orangutan" is quite unsuitable, because in Indonesia this word is also used to denote a madman or a savage human. Furthermore, "orangutan" is used to describe a defaulter, someone who does not pay his debts.

There is also something bizarre surrounding the history of the scientific name of the red ape. His first and correct subject name was Simia sativa. As the first orangutan, which appeared in Europe, came from Angkola in the north of Sumatra, American scientists thought the animal must have come from the African country of Angola, and consequently took him for a chimpanzee. As a result of this confusion, instead of *Simia sativa* a name coined later, *Pongo pygmaeus,* is now used.

The thus wrongly named creature is the only great ape in Asia and, as already mentioned, is also the largest tree-living animal on the planet. Science distinguishes two species: the Bornean Orangutan *(Pongo pygmaeus)* and the Sumatran Orangutan *(Pongo abelii).* Of course, the scientists are still quarreling, as some would like to have both animals—in appearance, behavior and genes very different—continue to be listed as mere subspecies and named as formerly *Pongo pygmaeus pygmaeus* (Borneo) and *Pongo pygmaeus abelii* (Sumatra).

The majority of scientists, however, seem to have committed themselves to the acknowledgement of two species and of the following three Borneo subspecies: the Northwest Bornean Orangutan *(Pongo pygmaeus pygmaeus),* the Central Bornean Orangutan *(Pongo pygmaeus wurmbii),* and the Northeast Bornean Orangutan *(Pongo pygmaeus morio).* (For more details on the phenotypes, their criteria, differences, and variants, see page 244).

While the other great apes spend the greatest part of their time on the ground, the red primates only extremely rarely climb down from their trees. They possess a heavy-set body, a thick neck with a large head whose lower part bulges out like half of a coconut. Their face is rosy at birth but will later become dark brown to leathery-black. The facial expressions are very much like those of a human. There is so much thoughtfulness and intelligence in their great dark eyes that the otherwise rather sober Environmental Investigation Agency (EIA), a London group of independent environmental investigators, went into raptures when explaining that they expressed "innocence and wisdom".

*Is this what an 'animal' looks like? Does a creature, in the law of many countries only a 'thing', have such eyes? Pensive gaze at the photographer of an orangutan girl from northern Sumatra.*

*Switch on the sat-nav! High in the canopy of a giant tree an orangutan figures out the quickest way to his destination—be it fruit trees, his nesting area, other orangutans, or drinking-water reserves in tree hollows.*

70 to 90 kg (155 to 200 pounds). The females are markedly smaller: head-rump length 78 cm (30 inches) at most, standing height up to 110 cm (43 inches), weight 40 to 50 kg (90 to 110 pounds).

Two orangutans from Honolulu Zoo show that these figures have to be handled with care, and also how the body measurements of captured orangutans can differ from those of their wild fellow-apes: the fully-grown ape male, Rusti, who celebrated his 27th birthday on 25 January 2007, weighed in at more than 140 kg (307 pounds) whereas his female companion Violet (who was 30 on 19 November 2007) weighed 53 kg (117 pounds). Unfortunately, the Hawaiian zoo keeps silent about the size.

According to statements made by Willie Smits, Rusti is by no means a heavyweight: Oki at Jakarta's Ragunan Zoo for example weighed more than 200 kg (440 pounds). And the largest orangutan on Beccari's list of victims measured 1.87 m (6 ft 2 in) from tip to toe, and his arms had a span of more than three metres.

As an outward sign of their "power" and dignity, dominant males possess large cheek-bulges, leathery and blown-up looking excrescences on the sides of their heads which they can move forward like blinkers, and large throat-pouches by means of which they can produce their characteristic sound, the "long call". More of this later when we talk about their reproduction.

Nature has given the animals everything they need for moving hand over hand at dizzy heights through the crowns of trees: long arms with spans of 2.3 m (7 ft 6 in) and more, as well as long hands and feet made for grasping, ideal tools for clinging on to round branches. Although at first glance rather gawky and asthenic looking, there is tremendous physical power in them.

Willie Smits has conducted tests with power-machines for fathoming out the muscular strength of the orangutan: he placed an ape

The scanty fur of long rough hair is of different shades, depending on species and subspecies, quite often also differing amongst members of the same genetic group: bright orange, rusty red, reddish brown, brown, and even brown-black like a gorilla. Both sexes have long beards. Orangutans are tailless.

Males reach a head-rump length of 97 cm (38 inches) on average and a standing height of about 137 cm (54 inches); they get to weigh

*Sunbathing ape-style. Effortlessly an orangutan hangs from a branch for more than half an hour and warms up in the rays of the morning sun.*

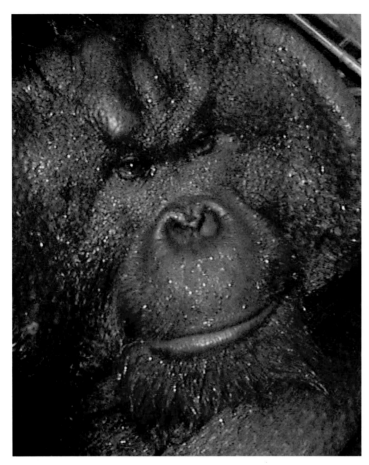

*Apes do not sweat according to the textbooks. The large orangutan male Marco, who was released into the wild by BOS in 1999, after fifteen years of cages and long suffering from tuberculosis, proves the theory wrong.*

male into a test machine he had built himself and modeled on those "torture instruments" from gymnasiums, and he showed him a bowl of fruit which the ape could only reach by pulling a weight to his chest with both arms. Result: the orangutan moved 240 kg (530 pounds) effortlessly.

Although further tests were not possible as the shaggy fitness novice demolished the machine during the very first trial run, Smits concludes that orangutans are about seven times as strong as average human adults. The main reason for this is that their arms and probably also their legs make much better "levers". In other words their muscles and sinews are probably attached to the bones in a way which slightly differs from that of humans, which is advantageous for developing greater strength.

If one sees how orangutans in the rainforest manage to hang on their fingers for hours, or how they unhurriedly break off arm-size branches when building a sleeping nest, one can conceive of how much strength they possess in their fingers. According to Smith's report, they have no problems in cracking fruit with their teeth, fruit that is armored with thick woody shells which normally can only be tackled by means of a hammer or machete. And for getting hold of hearts of palm, the "embryos" of those later palm fronds, they tear off the crown from grown palms, smash the trunk to smithereens as if it were made of sugar icing, and take the treat from its core.

One wild orangutan whose life was threatened also gave impressive proof of his tremendous strength: in Sangatta in East Kalimantan, the natives had driven the animal into an open-cast coal-mining area and set their dogs on him, dogs which were trained for wild-boar hunting. The red ape grabbed himself four of the attacking dogs and without any visible exertion tore their heads off. Just in time, BOS managed to save the primate's life; otherwise, his meat would have probably landed at the local market where orangutan is frequently on offer. Some buyers are convinced eating orangutan meat increases their own sexual potency.

The BOS founder has first-hand experience of the strength our cousins are blessed with: during the visit of a rehabilitation unit by an Indonesian minister, the big orangutan male Marco was irritated by the flashlights of the photographers. Annoyed, he grabbed through the fencing, snatched Smits' jeans with the tips of thumb and index finger, and ripped the strong material from his body as if it were tissue paper. Smits: "That hurt quite a bit, and I stood in my underpants in front of the minister!"

I myself at 2.03 m (6 ft 8 in) tall and weighing 90 kg (200 pounds) was unable to defend myself against two pushy ape-adolescents of about five years old in "Halfway House", a 10 ha (25 acre) area of forest where young orangutans have to give proof of whether they have accumulated those abilities required for a life in freedom. These two were not vicious, only curious, but their thin little arms which were pulling at me had the power of heavyweight wrestlers. Willie Smits had to "save" me.

One gets a first impression of the unique adaptation of the ape anatomy to life in the crowns of trees if one gives an orangutan one's hand. In the case of wild animals, one is well-advised not to do this, as, according to Willie Smits, orangutans have already pulled people's arms out; in "touristy" rehabilitation stations like Tanjung Puting, one is constantly greeted by the shaggy little pupils of the baby sta-

*To move through the canopy is a tight-rope act every time. The orangutan has to consider if the branches can take his weight and predict how far they can swing him in his direction of travel. The brain of the animal is thus considerably more active than that of a human going to the bakery or to the office.*

tion with outstretched hands and one can shake apes' paws to one's heart's delight. One can feel immediately that the finger bones are bent inwardly like little bridges. The normal position of such hands is a locked one—around a round branch. Special "foothold cushions" provide for further improvement of the grip (see photo page 156 top left).

Because of their prehensile feet, with big toes that, like thumbs, allow them to grasp a branch, the short bow-legs are certainly no disadvantage, either, when it comes to climbing. Only, when on the ground, the animals cannot cope so well. They are so slow that they cannot even run away from a four-year old, probably also because unlike other great apes they never learned to walk on their knuckles but rather, after a fashion, stalk around on their fists.

Their movements are so much more graceful when they are swinging through the maze of branches. Unhurried but full of inimitable elegance they swing through the green roof of the rainforest. They make use of their considerable bulk to bring the crown of the tree in which they are sitting into a swaying motion, and they carry on swinging until they get hold of a neighboring tree—then they make an elegant sweep over the gap. Primatologists therefore call them "four-footed swinging climbers". As a rule, three of the four feet are always holding fast.

In his book *Among Orangutans: Red Apes and the Rise of Culture* van Schaik writes that one can locate orangutans in the rainforest by listening for "tree-swishing". Why this is, the Dutch Director of the Anthropological Institute and Museum of Zurich University explains as follows: "The apes travel more or less like Tarzan does, except that like most movie-goers they've figured out that swinging on a vine doesn't necessarily take you to another vine. Therefore, orangutans climb to the very top of a tree and hang on as they throw their weight in the direction they want to go. When the tree bends to the point at which they are able to grasp the next tree, in the direction they're headed, they climb aboard and let go of the one they used to get there, at which point—swish!—it returns to its original position."

Traveling in this manner, by means of tree catapults, as Willie Smits points out, requires some fairly sophisticated calculations. For example: "If I start the tree on which I am sitting now swinging so that it sways so far that I can take a grip on a branch of the next one, at what height and how hard will I land on that one and how far can I get it to deflect with the least possible effort so that it swings far enough for me to get hold a branch of its neighbor?"

It goes without saying that these acrobats of the air also have to be make sure their catapult as well as their landing place can cope with their accelerated mass, and do not give way more than intended, let alone break. In nature, Smits has frequently watched orangutans spending a long time on such estimates. Just as in the case of human beings, their faces mirrored their concentration and mental strain, and later also the relief when they had worked it out.

The orangutans also require a lot of intelligence to find their food in the rainforest, because especially on Borneo, the supply of fruit is by no means so rich as Europeans imagine from their Garden-of-Eden pictures of the jungle, and the apes have to cover their considerable dietary requirements outside the fruit season for the most part with leaves and saplings.

Besides fruit (according to a rather theoretical figure which keeps haunting the entire range of publications on apes, allegedly around 60 percent of their nutrition), their menu comprises buds and young leaves, bark (which they chew and then spit out again "like an old man would spit out his quid of chewing tobacco", as it says in Grzimek's Encyclopedia of Mammals), tree sap, roots, flowers (orchids included), mushrooms, honey, termites and ants, spiders' webs, earth rich in

*Orderly chaos. What looks like 'green hell' is as clearly arranged to an orangutan as is a shelf in the supermarket to us. Only from the air can we see that concentric circles are formed around the 80 meter (ca. 90 yards) high Honey Bee Tree (Koompassia excelsa, yellow crown at bottom left in photo).*

*The life of a young orangutan literally hangs on his mother, and he never lets go his grip of the shaggy fur of his progenitor. This baby from Sumatra is about a year old and is still very afraid of his unknown surroundings.*

tures—were coddled by their perverted keepers with sushi and lobsters. Quite often, the anthropomorphized kings of the jungle rinsed down their un-ape-ish meals with alcohol.

In the rainforest where nothing is "dished up" without effort, orangutans are forced to get hold of their food with the least waste of energy possible. Therefore, it is in finding, not searching, that our cousins are world champions. They know their territory "like the back of their hands" and they know exactly where and when something tasty is ripe. For this, according to Smits, they use "invisible" deer passes whose course is three-dimensionally stored in their memories.

"When an orangutan passes a tree full of half-ripe fruit," says Willie Smits, "he will make a mental note of its position and he will head for this tree directly on exactly the day when its fruit is ripe. In an area of about 300 ha (740 acres), he knows each tree and knows when the most favorable time for harvesting has arrived. This works so well that it seems as if orangutans possessed satellite navigation."

It is documented in practice that, again and again, young orangutans are taken from the rehabilitation station of Nyaru Menteng to "Halfway House", 2 kilometers (1.2 miles) away and a last testing station before re-introduction into a 10 ha (25 acre) forest area, and each time, their carers cannot believe that their shaggy pupils—brought by car from the station via complicated diversions to their new quarters—find their way back to the station in a straight line through forest which is completely unknown to them. They are faster than the car and they are already waiting when the BOS people start to turn up.

However, the secret of their super-orientation has nothing to do with GPS. The animals possess a "visual ability" which is clearly superior to that of human beings. They also have an ability to learn

minerals, caterpillars, birds' eggs, and nestlings of birds and squirrels as well as small tree-dwelling vertebrates.

According to information from Willie Smits, visitors to Tanjung Puting once observed how orangutans fed on a plumpuro, a small prosimian, and he has heard reports, according to which orangutans kept as pets—poor, overweight, Coke and nicotine-addicted crea-

*Absolute trust. When the baby is close to his mother he feels totally safe. Even though he is hanging from a few tufts of hair at a great height, he looks at the photographer in a relaxed manner. It will not be long before he uses the long arms of his mother as a 'bridge' to move from branch to branch.*

*Three-point-safety twice over. An experienced orangutan does not take unnecessary risks when climbing at dizzying heights: it always holds on with at least three hands or feet.*

and to memorize "which is greater and longer lasting than that of an average human being," says Willie Smits. The animals had even outdone scientists who had wanted to sound them out intellectually as their "testers".

"In their spatial awareness and in their orientation ability, orangutans beat the pants off us," confirms the American psychologist, Anne Russon, professor at York University of Toronto. "Their world is more three-dimensional than ours is, and animals who had only spent two days in Wanariset knew about things right from the start while I spent years erring around between cages!"

After Nyaru Menteng, Wanariset is the second-largest BOS rescue station and re-introduction center on Borneo, and, as I know from my own experience, getting lost is pre-programmed in the maze of paths which meander in an approximately 2 ha (5 acre) grove of fruit-trees between about 70 ape-houses. Anne Russon, who carries out research at different BOS locations, is an author and connoisseur of orangutans.

Many trees at the Wanariset Centre were grown from seeds that Willie Smits obtained from orangutan feces. This way, he can be sure that first of all, his apes like the fruit from those trees growing around their cages, and secondly, that they get to know them as their nutrition. He underlines the role of the animals as "gardeners of the jungle". That is to say, a great number of fruit seeds only start germinating after their passage through the intestines of the orangutan. Trials with humans resulted in their being far less suited as "germination promoters".

Forest biologist Smits is convinced that numerous species of fruit-bearing rainforest trees will disappear if orangutans die out because their seeds can only be spread through the apes' feces. This triggers off a domino effect and many other species—hornbills and gibbons which also act as "seed carriers"—would be decimated.

All in all, the shaggy sweet-toothed creatures enjoy 300 varieties of fruit, if available. Beside numerous kinds of figs, which are mainly to be found on Sumatra all through the year and which they can also enjoy while not quite ripe, they are in particular fond of fruit varieties which are also regarded as delicacies amongst humans: mango and mangostane, litchi and rambutan, jack-fruit and durian, and countless types of fruit of which most Europeans have never heard.

Although their muscular strength and their strong teeth are ideal for breaking open tough-leathery fruit shells and for cracking nuts which are hard as iron, there are a few delights which nevertheless present a problem. The fruit of the neesia trees ranges amongst those difficult delicacies, a gigantic, woody fruit with a shell almost 2 cm (0.8 inches) thick, hard as stone. When it is ripe, it bursts open at five predetermined breaking points along its longitudinal axis. It then reveals its delicious kernels, which thanks to their high protein and fat content are very nutritious and, as the American evolutionary biologist and ape expert, Michelle Merill, tells us, "taste like sugared cashew nuts and coconut milk."

Big orangutan males are able to crack open the neesia nuts with their ox-like strength and they scoff the kernels from the shells like chocolates from a box. All other orangutans, however, females, adolescents, and young adult males, have to pick out the treat through the gaps of the armor-like shell using their fingers if that is possible at

*It is hard to understand why the red primates thought it necessary to invent tools when we can see how easy it is for them to crack a coconut without any technical help. For humans it would be impossible to open the fruit without the help of a machete or a similar tool.*

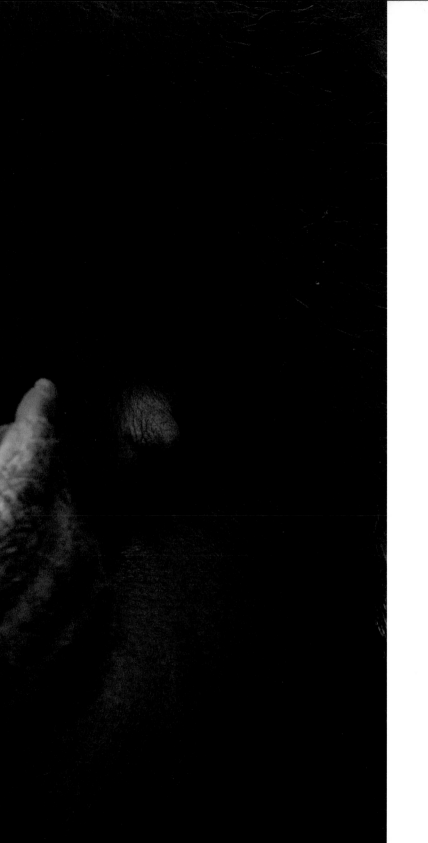

all. However, the inner fruit is lined with bristles, crystals of calcium oxalate, which bore into the apes' fingers and bite and itch terribly. Carel van Schaik calls them "Plexiglas needles".

By sliding a thin stick into a crack in the fruit, orangutans can get the seeds out without having to handle the prickly husk. "Here is an example of how technology makes it possible for animals to make a much better living," says van Schaik.

Because their menu comprises several hundred kinds of fruit and because it is not only during low fruit-yielding periods that they feed on leaves, we must conclude that orangutans possess a well-founded knowledge of botany, because a random consumption of leaves in the rainforest would not exactly lead to a ripe old age: a great number of the plants are toxic. Willie Smits also believes that each orangutan is intimately familiar with 1,000 jungle plants—edible, inedible, poisonous, and beneficial—and that he or she uses about 500 for nutrition. Other sources even estimate the botanical repertoire of the red ape at 4,000 plants.

*Danger is near. Even though the baby does not know exactly what danger his mother has seen he does understand that something is wrong. The mother holds on tightly to her baby and threatens the approaching stranger—possibly another orangutan female—with her eyes. It is not at all infrequent for pregnant orangutans to try and steal a juvenile.*

The rainforest gets its name from the high level of humidity present. In the (to humans) impenetrable and permanently wet jungle an orangutan knows the territory like the back of its hand—to use a human simile. He orientates himself effortlessly by using an internal three-dimensional map of his habitat. He knows every useful tree and how to get there in the quickest and shortest way possible.

Deceptive idyll. It all looks wonderfully natural on this picture. However, the opposite is the case, as three things are wrong: an orangutan mother is sitting on the floor instead of on a tree, and is eating a watermelon that is not naturally accessible to her. Furthermore she has washed the watermelon— an activity she has copied from humans. All this is given away by the small piece of watermelon peel in the picture at bottom left.

A walk in the swampy forest. For us humans it would be a feat worthy of a circus artiste, but for the red ape it is a relaxing pastime—even over crocodile-infested waters, such as here on the flooded island of Bangamat, close to the BOS station of Nyaru Menteng (Central Kalimantan).

51

The special manner in which orangutans move through the rainforest requires huge strength. It is partly for this reason that an average red ape is seven times stronger than an average human.

*For orangutans who know the laws of the rainforest, the fridge is never empty. Their menu includes young leaves, medicinal herbs, blossoms, twigs, fruits, buds, roots, bark, and much more. This diversity is not a luxury however, but necessary for survival.*

# Medication against migraine and malaria

## The "green pharmacy" of the ape field botanist

*The BOS staff use the small purple flowers of* Fordia splendissima *as an energy booster. Willie Smits first recognized the extraordinary properties of the plant by watching the orangutan female Tuti eat it in the rainforest of Sungai Wain. The plant is effective against migraine, and is a stimulant like caffeine.*

Smits is convinced that orangutans know a multitude of medicinal herbs and "take" them when required. "They eat plants which kill parasites and which are a remedy against malaria," the BOS chief comments. And against migraine: at one time in the rainforest he watched the orangutan female, Tuti, who was quite obviously tortured by a headache. She sat there all slack in her misery and held her head in her hands. Finally, she made an effort, dragged herself to a shrub with the botanical name of *Fordia splendissima,* ate a few handfuls of the mauve blossoms, and seemed after half an hour to be free of complaints.

Months later in the rainforest, Smits, at that time fighting his frontal sinus problems, was seized by a really bad headache. He suffered for some time. Then he remembered Tuti's self-medication, plucked a few blossoms of the plant and ate them—and promptly the pain in his head disappeared.

Meanwhile, BOS staff have discovered possible further uses of the miracle plant, which far exceed those of a "natural aspirin": a few petals, they discover, act as an energy-kick like two double espressos—but are relaxing at the same time. Meanwhile, near almost all BOS stations, a few bushes of *Fordia splendissima,* energy "filling stations", can be found.

"The orangutans had millions of years at their disposal during which they were able to acquire botanical knowledge for themselves," Smits said. "This is passed on from mother to child. This is a kind of culture!" And, justifiably, orangutans can be described as the "best field botanists" in the world.

The red primates would show signs of great surprise if they witnessed one of their conspecifics eating a plant which they themselves considered inedible. Thus the orangutan male Paul was flabbergasted when in front of his eyes orangutan female Sariyemm peeled off the bark of *Artocarpus cempedak,* a kind of a fig-tree, and licked off the juice. Smits: "One could clearly see what Paul was thinking: 'Crikey! You can eat that? I didn't know that!'" Impressed as he was, for the rest of the day, Paul slurped nothing else but the gluey white liquid.

*On the hunt for larvae with a 'toothpick'. This young male is using a twig to spear a brood of termites—an important source of protein in the jungle.*

*When fruit is rare, the orangutans have to feed on leaves. Old leaves—as shown here—are eaten only rarely. Young leaves are preferred.*

*Insects, such as these ants, are a welcome delicacy in the jungle. Orangutans enjoy robbing the nests of these creepy-crawlies, as well as the honeycombs of woodland bees.*

The tropical forest ecologist deems it possible that orangutans, whose sense of smell is in general not well pronounced, recognize and differentiate plants by the green of their leaves, and that they are able to tell apart 10,000 different shades of green and classify them. Smits, who cannot pass a single rainforest plant without quoting its botanical name, cannot give proof of this by primatological studies but only by his unique experiences with apes and their botanical knowledge. There will be no relevant studies in the foreseeable future to determine the extent of the botanical knowledge handed down by wild orangutans from generation to generation; how on earth could you devise a suitable experiment? That being the case, Smits' opinion on the matter is authoritative enough for me.

The daily routine of the shaggy-haired jungle botanist looks roughly like this: At about 7 o'clock, they rise from their airy tree-nests and look around for breakfast. This puts the orangutans amongst the late risers because most of the animals of the rainforest have by this time already been active for a whole hour. After having fed for two to three hours, sometimes hanging head-down in the trees, it is time for a nap. For this, they usually build a provisional nest.

In the evenings, they take a bit more trouble. As already mentioned, they bend strong branches to form a frame, line it with broken-off twigs and foliage and thus create for themselves a springy "mattress" of green material—and depending on their requirements also with a rain shelter or sunshade.

On the occasion of the "Orangutans Compared" Workshop of 2002, on which culturally "inherited" behavior patterns of the different orangutan groups of Borneo and Sumatra were discussed and collected (more of this later), it became public that the red apes in the National Park of Tanjung Puting on Borneo adorned their nests in interior-design fashion by means of decorative twigs. The green ornaments were recorded in the minutes of the conference under "artistic pillows". The apes also created "playing nests", "bridging nests", and "bunk beds".

The design of the sleeping-places, however, goes far beyond just aesthetic aspects (as was discovered only in October, 2006): Anne Russon and Willie Smits have found out that the orangutans also consider anti-insect measures because they want to rest without being molested by the swishing of the blood-suckers. Therefore, as a last detail of furnishing, twigs of the *Campnospermum* tree are put into the nest. Is it a coincidence that the leaves of exactly the same tree are also used by the Dayaks to fight off mosquitoes?

The nest-building drive seems to be immanent in the genes of the animals. According to Grzimek's Encyclopedia of Mammals, orangutan Jacob, who had fled from London Zoo into a tree of adjoining Regent's Park, made himself a sleeping-nest by every trick in the book, even though he had never watched members of the same species during the construction of nests in his entire life and although—to the eternal shame of the zoo—he had never had any experience with living branches!

After their siesta, the orangutans move on. As is their nature, they do this calmly and leisurely. A whole series of Ph.D. students and "finished" scientists have attempted to document how far the red apes cover during the day, and they came to results of between 90 and 3,050 m (98 and 3,335 yards). The average wandering distance of 790 m (864 yards) per day, published in some sources, is doubtless scientifically just as worthless as other ape data because just like

*Too tired for more hard work. With a blanket of fresh layers of leaves this Black Orangutan* (Pongo pygmaeus morio) *can reuse an old nest. This is normally frowned upon by primates as used nests usually harbor pests.*

*The construction of sleeping nests is firmly based in the orangutan genes. For training purposes, the young animals build their nests on the ground from time to time, as in this photo.*

housewives between those supermarket shelves, the orangutans will not walk so much if they can quickly find what they are looking for; they will do more walking around if this is not the case.

In any case, between dawn and dusk, grown-up animals only rarely cover more than one kilometer (half a mile). First, there is no necessity most of the time, and secondly, it must be rather burdensome having to shift 80 kg (176 pounds) through the crowns of trees.

As said before, orangutans usually walk on their own. Mothers climb through the branches with their baby, sometimes accompanied by adolescent siblings of the little one. This way, young female apes can learn the secrets of baby care by visual instruction. Other "traveling groups" are formed by several young males or females without a territory of their own that collectively move from one food-supplying tree to the next, or by a pasha with his current lady-love.

Sometimes, the chief ape and an ape female stay together for days, weeks, or even months after their first copulation, whereas other couples part as soon as the female has become pregnant. Why the paths of the animals separate—sometimes quickly, sometimes not—no one can tell for sure. Could it be that—just as in the case of human beings—empathy and harmony also play a role besides sex?

In Grzimek's Encyclopedia of Mammals, Kathy MacKinnon reports that during wanderings alliances are often formed between "young adult" males (aged ten to fifteen years) and a mother with a child. These enter into a community of interests because the male will protect them against enemies. "Young adult" males (as opposed to older orangutans) are acceptable as traveling companions because they do not require so much food and still leave enough for the mother.

However, this is one of those typical "instant photos" which is only mentioned for the sake of completeness. Probably, orangutans of all ages and of both sexes have on occasion moved through the rainforest in every grouping imaginable. Two cheek-pad-ornamented territorial chiefs, however, cannot be imagined as "chums", as the high level of sex hormones counteracts any kind of benevolence or obligingness. If two of the "pashas" meet, showing off is the order of the day: yelling and shaking of the fur, "nasty" looks, broken branches fly about, and the throat pouches are blown up to great effect. Most of the time, things go no further.

Little is known about the size of the territory. According to one source, the territories of "sedentary" females range between 3.5 and 6 km² (1.4 and 2.3 square miles) and are situated within the considerably larger territory of a "pasha" who is favored by the females for mating. Other publications state 1.5 to 5 km² (0.6 to 2 square miles) as an average size for a female territory and 2 to 10 km² (0.8 to 4 square miles) for the sovereign territory of a dominant orangutan male. It is certain that the size of territory also depends on the food supply; if the food situation is positive the territory is small, if not, the territory has to be correspondingly larger.

A kind of dangerous glitter gets into Willie Smits' eyes when he says that the food-determined hermit life of the red ape is still interpreted as due to contact problems, eccentricity, and maverick behavior. "This is a disastrous misunderstanding," he fulminates, "and it has led to too much animal suffering. As one usually meets orangutans alone in the wild, zoologists have for decades believed that it would present no problem to keep them in solitary confinement. But orangutans are only alone for the simple reason that two of them together would not find enough to eat."

Although they only share three to five percent of their time with other red apes, for example when they happen to come across them in overlapping territory areas, "they have a great need for contact with orangutans." Babies play with each other, and in fruit trees with large yields, two dozen orangutans often celebrate "a giant gluttonous banquet".

Therefore, surveys on orangutan density therefore only possess anecdotal (and unfortunately more and more nostalgic) value. They

*Orangutans are wrongly regarded as loners. When there is enough food, they like to meet in large numbers for a convivial feast.*

range from a "normal value" of one ape per km² (250 acres) of rainforest to superlatives of more than ten companionable and sociable animals as counted by van Schaik in Suaq Balimbing on Sumatra, a world record.

"They sought active contact, traveled together from tree to tree and even shared their food," the anthropologist reports, "mating associations lasted much longer than elsewhere, and mothers suckling babies often traveled in little groups, usually accompanied by their older and already independent youngsters, who played vigorously with each other." No sign of contact problems.

It is amongst the worst perversions in the history of suffering of the red ape (so abundant in atrocities) that in Taipeh, the capital of Taiwan, the average orangutan density must in the eighties have been higher than on Borneo: after the broadcasting of a TV soap-opera in which an infant was presented as an ideal domestic animal for cuddling, and which took the hearts of the audience by storm, there was a brisk demand for "sweet" little orangutan babies. The animal mafia did not have to be asked twice, and hundreds of the live fashion-toys were smuggled to Taiwan, most of them to the capital.

According to the Honolulu Zoo, unscrupulous wild-animal traders carried off a total of about 1,000 young orangutans to Taiwan between 1985 and 1990. As during catch and transportation of the primates intended for export—as described, per surviving animal a whole number of ape mothers and babies, practically collateral damage, has to die, the Taiwan exports, based on a "conservative estimate", led to a decline in the number of free-living orangutans in Borneo and Sumatra of around 3,000 animals. Grzimek assumes that for every baby which is traded, five to six will die. Thus, the soap opera exterminated five to six thousand orangutans.

*Botanical studies. To date nobody knows what criteria orangutans use to judge whether a plant is good to eat or to be used as a medicinal herb. Willie Smits suspects the color green. He believes that the apes can distinguish between around a thousand shades of green.*

For years, the red apes were omnipresent in Taipeh; one could even see them in the "Snake Alley" red-light district. There were given drugs there and, for the amusement of the spectators, they were allowed to decapitate tortoises with an axe. Afterwards, they had to let the blood of the headless reptiles run into a glass with the snake gall of freshly killed cobras, then stir the ingredients and offer them to the visitors.

The National Chinese authorities only stepped in when it was becoming impossible to close their eyes to the consequences of the ape imports: orangutans whose owners had difficulties coping with them and who were therefore thrown out of the house were wandering around the streets of the capital in increasing numbers. In 1990, the government prohibited the keeping of the animals. Many of the red apes were confiscated if they were lucky and ended in a rescue station.

Daidai was one of the 45 animals who saw their home again. The orangutan female had lived with a Mrs Chang in Taipeh and was acclimatized as perfectly as might be possible for a jungle dweller in the hands of humans. She ate anything that was put on the table and understood Taiwanese perfectly. She faultlessly carried out orders like "Get me the yogurt in the blue plastic mug from the fridge." She was able to say "Hai" (Yes) and apparently even tried to speak "properly".

However, under the care of Mrs Chang the ape female must have forgotten the few things she had learned from her mother when she was a baby before her mother was murdered: she did not manage to cope in the rainforest. Following her first release in Sungai Wain, a more than 10,000 ha (40 square mile) BOS protectorate near Balikpapan, she was kidnapped by the dominant orangutan male Charlie and was practically kept prisoner for one month. Because she hardly knew how to find nutrition in the rainforest and because her territory-boss was eating all the laid out food, she nearly starved to death.

She was recaptured and underwent an extremely comprehensive second re-introduction training. However, it seems that the human

The bark of the Cempedak tree provides a sweet amber juice that the red apes appreciate just as much as the delicate fruits and the young leaves of this forest giant.

Right: At the salad counter. Large orangutan males often climb down their trees to fill their stomachs with greenery. This is similar to the behavior of the African western lowland gorilla.

64

*Charcoal works. Like humans, orangutans use charcoal to soothe an upset stomach.*

beings had spoiled Daidai for the world of the apes. She was unable to cope with members of the same species and had great difficulties in acquiring for herself the requisite know-how for a life in the jungle. After a long time, she was again re-introduced into the Meratus Mountains. She disappeared immediately, and nobody knows how she got on.

Anne Russon is a pessimist: "It is sad but I believe that her survival chances were bad because she could not cope in the forest. She might have managed and I hope very much that this is true. However, if one looks at it soberly, she did not even know how to find food and to keep up orientation in the rainforest. She was not even able to climb properly: for example, she stepped on dead branches and crashed down!"

Willie Smits: "Daidai returned twice to Wanariset, once with a deep wound in her stomach, once with a heavy affliction of parasites. She learned a lot from Charlie and improved her climbing technique a great deal. In 2002, some months after Daidai's release, a pregnant orangutan female looking like Daidai was seen east of Camp Meratus.

The fate of re-introduced primates is hardly predictable: orangutan female Tuti, quite inexperienced in the forest, disappeared two days after her release in Sungai Wain without leaving any traces and only turned up again three years later after the search parties included previously ignored nooks and crannies of the 10,000 ha (40 square miles) into their program. Fully nine years after her re-introduction, the pregnant Tuti showed up in front of her BOS custodians again. She had been thought dead because her hand had been paralyzed.

However, back to the subject: numerous aspects of the reproduction of orangutans still remain a mystery for the investigators, amongst them such basic things as the beginning of sexual maturity or the duration of the female cycle. Because in red-ape females—as opposed to chimpanzee ladies—an unmistakable swelling of the genitals cannot be detected, observers in the rainforest would have to be

clairvoyants if they wanted to recognize the beginning of puberty or the duration of the menstrual cycle.

Therefore, and because puberty obviously seems to set in earlier in captured orangutans than in free-living ones, the relevant figures in ape literature are in wild disorder: statements on the age at which females can conceive vary between 5.8 and 11.1 years, those of the duration of cycle between 22 and 30 days. In the case of captured ape females, menopause sets in at 48.

One thing, however, seems to be certain: orangutan females in the rainforest—no matter when they start to become sexually mature, will have their first child when they are about 15 years old. Gestation ranges between 237 and 270 days. Other sources limit this to eight and a half to nine months. The birth weight of the individual baby is about 1,500 g (3.3 pounds).

Twin births are extremely rare. As the milk of the mother is only enough for one baby, only one little ape has a chance to survive. During the entire time in which orangutans have been confined, only three pairs of twins, born in zoos, survived the first weeks. Currently, the "Parrot Jungle" in Miami is keeping the twins Peanut and Pumpkin. In the spring of 2006, the sisters were two years old.

*French kiss with a taste of mushy leaves. Juvenile orangutans pass on tasty morsels to each other as their mothers used to do. No sign of their being "solitary animals", as many researchers see them.*

*The habitat of orangutans is one large pharmacy. Almost half of all medicines swallowed by humans originate from the tropical forests. Many of these plants would become extinct were it not for the orangutans who 'garden' the forest. This orangutan who is suffering from malaria is chewing on the root of* Euricomia latifolia *as first aid against the fever. The Dayak, too, use this plant for medicinal purposes.*

*Bitter morsel. This orangutan female is not enjoying eating the twig of the plant of the genus* Melastoma. *This plant, very rich in tannic acids and hence very bitter, is used by the Dayaks, the local former headhunters, as a cure for diarrhea. Do orangutans do the same?*

*The large leaves of the* Dillenia *tree have many uses for orangutans—as a salad and a sun-screen.*

*Bamboo is not only eaten by panda bears. The tropical grass is also on the menu of the red apes.*

*Left: Stuffed! Happy and with a full stomach, this orangutan is resting after the exertion of eating his meal. His dessert consisted of a little bit of clay. Scientists assume that the mineral neutralizes potentially poisonous substances in the leaves. Above: The menu of orangutans is enriched by flowers.*

# Seven years of training, five years of mother's milk and eternal ape-love

## The sheltered childhood of the orangutans

*The bond between mother and baby is closer than that of any other animal in the world.*

The little orangutan depends on his mother for a longer time than any other animal and receives his training from her for seven years, which gives him the requisite know-how for survival in the rainforest. This includes everything an ape has to know, from climbing all the way to botany. For one year, the baby is in permanent physical contact with his mother, for about five years (the information here is once again self-contradictory) it is breast-fed, although it would already during its first year of life start to nibble at leaves and fruit.

The uniquely well-protected childhood of the little ape leads to minimal infant mortality; "Cases of death by natural causes are extremely rare in wild-living animals," says the web page of Honolulu zoo, "because orangutan mothers are very good at raising their infants." Decisive for the low infant mortality is "the fact that the mother keeps her child with her for an average of eight years."

Taking an average of all the information available, the childhood of the little orangutan lasts up to his fourth or fifth year. Already at the age of two, the baby can undertake its first excursions but will always stay in eye contact with its mother. A little later, the offspring—according to the National Primate Research Center of Wisconsin University—moves hand in hand with its mother or other members of its species—through the branches: "buddy travel".

Between the ages of four and eight one could call the ape infant an "adolescent" (although in individual cases its mother will still allow it her breast at the age of seven); then in general, puberty sets in, and at the age of about eight, the young ape becomes independent of its mother and starts to go its own ways.

The longest childhood of all animals goes hand in hand with a very low fertility rate. However, this is not only due to the self-sacrificing nursing; weather phenomena also play an important role. Why this is, explains Willie Smits: "Every four years El Niño provides an abundance of nutrition for the orangutans. This makes the female ready for conception. But because a baby remains with the mother for seven to eight years, every alternate fertile phase passes idly, so to speak!"

And this is how it happens that on average only one baby comes into the world every eight years. "Thus, on statistical average, every orangutan female has no more than three children. This is the lowest birth-rate of all land mammals."

While this applies to Sumatra, the interval between births on the neighboring island of Borneo seems to be smaller (see page 244). It is even smaller in zoos, where according to Grzimek several ape females have given birth to eight children. An orangutan female from Philadelphia zoo even had nine offspring. She must have been quite an unusual animal as it seems (in the case of "wild catches" the date of birth is always a guessing game!) she lived from 1919 to 1976, which made her 57 years old at death. Her mate, probably also born in 1919, died one year later and at 58 years, he is the record-holder in terms of orangutan longevity. In the wilderness, the animals rarely

*A young orangutan closely observes its mothers every movement, thus learning for the future.*

seem to make it past forty (but no one knows this with absolute certainty). There is a male in Ketambe on Sumatra, however, who is almost sixty.

Owing to the low birth frequency—scientifically called "interbirth interval" (IBI)—the red apes, according to Smits, "are extremely prone to disturbances, loss of habitat, and killing." The PHVA study had shown that orangutan stocks can bear hunting losses of one to two percent only with difficulty, three percent, however, is no longer tolerable and leads to an extinction of the population.

In other words: if of 100 orangutans only three animals fall victim to poachers, the entire stock will in the long run have no chance to survive. Looking at it from this angle, it is almost a miracle that the red apes have remained alive at all until today.

At the age of about twelve, male orangutans become sexually mature (care is also required with regard to this figure as there is such confusion in the data); the University of Wisconsin quotes the generous age-span of eight to 15 years. Physically mature and ready for procreation, the young ape males enter into a strange transitional phase as they can only gain their "social maturity" when the territory of a dominant pasha becomes vacant and they can take over his job, or if they manage to push a red regent from his throne.

Until the time is ripe, they are "men in standby position", and cheek-pads and throat pouch, insignia of the pasha, are still missing. Scientists have coined the term of "bimaturity" for this two-level maturity.

Quite obviously, their reserve is not completely voluntary because as it seems, the "young adults" are "acoustically castrated", so to speak. How this is possible, the National Primate Research Center

*The demand for absolute domination causes the ape-machos a lot of grief in zoos. All the stunted alpha males that cannot live with each other are forced into a life of solitary confinement. Oki is doing time in the Ragunan zoological park in Jakarta.*

*Above: The job as pasha exhausts the territorial chiefs swiftly and thoroughly. When the kings are toppled from their throne their previously impressive cheek-pads shrink. Once the monarchs have lost their rights they are a heap of misery. Left: A pasha brimming with strength. Even though Romeo, a Black Orangutan, was smuggled from East Kalimantan to Taiwan and returned with hepatitis B, he is an image of male power in his cage in the BOS center Wanariset. He is currently waiting to be released onto the BOS island of Lapetan (approximately: "island of giants") where he will be spending the rest of his life in freedom.*

*Please, mummy, can I have another sip of milk? Even though the young lad is already more than five years old he cannot refrain from drinking his mother's milk. He persuades his mother with a kiss to allow him to her breast, which still has milk.*

*Success! The campaig worked and th nearly grown-u "baby" is allowed t have some mil*

*The cheek-pads of the orangutans from Sumatra are not as bulging as those of the males in Borneo and they often grow a beard.*

Stephen Hart of the "Animal Communication Project" describes the call as follows: "It begins with a low soft grumble, modulating in pitch like a string bass player using vibrato. It builds slowly to a roar audible a mile and a quarter away through the dense Borneo jungle. The third movement falls back to a soft series of mumbles and sighs."

On the internet, the "long call" sounds like a mixture of saurian roars from the primeval film shocker, *Jurassic Park,* the bawling of an ox and the squeaking of wild boars. It is noticeable that the orangutan not only breathes out during his roars; quite obviously, he also breathes in.

The functions of the call of the pasha are a matter for discussion by the scientists—how else could it be? If one puts aside those scientific blinkers, it becomes clear very fast that the egomaniac presentation probably has one of the following three functions, maybe even all three of them together: acoustic delimitation of the territory and expulsion of rivals, manifestation of presence and location report for his "subjects", and mating-call addressed to ape females able to conceive.

If a grown-up male (usually 15 to 20 years old) manages to leap to the position of boss of the territory, his hormones run wild, and within a few months the insignia of power, thick leathery-black cheek-pads and a throat-pouch, will start growing change his appearance completely. For Willie Smits, the change means that he is forced to re-identify clan chiefs who suddenly turn up on his journeys because the blown-up cheeks and other metamorphoses make the former "young adult" unrecognizable.

For the new clan leader, the comfortable bachelor life is now over and his new life is comparatively hard. A fully grown orangutan has to find great amounts of nutrition for his heavy body, and further-

of Wisconsin University reports by referring to a study of 2000 in which Carel von Schaik also participated: there is some evidence that the "long-call" plays an important role in the suppression of development among adolescent and sub-adult males. When adolescent males hear long-calls, "stress hormones are induced and rather than developing secondary sexual characteristics, their development is arrested."

*Instructions in fruitology. The mother patiently shows her offspring how to eat what fruit. She knows she has the attention of her child.*

*Hold on for the rollercoaster ride. As the mother steams through the rainforest on her back, always maintaining her orientation, her small passenger hangs onto the fur on her belly.*

84

more has a job with a lot of "responsibility" and pressure with the defense of his territory, deterrence, care for his renown, and courtly-love service. Scientists have found strongly increased levels of stress hormones in the blood of dominant orangutans.

"Most of the time, the pashas are burned out after a few years!" says American anthropologist Cheryl Knott of Harvard University. If a top-ranking orangutan loses his position of power to a younger and stronger rival, his "cheek-pads" also recede. It is almost like an officer on discharge removing his uniform and decorations. Knott's husband, the photographer Tim Lamann, has documented resignation and apathy in the faces of the former chiefs after their abdication.

It is even worse when lack of nutrition and sheer hardship ravish the dignity of the ape sovereign. Lone Dröscher-Nielsen has seen territory owners wandering half-starved through oil palm plantations after being driven away by humans. "Hunger has shrunk their formerly fat cheek-pads to empty flaps of skin!"

By means of the pasha metamorphosis, the orangutan male completely re-organizes his copulation strategy. If until now he had been permanently on the move, always looking for females he'd tried to court with little presents (most of the time without success), or, if he met them alone, raped them without much ado, he now wanders through his territory, waiting for willing ladies attracted by his martial call. His only "advertisement" is his appearance, which ape females on heat seem to find irresistible, and the "long call", practically his advertising jingle.

This strategy has been successful for aeons now. As it seems to a number of observers, females also like to be close to the territorial chief because this protects them against the attacks of violent males. Those rowdies with no territory of their own are surprisingly successful progenitors: a group of scientists working on Sumatra under the guidance of Suci Utami, biology professor at Jakarta University, found that males without cheek-pads fathered almost half of the ape babies in the group she monitored. The pasha sired the other half.

If one believes the information on the website of Honolulu zoo, there are major differences in the sex lives of the orangutans of Borneo and Sumatra. On Sumatra, as already mentioned, about half of the copulations were carried out on a "consensual" basis, that is to say by willing females visiting a territorial chief, while the other half came about by force. On Borneo by contrast 90 percent of the matings were performed by young adult males attacking lone females.

The results of the Utami study as well as the high proportion of rapes on Borneo are quite unusual. They seem to run counter to the theory of evolution because quite obviously, here the strongest animal (which among stags, stallions, and many other animals would normally have the sole right to paternity in the herd) passes on his genes surprisingly infrequently. Scientists have yet to unravel how this can be explained.

*Fun-hour in the zoo. Babies that are still in the care of their mother need never suffer boredom. Here mother Anne tickles her young one to keep her attention. Like all babies she is laughing with her mouth open.*

*First a bath and then a ride. Only the stroller is missing; other than that the way a female ape treats her baby is not at all different from the way a human mother treats hers.*

*In the never-ending rainforest where encounters with other orangutans are rare, mother and child are their own little universe.*

89

90

Above: Spitting image. In orangutans one can see family likenesses, just as in humans.
Right: Holding on with all fours. The baby, slightly more than a year old, has anchored itself into the shaggy fur of its mother with all its grasping limbs.

*Five years of cuddling. It does not matter if the baby is two weeks old (left) or more than five years (right)—the mother is always there.*

*One more sip from the bottle? The little milk fan is wistfully looking at the mother's breast and is wondering how to get another sip of milk (far right).*

92

# Brains, genius, or common sense

## What is inside an ape's head?

*There are hardly any problems in communication between humans and their closest relatives in the animal kingdom. Lone Dröscher-Nielsen, head of the BOS station Nyaru Menteng is talking effortlessly with one of her charges.*

Another one of the most important questions yet to be solved is: how intelligent are our shaggy relatives from the rainforest?

Scientists have serious problems when it comes to answering this because they come up against the limitations of their methods. They have to deal with a test object with which they can at best make a basic approach towards communication. Quite often, they have no basic knowledge of their experimental animals—tens of thousands of kilometers away from their native Indonesia—because they have never experienced one of the red apes in the wild. And quite often, the experimenters are neither sufficiently informed on species-typical characteristics nor on the world of the primates and are unable to make a proper evaluation of the gestures and body language of their experimental subjects. In addition, as if this were not enough, they present the latter with tasks solely designed according to human criteria, and then evaluate them equally anthropocentrically.

Numerous research papers create the impression that their writers were not interested one iota in the animals themselves, but exploited them solely as means of obtaining data for a publication in a professional journal. "Publish or perish"—this is the maxim of the academic rat race. And thus a considerable proportion of the published "facts" on the red apes are collected in grotesque circumstances, and with the "assistance" of confined apes.

This would be analogous to a team of Mongolian psychiatrists interviewing Albert Einstein (forcibly carried off from his Princeton study and very much annoyed about this) about the two-times table in a much-too-cold prison cell in Ulan Bator in a language (their own) incomprehensible to the genius, and then coming to the conclusion that the interviewee lacks simple numeracy skills. (Nothing against Mongolia: the analogy is only meant to indicate how far the level of understanding of the orangutans is removed from that of the humans, and that they are roughly as different as Mongolian and German or American).

And the results turned out accordingly.

*Quality control. An orangutan is scrutinizing the quality of a picture that a student has just taken.*

*A drawer full of milk. Using a technique that is thousands of years old—a water-storing sponge made out of the roots of orchids or leaves—a female ape is drinking milk in a BOS rehabilitation center.*

*The inventor and the opportunist. An orangutan has made a "fishing-rod" and is fishing floating fruit out of the River Rungan. However, his bounty is torn from him by a fellow orangutan that had, seemingly without interest, been watching his fishing efforts.*

The Orangutan Foundation International (OFI) owns a long list of research works on the intelligence of orangutans with authors of studies, titles, and often also in internet summary (www.orangutan.org). With comparatively few exceptions, the listing is a tragedy. Platitudes are sold as science because scholars conclude in their studies that "competent orangutan mothers" are important for the ability of their children to climb and to find their nutrition. Research is carried out into whether the red apes are intellectually able to understand what it means when a human test supervisor points his finger to a container with food. We can discover in which direction primates imprisoned in zoos most frequently look, and solutions are offered to the question of whether zoo apes, stunned and caught specifically for this test, recognized themselves in the mirror.

The best suggestion is to forget this kind of "research" immediately, just like all those other aborted projects which have aimed at clarifying the intellectual abilities of the apes, e.g. the attempts to induce domesticated orangutans by means of human deaf and dumb language to "give away private secrets" or (after their release) to "interview" wild members of their species or to "translate" for the scientists. There is a fatal resemblance to the likewise miserable failure of the Hawaiian experiments of the American physician and psychoanalyst Dr John Lilly (d. 2001), who tried to decipher the language of the dolphins. Dolphins are also intelligent mammals whose mental abilities cannot yet be assessed by science.

If—like Willie Smits—one believes, on the basis of decades of observation, that orangutans in the rainforest have a mental storage of the most important properties of about one thousand plants, one obviously cannot be further impressed if red test-apes were able to memorize seven different terms during one year, as was documented by Karyl Swartz, psychologist at New York City University, using orangutan female Iris as an example.

For some years now, Anne Russon has endeavored to examine the mental powers of our long-armed cousins according to the traditional modus operandi with orangutans in a zoo. In the process, the disadvantages of this method became more and more obvious to her. "Unfortunately," she writes in a publication of BOS USA,

*A problem shared is a problem halved. The robbed fruit-angler is complaining to his friends about the theft.*

*Drop-catcher. His mouth wide open, an orangutan is chasing beautiful drops of water that are falling from the top of the rainforest after some rain.*

*This orangutan from the BOS island of Kaja again and again makes attempts at spearfishing in the Gohong River, as he has seen the native men do. He is not enjoying any success with his clumsy tool, so he changes tactics and uses his stick to pull the laid-out fishing lines from the water (see picture bottom right), thus stealing the hooked prey, as shown in the picture on page 100.*

"the major part of research on the intelligence of giant apes was carried out with captured animals. Scientists determined their tasks and decided when the apes had to work. However, most people —and most apes—do not enjoy fulfilling tasks which others have thought up, and then having to do all this under pressure instead of according to their whim. This way, positive results only rarely come about."

At the same time, world-class research is more important than ever: the more carefully one scrutinizes giant apes, "the more we realize that they are able to carry out complex intellectual feats," Russon writes. "Language, production and use of complex tools, disguise, self-knowledge, and forward planning are all of them high-ranging accomplishments we once deemed to be exclusively human heritage. But now we are recognizing that orangutans and the other giant apes— chimpanzees, gorillas, bonobos—also possess these abilities. Their achievements might be less progressive than ours might, but they have moved much closer to our state of understanding than we had ever considered possible."

The professor of psychology drew the consequences: instead of carrying on working with jail-primates, she went to Borneo and studied re-introduced red apes. "These are very special animals." They had learned a lot about humans and their world but now they had to master life's difficulties in the rainforest autonomously. "Here, I can

watch orangutans as they solve problems they have set themselves." And because they are animals who are used to human beings, she can do it from very close up.

Together with the use of tools and the ability to learn, the solution of tricky tasks represents for Anne Russon the most important proof of their intelligence. She has no doubts at all that a lot is happening inside the heads of the red apes. "Orangutans are very patient and thoughtful," she said. "They plan, brood and think in advance. There are numerous cases in which they have proved to

*Bigger is not always better. Using unimaginable strength this orangutan manages to keep the far too heavy spear horizontal. However, he still does not catch anything.*

*Mouthwash in the morning. This orangutan, only holding on with a few fingers, is hauling water out of the river with practiced swoops.*

*An understanding of technology can fill the stomach. On the BOS island of Palas this orangutan has waited until a fish has taken the bite on the stationary fishing rod of a native. Now he collects the prey—after one failed attempt—with a self-made tool.*

be mentally superior to their keepers. Theft from the fridge of humans where they lived was usually only discovered after three to four days. This is how long it took until the keepers understood how the apes had managed to do this." One ape made a lock pick out of a paper clip, which he used to open the lock of his cage. As he kept it underneath his tongue, the attendants only found out with difficulty.

The learning ability of the orangutan is documented by an abundance of imitations of complex human behavior patterns, which are based on a learning process. Mrs Russon herself has experienced this or heard from other scientists of her acquaintance: "In my study I found ex-captive orangutans doing many things they must have learned by imitating humans. They chopped firewood, washed laundry and dishes, weeded and swept camp paths, sawed logs, sharpened axe blades, hung up hammocks and rode in them, and siphoned fuel. One even tried to make a fire and almost succeeded; she tried every single trick she had seen the camp cooks using daily.

"In all of these cases, orangutans did the jobs the same way humans did, yet no one had taught them—you'd have to be a fool to show a free-living orangutan to make a fire or wield an axe—and these tools were even hidden from the orangutans. So we concluded that the only way they could have learned all of these skills was by watching humans."

This is a very advanced ability because the imitator has to make a sort of 'mental video' of the model's behavior, then use that video, and nothing else, to invent new behavior. "In fact, imitative learning is one of the abilities that we have claimed to be uniquely human."

It would go beyond the scope of this chapter to portray all the many spectacular examples of orangutan imitation. We would like to mention just one: The ape female Princess, released in Tanjung Puting National Park, who had most of the time loafed around close to humans, had made up her mind to do the washing. She untied a canoe, rocked it from side to side to let the bilge water slosh around, rowed it to a raft on which the Indonesian staff believed to have secured wash-tub and washing powder from the grasp of the primate, and started to act as washerwoman. (Princess is one of the apes intended as an "interpreter": the American zoologist, Gary Shipiro, taught the very clever animal a considerable vocabulary of the US sign language Ameslan—however without the desired success.)

For better understanding, it has to be mentioned that orangutans do not swim and that therefore rivers present unbridgeable obstacles for them. And a raft which is anchored a few meters away from the riverbank is normally absolutely inaccessible.

*Above: Using a coconut-bowl that he fished out of the river, this ape is collecting water. Right: Finally made it. The shaggy hunter is giving his best to prevent the slippery prey that he is holding by the tail from escaping.*

100

*It all begins with twigs: Small twigs and branches, of which there is no shortage in the jungle, are used by orangutans in many different ways—as locust swatters (top), as chewing gum (middle) or as tooth-picks.*

However, Anne Russon has observed the first swimming trials carried out by the red apes of Pulau Kaja near Wanariset—"and some orangutans are not so bad at all at swimming".

Autonomous "sensible" actions of orangutans in situations in which they cannot refer to any learning-by-watching behavior pattern are to be evaluated more highly as proof of their intelligence than the most complicated imitative action.

One example for this is the "insight" of the ape female Bonnie from the National Zoo in Washington. By the end of the eighties, five young orangutans were bustling about in an enclosure, which was baptized "Think Tank" due to the mental abilities of the inmates. One keeper had rolled an empty barrel as an amusement for the apes into the enclosure. Suddenly Bonnie grabbed the toy, dragged it to the electric fence, and placed it there in an upright position, climbed on top of it, then climbed over the fencing and, her baby Kiko in her fur, strolled through the group of perplexed spectators of the well-attended zoo. Somehow, she had realized that the electricity had failed and that the top of the fence was unable to distribute painful electrical shocks.

Bonnie snatched the picnic icebox of a zoo visitor who, to be on the safe side, had taken to his heels, and placed herself in a flowerbed, her back resting against the glass façade of the "Think Tank". She held a chicken's leg in one hand; in the other she held a bottle of ice-cold Coke.

It took some time for the zoo vet to reach the scene of the crime, the stun-gun in his car. Bonnie waited calmly until the vet got out of his car with his gun. Then she dropped the bottle whose contents she

*A world exclusive photo. A swimming orangutan. For a million years rivers were insurmountable barriers to the red apes. However, a few inhabitants of the Kaja Island have now learnt to swim and they go to gather juicy fruits on the other side of the river.*

*A new way of life is holding sway. As the "creator" of the revolutionary hunting technique obviously enjoyed success, imitators quickly arrived. They are now enriching their normally protein-poor diet with precious fish-protein—close to an evolutionary great leap forward.*

Gorillas follow in fourth place, ahead of surili langurs, macaques, and mandrills.

Now at Grand Valley State University in Allendale, Michigan, Deaner is continuing his research into orangutans. One result is a study produced by the psychologist James Lee of Harvard, which appeared in the American academic journal *Brain, Behavior and Evolution* in April 2007. Once again the orangutans come out on top, as, according to Lee, they have the greatest capacity to learn and solve problems. They are followed by chimpanzees, spider monkeys, langurs, macaques, and mandrills. In this study, the gorillas are also-rans.

had used to rinse down the last bite of chicken, and went back into the enclosure—just as if clever giving-in were the most natural thing in the world.

It was not until the summer of 2006 that a study appeared which to a certain extent does justice to the intelligence of the red primates. In an evaluation of existing papers on the mental faculties of the hominoid apes, Carel van Schaik and the psychologist Robert Diener came to the conclusion in the American journal *Evolutionary Psychology* that orangutans were the most intelligent members of the superfamily. Deaner, whose analysis is based on his research at the Medical Center at Duke University in Durham (North Carolina), justified placing them above chimpanzees thus: "Orangutans are more patient and deliberative. And they're the master escape artists from zoos." In the primate-intelligence league table, orangutans get in ahead of chimpanzees and spider monkeys of the genus *Ateles*.

*Above: The watched watcher. With interest an orangutan is looking at the notes that a student makes of one his fellow apes.*
*Right: Well done! After a successful fish-catch the hunter is looking at his reflection in the water. To be able to look at himself in the mirror he performs a major acrobatic feat.*

# Alma and the tin-opener, Unyil's "rope trick", and Uce's love for symbols

## Encounters with orangutan intelligence

*Alma arrived in Nyaru Menteng recently with serious mercury poisoning. She often falls into a state of physical and mental inertness; this, like her hair-loss, is a consequence of the poisoning. She drank the heavy metal in the house of a gold-washer, where it was standing around in a bottle.*

There are plenty of examples of the use of tools, a talent for combination, and memory, which provide considerably more evidence than the complete academic studies on the "cognitive potential" of the orangutans. I would like to limit myself to three of them: one report by Lone Dröscher-Nielsen and two by Willie Smits.

The first story is one about the orangutan girl, Alma, who had come from Ketapang, a small town in West Kalimantan to Nyaru Menteng in the middle of 2002. For three years, Alma had lived with a gold washer. Because she had always been particularly curious and never caused any damage, she had been allowed to run freely about the house. One day, she had discovered a bottle of mercury on one of her rambles—and had drunk it. Gold seekers use the poisonous liquid metal for separating the gold from sludge and sand.

When Alma was confiscated two months later, she was already terminally ill, only skin and bones, and her hair was falling out. Lone Dröscher-Nielsen "adopted" her. When the "kindergarten" into which she was integrated because of her illness was closed early in the evening, Alma was allowed to accompany her home and to sleep in her bed with her.

The little ape had developed a particular fondness for the her hostess's kitchen—not because she was hungry (she ate practically nothing), but because there were so many interesting things here. Quite often, Alma opened a cupboard door or a drawer, got the contents out piece by piece, placed the items carefully in file on the floor and opened anything that could be opened. If she could

not manage, she asked Lone Dröscher-Nielsen for help. She was never untidy.

One day, Alma came across a tin opener. She considered what purpose the item might serve and concluded that it was useless as a hammer or a fan, and put it aside. Shortly after this, she discovered a tin of sardines in tomato sauce. She took it to Lone who turned it around and playfully bit into it: "No, Alma, it won't open". Alma

*The mercury also damaged Alma's digestive organs. As nothing worked to cure her serious diarrhea she is now getting the traditional medicine: a drink made from the leaves of guavas and papayas.*

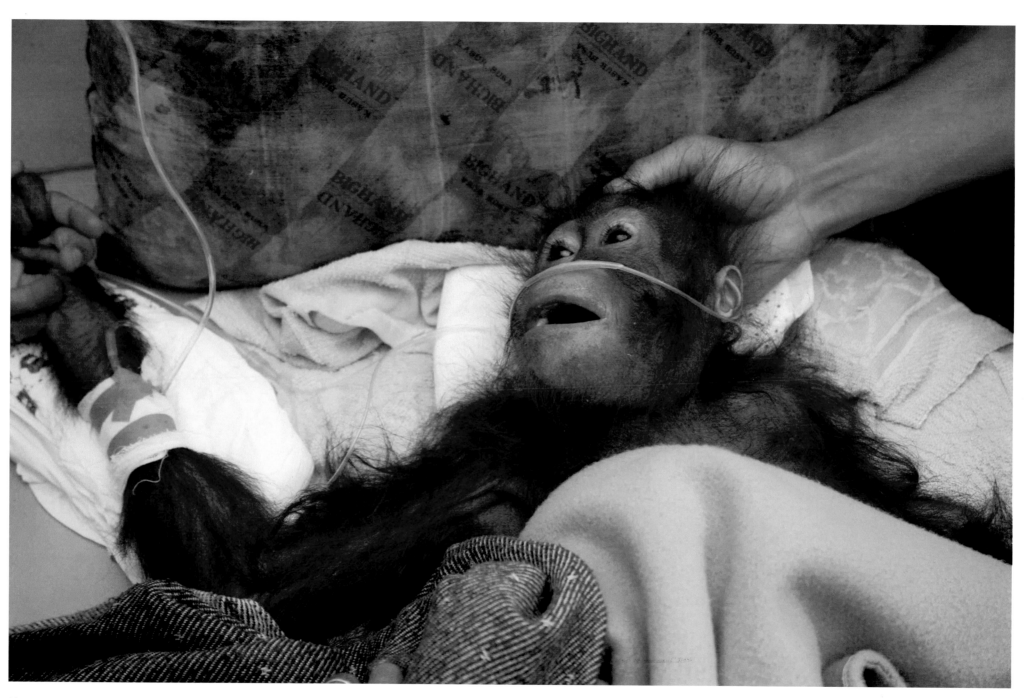

*The young orangutan is fighting for her life with a lot of courage. She endures the many infusions without fuss or complaint. When the pain gets too much she bites onto a small twig that she has placed between her teeth. A nanny is holding her foot to comfort her.*

107

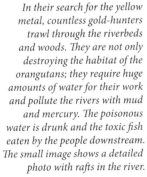

In their search for the yellow metal, countless gold-hunters trawl through the riverbeds and woods. They are not only destroying the habitat of the orangutans; they require huge amounts of water for their work and pollute the rivers with mud and mercury. The poisonous water is drunk and the toxic fish eaten by the people downstream. The small image shows a detailed photo with rafts in the river.

carried the tin back. After a few minutes, however, she returned and took Lone by the hand and pulled her into the kitchen where she once again put the tin into her hand. "But Alma, I have told you already, that can't be opened!" she repeated.

"Alma looked deep into my eyes as if she wanted to find out whether I was really telling the truth!" Lone reports. "Then, still looking into my eyes, she gave me the tin-opener. I do not know whether she could read in my eyes or in my face when I smiled about her cleverness—in any case, she was beaming because she knew she had hit the jackpot. I gave in, positioned the tin opener and turned it a bit. Alma watched this with a grave countenance, and when I gave her the tin, she turned the tin opener—just as I had done. She managed to cut the tin open without spilling one single drop of tomato sauce. She was so happy." The young ape died of mercury poisoning after six months of suffering.

Willie Smits first story is about the female ape, Unyil, who was liberated by BOS after twelve years of torture as the "pet" of a colonel

of the Indonesian army. Almost her entire life, she had been put in a much too small wire cage through which her arms and legs had grown, she had been permanently tortured and when confiscated, suffered from infectious tuberculosis of the lungs. (Smits describes the deliverance of the animal on page 299). She was taken to the quarantine ward of Wanariset and administered three different antibiotics at the same time.

"About two weeks after Unyil's arrival I heard for the first time of a worrying development in the clinic and quarantine station. Mangoes, apples and other (expensive) fruits were disappearing from the isolation compound. The quarantine station consists of different compartments for different diseases and each compartment of two rows of isolation cages, separated by a three-meter (three-yard) aisle in the middle.

"In the morning we would give the orangutans leaves to eat, and as a kind of stimulus to finish their 'greens' we would lay some juicy sweet

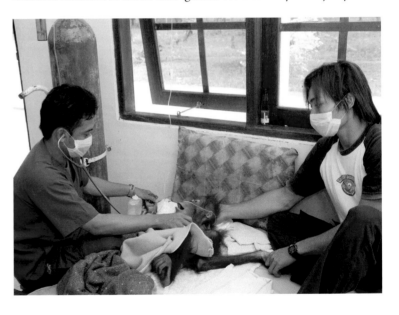

Alma's chronic poisoning plagues her with a continuous up and down of her health. One day she is doing as well as can be expected; the next she requires assistance and care around the clock. In these moments only constant infusions can save her.

Only orangutans understand this game. In Jakarta Zoo a red ape has gathered stones into a bucket and is stirring them with two twigs. An imitation gone wrong? Is he playing cook?

*World exclusive. After several failed attempts an orangutan beats a fish that was swimming past with a baton and eats the prey. This is previously unseen proof that the red apes use tools to hunt.*

*Group photo with Licuala palm. When Uce sees Willie Smits she remembers her release in 1992 and the Licuala palm leaf she received as a good-bye present from Willie. On this picture showing Uce with her second son Bintang and his father Dodoy, she is reaching for this plant: Willie Smits is the photographer. Uce and Dodoy are the first two orangutans that Willie Smits saved. BOS started with them.*

*When testing new plants orangutans proceed methodically in three steps. First, the new herb is felt (large photo, left). Then the "tester" smells the research object thoroughly. After this the ape checks whether the plant has an unpleasant effect on lips or tongue (above left). Finally the ape analyst chews the new leaves and inspects the result with great care (above right).*

fruit in the middle of the aisle. Those orangutans that had finished eating up their 'greens' would be given the fruity desert awaiting them in front of their cages but out of reach of their long arms.

"Suddenly, some of these expensive appetizers went missing each day. The keepers started accusing each other of theft and the good team spirit amongst the colleagues turned sour. As I could not tolerate this, I asked my assistant of many years, Udin, the head keeper, to find the thief and to fire him. However, one week went by and despite all investigations, we were unable to identify the culprit and the thefts continued.

"Because Udin was at his wits' end, he climbed up on the roof of the quarantine station one morning and watched through a small hole what was going on inside.

"Everything seemed normal, the vets made their rounds, medication was distributed. The cages were cleaned, leaves were brought into the cages and the 'appetizers' were placed in the middle of the aisle between the rows of cages. To Udin's disappointment, the keepers left and for about 20 minutes, nothing happened. Had the thief found out about his presence on the increasingly hotter roof?

"Then Udin noticed something strange. Unyil, who normally crouched lethargically in the corner of her cage, as was to be expected of a very sick and heavily drugged orangutan, suddenly moved towards the bars of her cage looking very attentive. After a few minutes, she sat down and started pulling out hairs from her shoulders. Hairs that never had a chance to break and shorten, because of the confinement in the rusty cage that had surrounded her. Within

113

*Oral hygiene for apes: the use of tools is widespread among orangutans. This includes the spontaneous use of twigs to remove the tough fibers of wild mangos from the teeth.*

*Rain-protection. In the Tanjung Puting National Park an orangutan is waiting for visitors. The tropical downpour is not putting him off—he is using a piece of carpeting as an umbrella.*

minutes, she produced a rudimentary rope and looking around her cage found a banana peel, which she tied to the end of the tiny rope. Sticking her arms through the bars, and with great concentration, she threw the banana peel behind the apples and mangoes, making sure not to let go of the other end of the rope. Very carefully without breaking the rope, she pulled the apple towards her with the banana peel, repeating the throws several times until she could grasp the apple with her hands. Having finished several more of the juicy fruits, carefully hiding the mango stones in her toilet, she sat back in the corner of the cage, lethargic as before…"

I have told this story in full as it documents, in a unique way, how clever our shaggy-haired cousins are. Unyil not only thought up a tool and manufactured it, she also thought up a utilization strategy and put this into practice, but she also made sure to get rid of the mango stones which would have given away her petty larceny of food to the keepers. The history of crime is full of human villains who have acted in a considerably more stupid fashion.

Another story makes one very thoughtful. A story Willie Smits experienced with Uce, the ape female he found at the end of 1989 as a dying baby on a rubbish heap at the market in Balikpapan, and whose "fault it is" that he underwent his great transformation from a forest scientist to a protector of orangutans (see page 204).

On 23 May 1992, Uce was supposed to be released from Sungai Wain. The day of her re-introduction coincided with the inauguration of the new BOS open-air enclosure. However, Uce did not feel like celebrating—she felt miserable. The other seven orangutans that were to gain a new home in the forest area together with her had already disappeared into the thicket. However, Uce still sat on the roof of her cage and flung her long arms about herself as if she were looking for support. She was frightened of the new life in freedom.

Willie Smits took his fosterling into his arms, comforted and stroked her. Finally, he led her from the clearance into the forest, cut off a leaf of a plant, a member of the palm family with the botanical name of *Licuala repens,* and gave it to her as a good-bye present and comforter. She took it and went off. She managed to acclimatize well.

In October 1998, Smits met Uce again. He had visited her a few times after her release but for the last three and a half years had simply never found her again in the forest.

After the exchange of greetings, Uce pulled her rescuer by his hand into the forest. Determinedly, she went to a shrub of *Licuala repens,* bit off a leaf and held it out for him. Smits is certain: "She wanted to say that she had not forgotten what I had done for her!" Is this evidence of an excellent botanical memory—or of a lot more? Is this possibly a case of empathy, the ability to put yourself into the shoes of somebody else? According to Dutch primatologist Frans de Waal, "Empathy is part of our primate heritage. It is also the least studied topic in the world." Is an animal able to understanding the meaning of a symbol, and can it by means of such a symbol—in a roundabout way, so to speak—convey emotions? Is it possible at all for the animal to have the idea to do something so "human"? Or was it just coincidence?

The incredible occurrence with Uce's Polaroid photos (see pages 256ff) argues against this. As does Bruno's present (see page 272).

*Water games. Just as in Goethe's* Sorcerer's Apprentice, *the five-year-old male orangutan, resident in Ragunan Zoo in Jakarta, cannot control the waters that he summoned. He is playing and fighting with the spout of water coming out of a tap that is normally switched off.*

114

*Despite his enormous strength and the vise-like grip of his fingers the soaked ape does not manage to stop the floods coming out of the tap.*

*Ape-bath. As the water coming out of the tap is continually going in unexpected directions, the shaggy player in the water is getting wetter and wetter. When his efforts to stop the water using his immense strength fail—and embarrassingly he is watched in his failure—he starts 'washing' a towel, as he has seen the staff of the zoo do. The employees do not get that wet, though!*

118

# Ape culture

## Could this be possible?

*Eman has not understood yet, and gives the "other" orangutan a shy kiss. However, it only takes a few seconds for the four-year old primate, who lives in the BOS rehabilitation center at Wanariset and is now looking into the mirror for the very first time, to realize that he is kissing himself. He then understands and uses the new toy to inspect his teeth.*

According to the conception of Carel van Schaik, a very special driving force—culture—lies behind the intelligence of orangutans. In a simplified way, this means the ability to develop new behavior patterns which will become the common property of a whole group of apes and will be passed on in this population from generation to generation—exactly as happens in humans with the various forms of music and painting, architecture, language, and technology as created in various cultures.

With the red apes, too, technology is one of the key-words: by the invention—and non-genetic "inheritance"—of innovative processes and tools which enabled them to make use of new and especially nutritious food sources like the already mentioned neesia fruit (see page 44), especially clever apes secured an important evolutionary advantage for themselves.

Besides creativity, social intelligence and sociability are preconditions for this ape culture, which was for a small eternity identical with that of our animal ancestors. The Dutch anthropologist writes, "Now we know that the origins of orangutan culture date back around 14 million years, we can see that the cultural 'roots' of the humans also reach considerably further back into prehistoric times than one had imagined. Until now one had assumed that culture was an exclusive property of human beings and of chimpanzees, and that it was created about 7 million years ago," writes the Dutchman, then working at Duke University in Durham (North Carolina), in a spectacular series which was published by the magazine *Science* in January 1993.

(For an explanation: scientists believe that the ancestors of today's orangutans, who were also our predecessors and those of the chimpanzees, possessed even then the seeds of culture. Around 14 million years ago, the original orangutans branched off from the hitherto common hominid path; on the evolution highway to Africa they took the side road to Asia so to speak. By the 1960s, it was known that chimpanzees used simple tools. Today, some 40 different aids have been registered. Until the nineties, it was believed, however, that orangutans were completely ignorant in respect of craft and technology. One has to ask oneself: "Where were scientists looking all these years?"

And it is quite the same with wild gorillas: here, it was only at the beginning of 2005 that two of the apes in the Congo were observed with tools—a "depth gauge" for stretches of water and a "bridge" over a swampy patch. On the other hand, in the case of about 370 gorillas in an American zoo, scientist Tara Stoinski of Atlanta Zoo found 48 behavior patterns passed on via culture, amongst them the use of tools. As she told the news agency AP in February 2006, among other things, the apes used a stick for sliding apart charged electric wires—which were used (one can hardly believe it) to "protect" the trees in their enclosure—to get hold of the juicy bark.)

*Dexterity and long arms pay off for one of the inhabitants of the rehabilitation island, Kaja, in the province of Central Kalimantan, Borneo. He is fishing fruits out of the Gohong.*

*After dinner you should rest or walk one thousand steps. This two-year-old fatty is following this Roman wisdom. If you walk upright with your staff all that food will settle.*

But back to the social component of intelligence now: the passing on of technical inventions demands social contacts which—as described—are rare especially on Borneo because of the scanty food supply and the resulting solitary life-style. It is only in social groups that apes are able to copy the use of tools from other apes. It is not surprising that van Schaik discovered the use of tools in the fertile swamp rainforests of the Gunung Leuser National Park in northwest Sumatra, where the orangutan density was particularly high. It is almost incredible that this only happened in the mid-nineties.

The anthropologist believes that by studying the red ape, mysteries of our own past can be solved. He dreams of finding out what provided the impetus after millions of years of comparative stagnation for the sudden cultural leap made by the human race, which ultimately resulted in nuclear reactors and space travel. Did everything start with the invention of a primitive tool for the opening up of a new food source rich in proteins and fats?

Van Schaik's search for our own origins would end if the orangutans and their behavior patterns were to become extinct. "An animal's environment and its mental abilities merely set the scene. Any new techniques will only catch on once a threshold of relaxed social contact is reached and maintained." This underlined the susceptibility and sensitivity of primate culture and technology.

"Once a culture has become extinct, it may be lost forever." Reduced habitat quality due to selective logging may already be enough to send the orangutans back to the hominoid equivalent of the dark ages.

After the orangutan scientists had spent a long time collecting their data according to their own discretion and homemade guidelines, paying little attention to standardization and comparability, the eminent authorities on apes finally got together for the "Orangutans Compared" workshop in San Francisco from 14–17 February 2002. In his welcoming speech, the organizer, van Schaik, described the meeting as "overdue" and expressed his hope that the conference—the basis of the subsequent article in *Science*—would lead to an improvement in cooperation amongst the colleagues.

The scientists who had gathered here compared documented orangutan behavior patterns in six monitoring areas, four on Borneo, two on Sumatra, which they regarded as culturally handed down.

The result was spectacular: despite an admittedly fairly low monitoring intensity, the scientists had gathered 36 "behaviors". On Borneo, they counted 25 behavior patterns of which 12 occurred only on this, the third largest island of the world, and 24 on Sumatra, of which nine were observed only there. Fifteen "behaviors" were found on both islands.

Nineteen usages were concerned with tools and their utilization. Here too, Borneo led by eleven to seven, although international primatologists had for decades unanimously denied the local orangutans had any affinity for tools or capability of using them, and many still do so today. Willie Smits, however, has always claimed that the red apes were using "far more tools than chimpanzees," who, for whole groups of primatologists, represent the "tinkerers" amongst the giant apes.

Thirteen of the culturally handed down behavior patterns were concerned with eating and drinking, eight with the construction of

*One could be an eye-witness of evolution. The way in which the female ape Ingrid is walking upright with her baby Indonesia is identical to the reconstruction of the world-famous hominoid fossil 'Lucy,' discovered in East Africa by the famous Richard Leaky.*

*Having a bath with foam on the mouth. Orangutans that have been in the care of humans are far less shy of water than their wild counterparts—and they love soap. However, not as a cleansing material, but as a delicatessen. In the Tanjung Puting national park, and many other places, soap is stolen in abundance as a high-quality snack.*

nests and with sleep, five with body and fur care. Four were connected with play and showing off, three with the production of noises, two revolved around sex, and one was linked with hiding.

Here is a small selection of the most typical ape customs. The red primates from Tanjung Puting National Park gave dead wood a heavy shove and then slid downwards on the overthrown tree-trunks like children on banisters. Only just before the impact, did they bring themselves to safety. Others bit through lianas in order to make use of the loose end to swing boastfully, Tarzan-like, through the air.

In order to enhance the volume of their characteristic kiss-smacking, the primates used leaves, the palm of their hand, or their fist, forming an acoustic horn. They rolled leaves to make drinking straws, applied little sticks as "tin-openers" for termite nests in rotten wood, as "fruit knives", scratching tools and sex-toys, or for licking "insect lollipops". They made "gloves" from leaves which allowed them to touch prickly fruit, used them as ladles and drinking-sponges, and as napkins for wiping off latex juice from their mouths, and they rubbed their fur with leaves as with a face-cloth.

Carel van Schaik is convinced that the apes have understood the basic principles of construction. If they were not sure how long a tool had to be for the optimum fulfillment of its purpose—like for example the "honey spoon" which they used for scraping the

honey from honeycombs—they took a slightly too long little stick with them on their climbing excursion into the bee-tree. This meant: they were wholly aware of the fact that they could shorten their extraction instrument according to requirements, but not lengthen it.

"One hardly dares to imagine what they would be capable of if given a credit card and access to a DIY store," is the comment of Harold V. Cordry, professor at Baker University in Baldwin City (Kansas) on the research results of van Schaik. There is no better way to clothe a thought in words.

Cordry's reference to the narrow limits nature places on the inventiveness of the orangutan by offering him mainly bark, wood, or leaves as raw material for tools, reminds us of the deep sighs of a lot of dolphin researchers: "The things dolphins could achieve with their intelligence if they only had hands!"

It is certain that these 36 documented usages represent only a small fraction of utilizations which are customary amongst orangutans. Willie Smits is convinced that they only constitute ten percent of all "behaviors"—whether they are culturally handed down or not, which is often difficult to determine. In any case, the lion's share was not registered because first of all, the red apes are only comparatively rarely observed and, secondly, the whole approach is often inadequate.

The national and international professors staying in Indonesia to study the red primates, as a rule, only carried out a minute fraction of the observations themselves. "Of all the many hours of field research mentioned in the studies, the personal contribution of these scientists is usually very low as they leave the strenuous field work to their students and assistants." But a lack of general knowledge of the field

*The apes that have been released into the wild but continue to seek the proximity of humans learn useful traits from Homo sapiens sapiens. In Tanjung Puting, Princess, who is famous for her talent in imitation, is not only busy as a washerwoman, she also sweeps the floor wherever she goes or rests.*

*Performance ape-style. This three-year-old 'clown' is entertaining his compatriots with his comedy that he must have copied from the humans in whose care he has been.*

*Open-air culinary aesthetics. This female orangutan is preparing her midday snack in half a coconut shell as if she were preparing a salad platter in the Hilton. She is even using a fork, as the art demands.*

*Make-up imitation. Using wood meal from a rotting tree this young female is making a facemask. The majority of Indonesians do the same, using rice meal however, to protect their skin from the sun.*

The cook and the water-collector. The two orangutans (above and right) are exercising behavior patterns that they must have copied from humans. The majority of activities that are copied are women's duties—the men are often not at home.

A bath a day. Normally hygiene and body care are unknown among orangutans; however, this female has copied the activity from humans.

*In Camp Tuanan some ten scientists are working on several dozen studies concerned among other things with the culture of the orangutans. The camp is situated in the Mawas area assigned to BOS by the governor—377,000 hectares (1,455 square miles) in Central Kalimantan.*

of the following trips (see page 110), In other words: twice in a row, he observed something which local researchers had never seen before. They had, however, probably never lain in wait for as long as Ullal had.

Unyil's "fishing rope" is also a tool, and it is one of the most refined ones—but not mentioned in any study.

Anne Russon attests to the red ape "numerous" fashions and usages. "They are like us," the professor writes in one of her countless e-mails to me. "They possess a repertory of behaviors, but they can at any time, if required, think up new abilities and techniques."

"The use of tools which we have observed in the case of the orangutans in its complexity definitely does not range behind chimpanzees," van Schaik adds. "One orangutan female used 54 tools for insect hunting and 20 for fruit. Each of these was specially made for a certain task.

Two of the ape customs documented at the San Francisco conference gave me special food for thought, although they are in principle unspectacular and have nothing to do with nutrition or primate technology: the already mentioned "artistic cushions"—decorative twigs for adorning the sleeping nest—and the orangutan custom, likewise observed in Tanjung Puting, of pressing a bundle of foliage against them during their sleep as if it were a doll.

Cuddly primates with a sense of beauty? Is that possible at all? "But of course," says Willie Smits. He has found hints for a well-developed predilection for aesthetics on the part of the red apes. Orangutans enjoyed playing with soap bubbles and seemed fascinated by their opalescent and transient beauty. They loved water games, tried out a rudimentary kind of make-up where, for lack of other cosmetics, sludge had to serve as lipstick. They liked to decorate themselves with leaves and flowers and with great devotion admired their reflections.

The BOS chief even considers it possible that our red cousins pay attention to the quality of the panorama when they, high up in the branches of a jungle giant, select a place for their sleeping nest. Smits:

on the part of these latter might result in them quite missing out on the subtleties of the "behavior".

This is probably how we can explain why photographer Jay Ullal was immediately successful during his first trip to Indonesia (where he was all alone, taking pictures for this book) when he made spectacular photos on Kaja island near Nyaru Menteng of an orangutan custom which had never been either photographed or even described in the specialist literature—namely that of catching fish out of the air with the aid of a stick. Perfectionist Ullal discarded the first pictures and took an even better series during one

"It could be that they would like to have a nice view when they wake up in the mornings!" This is not an assumption but an observation: Smits climbed up into lots of nests in treetops and judged that most of the time not only was the view of top quality but that also their "breakfast" grew right in the vicinity.

A daring theory? Non-scientific enthusiasm? No, rather a consequence of numerous observations. Anne Russon is also certain that orangutans possess a sense of aesthetics. "Quite definitely they have a sense of order," she writes. "They like it nice and organized. They make a bundle of equally long little sticks and lay them out all neat and parallel." They like to adorn themselves with leaves or even human clothes, "and one has the impression that they are very conscious of their looks."

"As far as the primates' sense of art is concerned, there is no need for research. For example, it is worth analyzing and comparing the drawings and paintings of various giant ape species. They have different predilections for colors, shapes, and for the arrangement of picture elements."

However, it will probably take a long time until research is carried out in this field, according to Mrs Russon "only a marginal object", maybe only after the extinction of wild-living orangutans. Science may have struggled through to granting the apes intelligence and culture—but aesthetics? Why not even a soul?

Regardless of the realizations of zoologists, anthropologists, and primatologists who often cannot see in front of their nose on account of their "objective" and materialistic science, it must have meanwhile become obvious to the reader what exceptional creatures orangutans are—and that we know frighteningly little about them.

While I have restricted myself to the physiology of our "co-apes" and have tried, despite a lack of research data, to convey an impression of their intelligence. Willie Smits has described the character and nature of the orangutan in his contribution "Psychograph of a Primate".

After all, even politically correct primatology grants our ape cousins the existence of a character. Benjamin Beck, curator of Washington National Zoo, has captured the nature of the red ape in a short but true story: "If you put a screwdriver into the cage of a gorilla, a chimpanzee, and an orangutan, the gorilla gets frightened, squats for a long time, scared, in his corner, then approaches the screwdriver only after a few hours—and tries to eat it. The chimpanzee immediately throws himself onto the toy, does a lot of silly things with it—and finally throws it away. The orangutan, however, starts by feigning lack of interest, then, sometime, he will hide the screwdriver—and unscrew the lock of the cage during the night."

Anne Russon has encountered personalities among the orangutans which differ in the same way as among human beings: witty, sulky, playful, loud, and gentle apes as well as lazy and workaholic, downright stupid, and studious ones. There can be few, if any, character traits which are found only amongst apes or only amongst humans.

*The researchers also study the eating habits of orangutans. Here we can see the fruits that one of the apes would eat in a day.*

*Laura is fascinated. In amazement the red ape, who is on one of the BOS islands in Samboja Lestari as she is suffering from chronic hepatitis, is looking at a digital photo that shows her with Willie Smits. The orangutans have no problems interpreting photos.*

*The Bagangtung BOS camp is connected by the longest wooden bridge in the world with Camp Tuanan, 23 kilometers (14 miles) away. The bridge was made from the wood of fallen trees. Chemicals from the decomposition of peat have colored the water nearly black.*

However, let us return to Willie Smits: I do not know anybody as qualified as he is to speak about the psyche of orangutans. Luckily, he is no primatologist, and his view is not barred by academic blinkers. He regards the apes as fellow-beings and not as experimental subjects, and he reports what he has seen—even those seemingly "unscientific" things like our red relatives' behavior patterns, traits of character and abilities which do not fit into the rigid pattern of zoology or a related science.

Or emotions. These are often swept under the carpet, on grounds summed up in verse by the German comic poet Christian Morgenstern: "For, they reason pointedly / That which must not, cannot be." "Students of animal behavior are urged to steer clear of emotions," wrote Dutch scientist Frans de Waal, professor of primate behavior at Emory University in Atlanta, Georgia, in the journal *Seed* at the end of 2005: "they would rather let their rats press down levers than attempt to find out what the rodents feel!"

But how do we cope with these sensitive and peaceful animals who are so similar to us, with what Anne Russon certifies to be "a much more complex intellect than we have ever experienced"? How do we treat the red apes who—according to the psychologist—make science wonder why they are so "mild" and so little resentful?

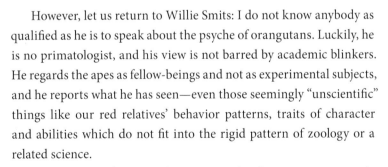

*Masturbation in the open. This three-year-old ape girl is fingering herself with a lot of concentration.*

130

*Facemask. Nobody knows why they do
this: the apes often smear earth and
other natural products into their faces.
Maybe they like playing Zorro…*

132

69, gay fellatio—you name it. Orangutans are intelligent mammals, and no sexual practice is unknown to them.

*Hopefully nobody is looking... If an orangutan male cannot find a partner, he may have to do the job himself.*

*Left: Swinging with the shade. On the island Palas, Central Kalimantan, this young ape lady is swinging backwards and forwards on lianas and is watching the shape of her shadow change on the surface of the water. A great-ape performance.*
*Above: Mirror mirror on the wall… In fascination, this four-year-old female is looking at her reflection in the water. Can orangutans be vain?*

*Left: Is this about aesthetics or fluid dynamics? For an hour this orangutan female has been studying how the water moves, gurgles and splashes.*
*Above: The circles of Archimedes. Highly concentrated, this shaggy scientist is watching how rings are formed in the water and how*
*they cross and fade. The researcher chooses several different dropping heights and various amounts of water.*

# From bush meat to a 50,000-dollar export article

## The history of a genocide

*Barbaric display. This 'window display' in a shop in Surabaya, the second-biggest town on the island of Java, proves the uselessness of laws that are only valid on paper, as their implementation is of little interest to the authorities. As in many towns orangutan meat is on sale; people, mainly Chinese, believe it increases their vigor. Using grisly trophies such as heads and hands the salesmen seek to prove the authenticity of their cannibalistic goods.*

Orangutans have few enemies—the remaining Sumatra tigers, clouded leopards, boas, Asiatic wild dogs, and wild pigs. And of course: humans. They are the ones who have been hunting them from time immemorial, who have killed them and eaten them as if they were not our "cousins" but just very ordinary bush meat like deer, hare or pot-bellied pig. According to Grzimek, the red primates have "for at least 35,000 years" ended on the spit or in the cooking pot of southeast Asian huntsmen. It was probably due to "overhunting by early *homo sapiens*" that no orangutans exist on Java any more.

Beside a fancy for ape meat—as Kathy MacKinnon further reports in Grzimek—later in time, a male ritual of the head-hunting Dayak tribe also brought about a bloodbath amongst the apes. As the white colonial rulers had forbidden the Dayaks to collect human skulls and trophies, the headhunters sought a legal substitute for a courage test. Young warriors who wanted to prove their manhood did not kill the inhabitants of the neighboring villages any more but measured their strength against an adult orangutan instead.

As they would not have had a chance against this opponent in a fair fight, the Dayak, according to the report, played a trick. The warrior stretched out his hand to the ape as if in greeting. If the orangutan took it, the Dayak slashed his machete into the arm of the animal—and used the confusion of the injured primate to deal him a deadly blow.

Despite hunting and male rituals, ape figures declined only very gradually. It was not until the middle of the second half of

*Ghastly souvenirs. The market men make Dayak head-trophies of orangutans—'authenticity guaranteed'—for ignorant tourists. The grisly skulls are even found on eBay. As proven by the pronounced bony ridge in the center of the skull, many of the victims were big orangutan males.*

My house, my car, my ape… In addition to the luxury villa and the Mercedes, a tame orangutan is mandatory as a status symbol of the Indonesian who has 'made it' and wants to show this off. The young primates that have been stolen from the jungle are stuffed with sweets and Coke and are raised to be chain-smokers. Everybody thinks it is chic when the clever creature jingles on the piano. When the 'pet' gets too big and strong it is locked away in a metal cage that stands in a dark back yard.

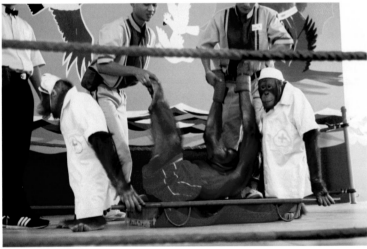

*Knock-out in round two. Two hundred orangutans are kidnapped out of the forests every year to be clowns in amusement parks and to provide cheap entertainment, such as here in 'Sea World', on the beach of northern Jakarta. Unfortunately, a lot of schoolchildren are watching the spectacle. The troupe of a dozen ape boxers, paramedics, ring-card-girls and referees was confiscated in the mid-2006 by BOS and brought to the Samboja Lestari rehabilitation center.*

the last century that three catastrophes befell the red apes in quick succession, which melted their numbers like ice-cream under the hot sun of Kalimantan.

The disaster started in the seventies with an increasing demand for small orangutans which got more and more out of hand. It did not take long until it was fashionable in society circles and in the officer corps of the Indonesian armed forces and police to show off with one of the oh-so-cute animals as a housemate. The red show-off objects were mothered, they were stuffed with sweets, filled with Coke, chauffeured through the streets on the passenger seat and given a light if they wanted to smoke.

If their owners could not control them, they were locked away. Most of the time, the former pets ended in some dark backyard where they had to spend the rest of their lives in a much too small cage or were sold to orangutan butchers for meat.

Orangutans as domestic animals, toys, and substitutes for children became an almost everyday sight. And there were certainly people who were prepared to carry cruelty to extremes. They made circus clowns out of the good-natured creatures and silly monkeys for stage shows, they kept them as sex slaves, shut them up in brothels and had them appear in US gay porn movies.

The misery of the animals was great and it often went on for many years; the blood toll during the catching, transport, and keep-

ing of the entertainer apes was high. However, it was far surpassed by the bloodbath which went along with the extensive destruction of the rainforests by ruthless and illegal logging as well as by slash-and-burn clearance in the eighties and nineties. The killing has even picked up speed once more and—since the turn of the millennium—has almost reached an apocalyptic extent with the explosive expansion of the oil palm plantations. What started as a hunt for pets has taken on the appearance of a genocide.

Borneo is the best example of the speed with which destruction closed in on both orangutan islands, and the extent which this destruction reached. The rainforest habitat—the orangutans' living room and bedroom, larder and pharmacy—disappeared so fast that it resembled the end of the world. Think of the oceans being drained

*Author with ape. Gerd Schuster with a young orangutan that BOS saved from a 'career' as clown boxer, child-ersatz or prestige-pet. It is good fun when one of the small rascals in the center of rehabilitation climbs up you as if you were a tree. But it is recommended you keep a tight grip on your cell phone, notebook, pen, hat, and glasses.*

The "Jungle Breakfast" attraction was a magnet for the public and brought a lot of money to the zoo in Singapore. However, for part of the cast it was deadly: many of the breakfast apes fell ill, some even died. After protests by BOS the zoological garden stopped the show in 2006.

143

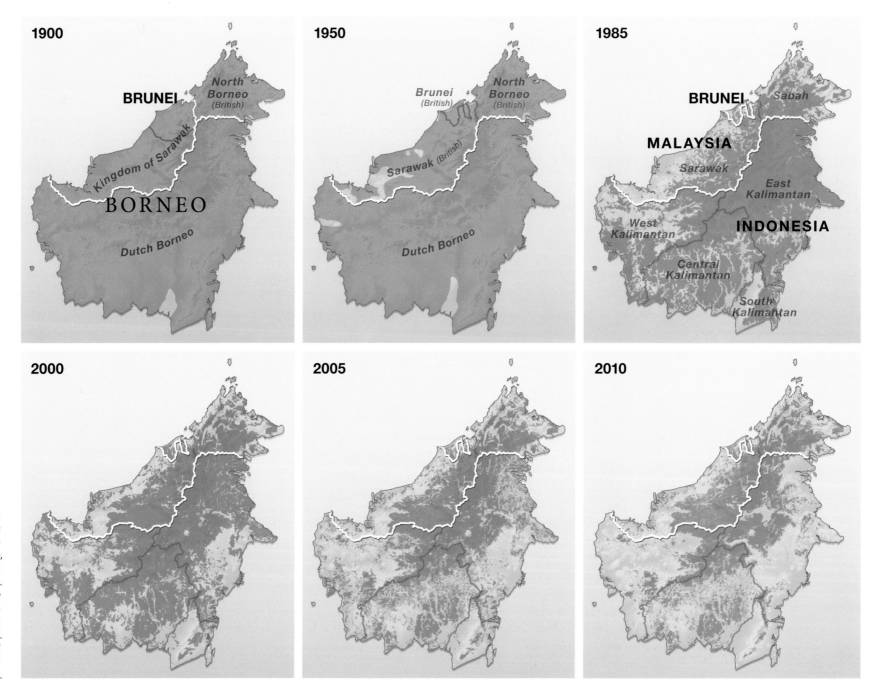

**1900**

BRUNEI

North Borneo *(British)*

*Kingdom of Sarawak*

BORNEO

*Dutch Borneo*

**1950**

*Brunei (British)*

North Borneo *(British)*

*Sarawak (British)*

*Dutch Borneo*

**1985**

BRUNEI

*Sabah*

MALAYSIA

*Sarawak*

*East Kalimantan*

*West Kalimantan*

INDONESIA

*Central Kalimantan*

*South Kalimantan*

**2000**

**2005**

**2010**

*Documentation of a decline. The WWF has mapped the continuous deforestation of Borneo, which has recently taken on ever-faster proportions. The green spots are mainly mountain forests and steep hills whose exploitation is not (yet) economical. Practically all lowland rainforests have fallen victim to chainsaw and fire.*

Martial masquerade. Often the police are nowhere to be seen when they are needed in the Indonesian rainforest. Instead of protecting the forest they restrict their activities to occasionally posing for photos. This officer is having his photo taken standing with his sub-machine gun next to a protected, yet felled Ramin tree. The 'operation', in which just one poor tree-thief was caught, only occurred because the foreign press happened to be present.

145

*Boredom and frustration. Daily life for orangutans in Singapore Zoo is spent being stared at and photographed.*

and its effect on the dolphins, and you have some idea of the disaster which befell the orangutans.

Even in the mid-1960s, Borneo was completely covered with rainforest and until the 1980s, the jungle was still two-thirds intact (see maps page 144). Between 1985 and 2005, however, the island—according to a WWF study—lost about 850,000 ha (3,280 square miles) of rainforest per year. In total, this amounts to about 17 million ha (66,000 square miles) which corresponds to the total area of Florida! By late 2005/ early 2006, half of Borneo was deforested. During the devastating forest fires of 1997 and 1998, one single major fire destroyed five million ha (20,000 square miles) of jungle and killed one-third of all the orangutans on the island. About 40 percent of the global $CO_2$ emissions at that time came from the burning jungles of Indonesia.

After the turn of the millennium, the deforestation speed increased: between 2000 and 2002, 1.3 million ha (5,000 square miles) of jungle disappeared every 12 months, this equals 148 ha (more than half a square mile) per hour or 2.5 ha (6 acres) per minute!

The living space of the approximately 50,000 orangutans that still live in the Indonesian provinces of West, East, and Central Kalimantan as well as in the Malaysian districts of Sabah and Sarawak, was totally fragmented by the beginning of 2006. The red apes lived—like castaways on an island in the ocean—in about 300 more or less small forest islands. The population of most of these areas amounted to less than 250 animals and was therefore too low to allow them long-term survival, even if

*Hunters of the lost apes. This palm oil worker is making some cash on the side by shooting desperate and half-starved orangutans that have sought refuge in his plantation.*

tree-felling and persecution suddenly stopped by some miracle.

However, the chain-saws carry on screeching, and the miserable patchwork carpet will soon be completely tattered. By 2010—an estimate by the WWF—all lowland rainforests will be cut down or burned: a death sentence for the red apes.

But not only the shaggy kings of the jungle die. Together with them (something which is often brushed under the carpet), an unparalleled variety of species will become extinct. According to the WWF study *Treasure Island in Danger*, the still intact rainforests of Borneo are home to 222 species of mammals, around 400 reptile and amphibian species (amongst them 166 snakes) as well as 420 sedentary species of birds, 19 species of fish and 40 of butterflies are endemic here; they exist here and here only.

No less breathtaking is the wealth of the flora: according to the report, the last untouched jungles of the gigantic island—around the size of Tennessee, North and South Carolina, Georgia, Alabama, and Mississippi together—harbor about 15,000 different flowering plants, amongst them more than 2,000 kinds of orchids and about 1,000 ferns. About 5,000 of the flowering plants, of which up to 240 species could be found on just one hectare (2.5 acres), are endemic. Around 3,000 tree species are scattered over ecologically unique forest biotopes—swamp forest, heathland forest, peat bog forest as well as winged-fruit forests in which the most venerable, oldest and most precious jungle giants prosper, the *dipterocarpacea* (winged-fruit trees), among which are the trees which provide the bangirai and meranti timber known in the West. About 155 of the tree species grow on Borneo only. By comparison: about 66 tree species have been counted in Germany, only six of them endemic.

However spectacular the number of species may be, they still do not do justice to reality, as there are whole genera of animals which no scientist's eye has ever spied. Solely between 1994 and 2004—despite the inexorable destruction—361 new species of animals and plants were discovered on Borneo. In 2005, WWF associates even photographed a hitherto unknown linsang species. With certainty, numerous plants and animals will be eradicated forever before any scientist can document their existence.

In their study, the WWF do not neglect to point out the great abundance of native tribes on Borneo which would be decimated or—like the orangutans—exterminated during further deforestation of the island.

On Sumatra, the situation is even more serious than on Borneo: here, 70 percent of the forest covering has already disappeared—and with it about 90 percent of the lowland rainforests, the habitat of the orangutan. Soon their last remnant in the north and northwest will have disappeared.

During the fifteen years between 1990 and 2005, the number of the red jungle kings of the island decreased by half, and it continues to shrink by 10 percent per year. By the beginning of 2006, only about 7,000 were left. According to the PHVA study their remaining living-space amounts to less than 9,000 km² (3,000 square miles), which is less than two percent of the area of Sumatra (473,480 km² or 182,812 square miles). According to the study, only seven of the remaining 13 populations hold more than 250 animals and could therefore be preserved for a few decades providing trees and apes were left in peace from now on.

But no such luck: in six of the seven territories, among them the largest orangutan populations in West and East Leuser as well as Singkil, every year, the chain saws of the illegal loggers get rid of 10 to 15 percent of the living space of the apes. There is a tiny glimmer of hope for the ape population of West Batang Toru. Here, the decimation

rate "only" amounts to two percent. The consequence: this population will exist longer than the others will, but will also be destroyed.

And this is the result of study which rates the future prospects of the Sumatran Orangutan as "extremely bleak". Probably, only a few years will remain for the animals.

This "galloping consumption" has reached such a dramatic pace that one can hardly keep pace in writing with the speed with which the red apes are being slaughtered, and that a lot of data is already antiquated when the printing machines start up. As a consequence of the destruction of the rainforest, which has got completely out of hand, there is a sheer glut of apocalyptic information on the territories which are being felled or which are subject to slash-and-burn land clearance. The figures range from 2.2 million to 5 million hectares (8,500 to 20,000 square miles).

Regardless of the correctness of the information (no one has very exact figures anyway) about which forest territories of this gigantic country fall victim to the chain saws during one calendar year, Indonesia has one of the highest deforestation rates in the world.

Outlining this criminal, abysmally stupid and self-destructive outrage with figures is truly depressing. However, it is at least the duty of the chronicler to give a brief description of the second catastrophe which has befallen the orangutans in the shape of whole armies of wood-cutters, because it is closely connected with the first (the ani-

*An honest fighter for the animals, Yunus Tondok, former head of the forestry police in Jakarta (above: in front of a load of confiscated animals; below: at his place of work). The 55-year-old policeman and lawyer was often the target of terrorist attacks from the animal mafia. The efficient Yunus has been neutralized as he was too inconvenient for the powerful.*

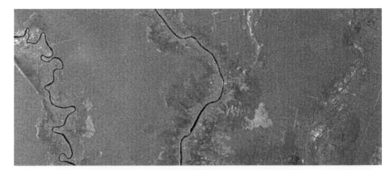

Decimation due to megalomania. President Suharto wanted to impress the FAO, so he had about one million hectares (4,000 square miles) of rainforest felled in 1996 to plant rice. The satellite images show the area in 1994 and 1997. As was predicted by the experts the huge project failed miserably. What remains is a desert (below).

*There goes the forest. On huge pontoons the vegetation of massive areas of forest is taken away. Orangutans and countless other animals used to live in these areas. The criminal overexploitation is supposed to still the hunger for wood in Java, and, when smuggled to Europe, Japan and China, to make the plunderers rich.*

*At the edge of most larger rivers in Borneo are countless sawmills, most of which are closed. The few that remain, such as this one at the Kapuas, close to the village Mantangai in Central Kalimantan, have to work on trees that are matchsticks compared to the forest giants from previous times. They come from the remaining forests that are now being totally destroyed.*

148

This drained and wrecked area in Central Kalimantan used to be, not so long ago, marshy rainforest, the home of countless animals and plants. In addition, they functioned as a store for water, which prevented floods further downstream. Now the thick layer of peat on which the forest giants used to stand is decomposing and large amounts of greenhouse gases are being released into the atmosphere. Such a large area of forest ruin brings misery and suffering to hundreds of thousands of villagers.

Villagers close to the tim
hamlet of Petak Putih wor
for a pittance to be woo
thieves and drivers. As
'bonus' they can suffer th
ecological consequences of th
deforestation—fire, smoke, ar
floods. The big money goe
to the unscrupulous woo
barons in the big citie

*Laws have no validity even for lawmakers. This Indonesian MP is keeping a large ape as a member of his household, even though it has been strictly forbidden to do so since 1942.*

*Pony was kept captive for years in Central Kalimantan. This photo shows the ape when she was freed, horribly obese and her entire body shaven. Since she has been living in the BOS center at Nyaru Menteng, she has slimmed down and her hair has grown back.*

mal trade) and the third (the palm oil boom), and overlaps with the other disasters.

In a nutshell, the publications of renowned institutions like the World Bank, the London Environmental Investigation Agency (EIA), which has published several first-rate studies on the subject, and serious environmental groups like the WWF, present the situation as follows: the illegal cutting of timber in all remaining forested islands, even in the national parks, has got completely out of control. At local, provincial, and national levels, corrupt government officials—unpunished for their deeds—enter into business with illegally cut wood. Police and military groups earn their bit, too, by protecting the tree thieves and by trade on their own account: according to the EIA study *Final Cut Update,* members of the military forces for a long time illegally moved around 100,000 m³ (3.5 million cubic feet) of tropical wood per month from East Kalimantan to its Malaysian neighbor East Sabah.

About 70 percent of the wood which is cut and processed in Indonesia originates from illegal sources. Year after year, millions of cubic metres are smuggled abroad where intermediaries profit from the immense increase in the value of the wood on export markets like Europe and the USA. For Indonesia, the country of origin,

*The ape traders show no shame and have no scruples when offering their illegal goods at the side of a road or a riverbank. The police turn a blind eye. If the officials do bother to go on an assignment, they make sure they get some extra on the side.*

apart from the destruction of the environment and its consequences, only scraps remain. The country is squandering its wealth. According to EIA investigations, the men with the chainsaws only receive two to three dollars per cubic meter (35 cubic feet) of luxury wood which can earn more than 1,000 dollars in the United States. According to a World Bank study, the developing countries lose national wealth to the value of ten to 15 billion dollars annually by illegal tree-felling.

The government in Jakarta has promised to cut out the illegal tree-felling in national parks but has not kept this promise and has not taken proceedings against "wood barons" like the filthy-rich Abdul Rasyid whose chain-saws have shredded large parts of Tanjung Putin National Park on Borneo. All attempts on the part of the Indonesian government to stop the smuggling, e.g. by quota regulations, for the trade in the luxury wood, ramin, have remained fruitless, as has the incorporation of the tree into Appendix III of the Washington Convention on International Trade in Endangered Species of Wild Fauna and Flora (CITES) in 2001.

The fault does not lie solely in widespread corruption and the fact that really good-willed and committed forestry ministers—those exist, too—often had brakes applied by their bureaucracy, but also in the fact that the buying countries did not support the Indonesian protection efforts, or even undermined them. Thus, the West has carried on encouraging imports of the "blond" ramin although the Indonesian government had imposed a trade prohibition. Another official Indonesian request has also been blessed with little success: the boycott of ramin sourced allegedly from Malaysia.

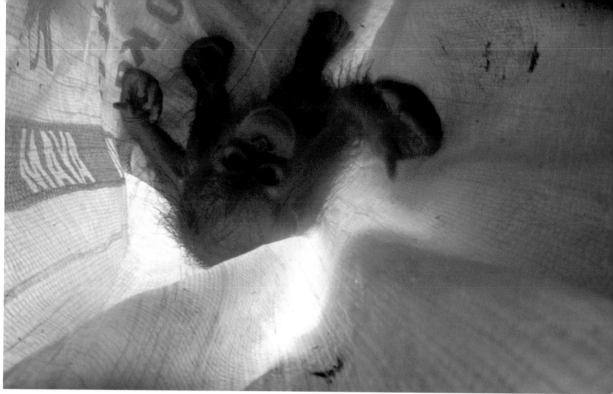
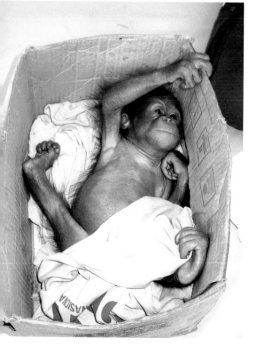

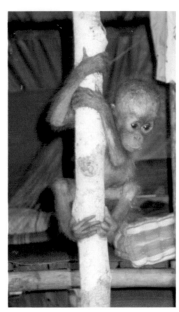

*Scenes of a hunt in an area of palm oil plantation. The misery of the apes that fall into the hands of the plantation workers is indescribable. Eyes that have been shot out, half-starved trading goods, a baby that is clinging on to the corpse of his mother, are an everyday occurrence.*

*BOS staffer Eko alone has rescued over 400 orangutans from human hands. The red apes were mostly kept in tiny dark cages.*

*You would not keep a chicken in a coop like this. Many orangutan babies kept in such conditions die before they can be sold or rescued.*

"Not a single one of the consumer countries has passed a bill which would make it possible for the criminal prosecution authorities to confiscate such deliveries of wood which are known to be illegal," states the EIA Report *Timber Trafficking*. The conclusion of the study: "By ignoring the problem, the consumer countries are becoming accomplices of the corrupt wood barons."

Germany must also take its share of the blame as the Federal Government has up till now assiduously ignored the demands of organizations for species protection like Pro Wildlife to enact a law for jungle protection in order to put the kibosh on the trade with tropical wood from the robber economy. But individual countries need to take action, said the Munich group on the International Day of Biodiversity on 22 May 2006, as the European Union was handling this matter "irresponsibly".

This was documented by spokeswoman Sandra Altherr as follows: On the one hand, the European Union passed directive no. 2173/2005 at the end of 2005 which was intended to combat the import of illegally cut wood. The weighty document, however, "was completely inadequate" as it merely provided for "voluntary agreements" with five countries of origin. For the tropical wood from all other countries, the gates of the European Union further remained wide open.

*The police, your friend and animal torturer. This official had tied his illegal pet so tightly to a rattan chair that the stalk grew into the flesh of the animal. When he was cut loose the baby bled heavily.*

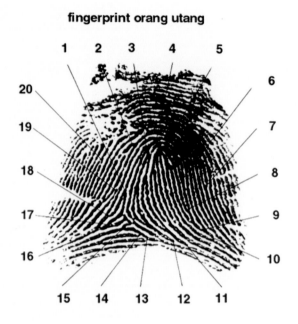

**fingerprint orang utang**

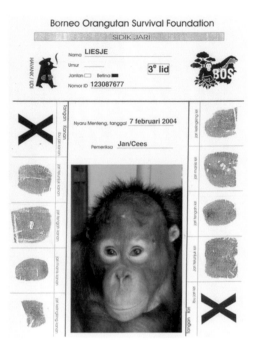

**Borneo Orangutan Survival Foundation**

SIDIK JARI

Nama **LIESJE**
Umur _____
Jantan ☐  Betina ■   **3e lid**
Nomor ID **123087677**

Nyaru Menteng, tanggal **7 februari 2004**
Pemeriksa **Jan/Cees**

*Using modern tracking techniques BOS is trying to stop the illegal trade in orangutans. The organization uses fingerprints, 'passport photos' and microchip implants for this purpose.*

It is also highly debatable whether "voluntary agreements"—known to be the shakiest of all shaky measures—will disturb in the slightest the well-organized timber mafia, which is willing to resort to violence and which is supported by politicians and the military.

When one learns about the kind of export goods the wonderful rainforest is being destroyed for, one feels sickened, because the trees in which orangutans and thousands of other animals and plants once lived are ending up as dowels, curtain rails, shutters and blinds, picture and window frames, parquet flooring, bedsteads, furniture, plywood yard goods, billiard cues, broom-sticks and toilet seats in our stores. As a rule, these items could be produced without loss of quality from oak, beech, and other native wood.

*Molecular biology can also help protect the animals. Using genetic fingerprints, which can be made from hair, bodily fluids and feces, the identity of individual animals can be established without a doubt.*

*Forced exile in Thailand. Hundreds of red apes are smuggled into the country. Despite the efforts of animal rights activists so far only a few dozen have been freed.*

*BOS is using a poster to raise awareness of the plight of kidnapped orangutans in Thailand.*

159

# The oil which nobody knows

## The palm oil boom and the end of the last rainforests

*It looks as if napalm bombs have hit the areas in which the palm oil companies are at work. Slash and burn is illegal in Indonesia; however, the fires that are started anyway eat up substantially larger areas than the concessions—which are often obtained through corruption—specify. Should one choose to believe the companies, the fires have started "purely by chance".*

The effects our consumer behavior can have on far distant ecological and social systems without our being conscious of it become even more transparent when we take the case of palm oil.

The fat which no consumer knows is gained from the plum-size fruit of the African oil palm *(Elaeis guineensis)*. In 2005, it became for the first time the world's most important plant oil after overtaking the front-runner soy oil with a production of 33.5 million tons.

Elaeis guineensis is an economic blockbuster: according to the WWF, no other domestic plant produces as much oil per hectare as the fast-growing and 20 m (65 ft) high tree, which allows first harvests just three years after planting.

Unfortunately for the orangutans, the "useful crop of the year" (dpa) only flourishes in the plain, the habitat of the lowland rainforests; at levels of 300 m (1000 ft), there is already a drastic decrease in yield.

The infructescences of the oil palm, often an agglomeration of several thousand fruits, are cut off and sterilized by steam in order to render harmless an enzyme which would make the palm oil rancid.

After the fruit is broken up and boiled, the oil is pressed from the pulp and then clarified. During this process, floods of waste water with a high proportion of organic matter occur, which during decomposing release gigantic amounts of the greenhouse gas methane.

Palm oil—colored orange-red by carotenes—is solid at room temperature, smells like violets and tastes pleasantly sweet. From the kernels, which are mechanically reduced to small pieces, the expensive palm kernel oil is gained. The residue of the pressing is called palm kernel grist and is sold as animal feed.

Palm oil is in thousands of everyday products. It is found in frying and cooking oils as well as in margarine, mayonnaise, ice-cream, chocolates and sweets, soups, flavorings, instant meals, bread and cakes, cosmetics, lipsticks, soap and other personal hygiene items, in candles, detergents, and cleaning agents, well, even in the milling grease for the production of the thinnest steel plate.

In 2005, Germany imported 887,300 tons of palm oil and, according to the information given by the Hamburg trade information service Oil World, occupied sixth place in the world and second place in the EU. As for palm kernel fat (imported quantity: 298,300 t), Germany is the international front runner in imports. 426,700 tons of palm kernel grist also have to be added.

But why does nobody know these fats? "Palm oils are so little known because, although omnipresent, they are hidden," says Markus

*A drop in the ocean. It looks spectacular and media-effective when planes and helicopters fight the fire. However, their efforts are useless. Often the flames are burning in thousands of places at once.*

*In the wake of the palm oil plantation comes an invasion of opportunist thieves who steal the remaining trees.*

Radday, who is charge of tropical forests at WWF Germany in Frankfurt. A forestry engineer, he is an author of studies on the ecological consequences of palm oil production, including the study *Deforestation for Breakfast.*

The exotic fats did not enter into the awareness of the consumers as there is no labeling obligation for them and because frequently it is not the original fat but chemicals produced from it that are used, for example "washing-active substances" for cleaning agents. One could, however, stick to the rule of thumb: "Wherever it says vegetable fat, in all probability it contains palm oil!"

"Definitely more than 80 percent of German imports," says Radday, stem from ecocidal cultivation: "We obtain 90 percent of our palm oil from Indonesia and Malaysia, and it is only in Malaysia that there are first tentative attempts at making production beneficial for the environment."

Switzerland has been much more progressive than Germany in this respect: about half of the Swiss imports originate from sustainable sources in Ghana or Columbia. The overall premium of the "good fat" is currently between ten and 20 percent, but the Migros concern, who started the initiative, want to push this down to zero.

Even the most hard-boiled consumer would have trouble with his potato chips and mayonnaise if he were to be shown the cruel ecological and social consequences of the palm oil boom: on Borneo and Sumatra, endless oil palm lines are spreading out like a deadly disease. In 1985, there were about 600,000 ha (2,300 square miles), in 1998

about 2.2 million (8,500 sq mi), in 2000 over 3 million (11,500 sq mi), and in 2005 already more than 6.5 million ha (25,000 square miles) of oil palms were covering former jungle soil. According to WWF information, a further 3.5 million hectares (13,500 square miles) of lowland rainforest were ruined during the establishment of the plantations.

WWF gives a laconic account of the procedure: "Normally, plantations are set up after the tree species which can be used in the timber industry have been cut down. After this, the remaining stock and the waste wood are burned in order to clear the area for the cultivation of fast-growing tree species, like acacia or oil palms. Sometimes, the fires get out of control, either deliberately or unintentionally, and they destroy expansive areas—not only the license areas of the plantations—as was the case during most forest fires in Indonesia in 1997/8."

At the same time, the application of slash-and-burn land clearance for obtaining plantation land has been forbidden since 1995, with a penalty of 15 years' imprisonment and a fine of $ 500,000. But nobody takes any notice of this law. The Ministry of Agriculture and Forestry has investigated the cases of 176 plantation and forestry enterprises—amongst them 133 oil plantation companies—because there had been fires on their concessions, but only five have been charged.

The plantations in which the monumental stumps of the felled jungle giants frequently still project out of the ground are green deserts in which no bird flies and no lizard creeps. Quite often, half-starved orangutans—often fleeing from unstoppable forward-moving wood-cutter gangs—lose their way in the oil plantations where nothing edible exists for them apart from the marrow of palm-trunks, and get gunned down as vermin when they tear the trees apart.

The people also suffer. The smoke from the burning jungles makes them sick. They suffer from thirst as together with the forest, their

*And when the locusts have moved on... When the loggers of the large companies have done their job and the palm oil saplings have been planted, the area looks like a battlefield. Incessantly the volcano of carbon dioxide, inherent in every palm oil plantation on marshy ground, is emitting vast quantities of greenhouse gases.*

*When night falls the forests burn. Under cover of darkness the palm oil companies start fires at the edges of plantations to enlarge their area of cultivation illegally and cost-effectively. As the authorities turn a blind eye a team from BOS (white off-road vehicle) is present to take on displaced animals.*

In his work, Willie Smits has described the "typical" downfall of a community losing "their" jungle, describing the fall and resurrection of Samboja Lestari (page 300f.).

However, there is currently a gold rush going on, and the name of the gold is palm oil. Although on Borneo and Sumatra hardly anybody profits from the boom, everyone is seized by its fever, and nobody spares a thought for apes, humans, or ecology any more. On Sumatra, a further 1.6 million ha (6,000 square miles) of jungle are due to be cleared, a million more on Borneo. According to industrial planning, the plantation area is to be extended to 16.5 million ha (64,000 sq mi) by 2020: plus 250 percent. The capital without which the vast expansion and the accompanying destruction of the rainforest would be impossible mainly comes from Europe, North America, and the Far East, according to WWF.

Those euros, dollars and yen are financing an ecological catastrophe of the worst kind. "We have already lost huge areas of orangutan habitat and tens of thousands of orangutans to the palm oil industry," complains Ian Singleton, Director of the Sumatra Orangutan Conservation Programme, "and we are losing many many more!" The loss of orangutans, mainly in Kalimantan, has never been greater than in the past three years," seconds Willie Smits, "and this is first and foremost to be blamed on the oil palm plantations!"

According to Singleton, the Indonesian government plans to set up the largest oil palm plantation in the world. In the course of this, an approximately 845-kilometer (525-mile) "oil palm fence" would be developed along the border to Malaysia, and lowland rainforests planned as orangutan protection zones would be destroyed. These biotopes are among the most biodiverse regions in Southeast Asia and are the home of numerous red apes. Singleton: "The problem really is an immense one."

Immense also is the responsibility of those who are financing the disaster. Unfortunately these are not just greedy insatiable millionaires

wells and streams also disappear, and they are hungry because forest fruit and meat from jungle animals is not available any more. Fish are also rare because the waste water from the palm oil factories has converted many rivers into sewers.

The often-heard argument that oil palms bring employment is wrong. There are studies according to which only 0.12 jobs are created per hectare (0.3 per acre) of plantation, and these are badly paid and dangerous because of the splashing-about with poison. Mechanization means these jobs will also soon disappear.

*Every pyromaniac's dream. Funnily enough, the fires mostly start at night when there are no patrols about.*

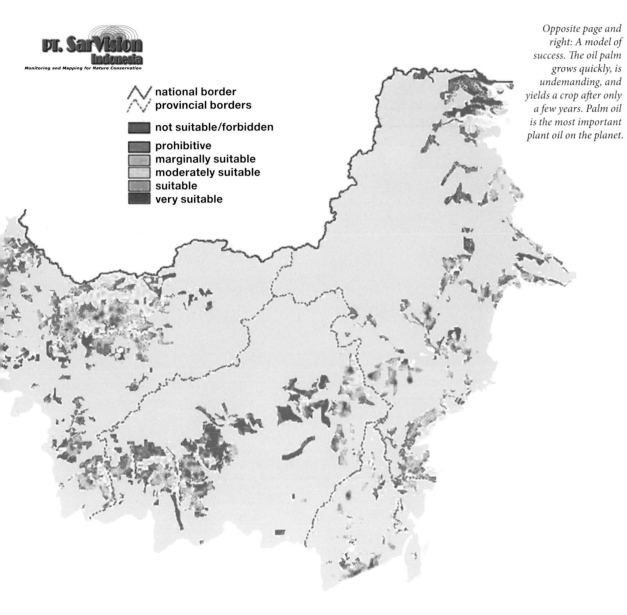

national border
provincial borders

not suitable/forbidden
prohibitive
marginally suitable
moderately suitable
suitable
very suitable

*Opposite page and right: A model of success. The oil palm grows quickly, is undemanding, and yields a crop after only a few years. Palm oil is the most important plant oil on the planet.*

*Proof over and over. New oil palms are planted in areas where the lie of the land is unsuitable, and that do not have the climatic conditions and altitude appropriate for this crop, and therefore do not provide an economical yield of oil (red areas). These areas are the home of the last orangutans. Only a few concessions are on suitable ground (green areas). The huge areas of grassland along the coast that are prime soil for palm oil plantations are ignored by the companies. One cannot steal valuable wood in areas where only alang-alang grass grows.*

Big capital and exploitation. The palm oil companies heap money into their machine parks, but they are stingy when it comes to wages. The workers are paid a pittance for their hard and often dangerous job (often they are exposed to pesticides without protective gear). Their wage is frequently significantly below the minimum wage.

*When the rainforest was still standing there was water in abundance. Today the local population (in the picture a typical Dayak longhouse) has to rely on trickles of water polluted with herbicides.*

who couldn't care less about ecology or orangutans, but, indirectly and involuntarily, you too, the readers of this book, and we, the authors.

"How come?" you ask. The explanation is sad and sobering, and it casts some light on the poor quality of our environmental policies. The associations seeking to combat this perversion of environmental protection deserve far more support.

The fact that Germans are among the most enthusiastic buyers of palm oil has been mentioned already. What is new is that the oil for which orangutans are dying has been in use for some time now not just for food and cosmetics, but as a fuel. Its use as heating oil is spreading throughout Europe at a breathtaking speed.

In Germany too, of course. The oil from the Far East is already being burnt in one-third of the thousand or so heat-and-power stations in Germany, and that figure is increasing. 1.3 billion kilowatt-hours of electricity are currently being generated in Germany at the expense of the rainforests, and—grotesque as it may seem—is being labeled as "green" energy.

Well-meant regulations with which the government sought to promote the sale of ecologically generated electricity through the use of non-fossil fuels are the reason why we are all accomplices, willy-nilly. The original intention of the laws is being taken ad absurdum by thoughtless and unscrupulous profiteers, and no one in Berlin seems to worry. A change in the regulations is overdue.

This is how it works. The Renewable Energies Act requires major power generating companies to buy in, from their unloved alternative rivals, power generated by wind, solar and bio-mass. For this they have to pay 11.5 euro cents per kWh. In addition, where applicable, they have to pay a 6-cent bonus under the terms of the Renewable Raw Materials regulations.

"The whole thing has two big snags," says Reinhard Behrend, chairman of the Hamburg section of the organization "Rettet den Regenwald"

*Oil palms as far as the eye can see. In never-ending rows the saplings in this mega-nursery are waiting to be transported to plantations.*

*Monoculture. On the over-exploited soil that used to be rainforest, the palms only grow with the massive use of agrochemicals.*

(Save the Rainforest). "Since the laws make no distinction between real green electricity and energy derived from environmentally destructive palm oil, they promote firstly the destruction of the rainforest, and secondly the major utilities have to pay far more for "alternative" energy than they do from that produced in coal-fired power stations, and they pass these costs on to the consumer. And so we all have to pay for the destruction of the rainforest whether we want to or not."

It was the coalition of Social Democrats and Greens, of all people, who pushed through the Renewable Energies Act, which has led to the absurd situation that many power stations in Germany burn South-East Asian palm oil instead of domestically grown rapeseed oil. The

171

*Orangutans are unwelcome pests in the plantations as they peel the bark off and eat the core of the plants. Using a stun gun special BOS teams are keeping watch to prevent the murder of the red apes by the workers on the plantation. Some palm oil companies pay a bounty for killed orangutans.*

palm oil is in monetary terms cheaper, because the enormous cost of the environmental destruction caused by the palm oil plantations doesn't figure in the account. Unfortunately, most heat-and-power station operators look only at the price, and don't give a thought to the destruction of nature, the suffering and the death which is the real price of this cost advantage.

"I simply couldn't believe it," groans Behrend, "when I learned that the Schwäbisch Hall city utilities, of all people, who supply energy to the 'eco' power supplier Greenpeace Energy, are building a palm oil power station with a capacity of five megawatts."

The combative forest advocate points out that the cheap new fuel is not only extremely unecological, but also questionable from the point

of view of the energy balance-sheet. "Not only does the palm oil have to be transported a long way, during storage it has to be kept at about 50 °C (120 °F). in order to keep it in liquid form!"

Thanks to the internet and the protest page www.regenwald.org, within a few days the Schwäbisch Hall city utilities and federal environment minister Sigmar Gabriel found themselves the targets of countless hostile e-mails. The successful outcome of the campaign: "Greenpeace Energy will not be buying any more electricity from Schwäbisch Hall," says Behrend.

Instead of just turning off the switch, minister Gabriel is trying to develop a certification system for eco-friendly palm oil. Behrend: "He really ought to know that certificates are often hardly worth the paper they're printed on. In addition, the palm oil corporations are not exactly strangers in the federal capital: they have received hefty subsidies for long enough."

One of these corporations is Sinar Mas, a cellulose producer which has gone over to planting the profitable oil palms. In the 1990s, the government under Helmut Kohl underwrote loans to the tune of a billion deutschmarks so that the company could build cellulose factories and deforest Sumatra. The subsequent Social Democrat-Green coalition approved a further half-billion worth of export credit guarantees for the supply of machinery to the cellulose industry in Sumatra.

The Deutsche Investitions- und Entwicklungsgesellschaft (German Investment and Development Society), wholly owned by the German federal government, has by its own account promoted several new palm oil plantations on Sumatra.

Research by the Indonesian environmental organization Walhi shows, according to Behrend, that the paper and cellulose industry on Sumatra has been building up a palm oil production capacity of its own on a grand scale since 2001.

The ploy of the corporations, including a number whose credit has been underwritten by the government, is this: they planted, sometimes via subsidiaries, oil palms in areas where they were supposed to plant timber to cover the raw-material needs of their paper production. But because they neglected the latter, these corporations had a raw-material shortfall, and covered it illegally in primary rainforests. The chain-saw gangs didn't even stop at the boundaries of national parks.

The warm rain of deutschmarks into the coffers of Sinar Mas was not a good investment: mismanagement and a collapse of cellulose prices drove APP, a subsidiary of Sinar Mas, into bankruptcy. In the aftermath, the corporation's debts were written off at the expense of the German taxpayer.

In their TV documentaries *Fette Beute* (Fat Spoils) and *Das verbürgte Elend* (Underwritten Misery), the film-makers Inge Altemeier and Reinhard Hornung have shown how German cash for Sinar Mas brought destruction to the forest and suffering to the people. The

documentaries made the struggle of the local environmentalists and their leading protagonists widely known in Germany, for example Feri Irawan of Walhi. The group demands a total ban on the export of tropical wood and also rejects the unecological "bio" fuels derived from palm oil. One of the targets of Irawan's attacks was Sinar Mas.

"The brave defenders of the rainforest in Indonesia have a right to our help," says Behrend. "After all, the cash for the deforestation is coming in part from European banks, so-called development banks, or direct from the German finance minister. So it is no more than right and proper that support for the environmentalists should also come from Europe!"

Similar goals to those of Feri Irawan are being pursued by Rudy Ready Lumuru, director of "Sawit Watch" (Sawit = palm oil). Since 1998, this environmental campaign group has set up a network of about 50 local partner groups in which small farmers, plantation workers, human-rights activists and environmental campaigners are involved. They work directly with some 45,000 families in 75 towns and villages whose livelihoods are threatened by palm

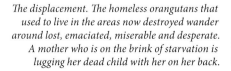

*The displacement. The homeless orangutans that used to live in the areas now destroyed wander around lost, emaciated, miserable and desperate. A mother who is on the brink of starvation is lugging her dead child with her on her back.*

oil plantations. Rettet den Regenwald has been supporting Walhi and Sawit Watch for many years.

Those who, like the two groups, are active on behalf of the preservation of the rainforests, their inhabitants, and social reform disturb the circles of timber and palm oil barons, corrupt politicians, cellulose and mining corporations and Western banks that profit from the destruction of the rainforests. This is why Feri Irawan is always nervous when his telephone rings. The 33-year-old father of a young child, he has often been railed at by anonymous callers, and has even received death-threats.

Reinhard Behrend stresses that, in view of the mass extinction of species and the decimation of the orangutan population, it must not be overlooked that the destruction of the jungles also takes away the livelihood of human minorities such as the nomads, native tribes and small forest farmers.

Rettet den Regenwald helps the poor, the powerless and the victims of frequent discrimination in their struggle against the rich, powerful and mostly lawless. "Without assistance from abroad, the rainforest people are lost," says the activist from Hamburg. "We inform the public about German involvement in rainforest destruction, name the perpetrators and seek to influence the government's overseas development policy and the business dealings of banks and corporations."

According to Behrend this is urgently necessary, because: "Our timber merchants dictate the wording of laws and regulations to the bureaucrats in Berlin, as the magazine *Monitor* revealed at the beginning of 2007. What emerged was the federal government's new timber-procurement rules, which were criticized in February 2007 even by the Council for Sustainable Development that is appointed by the government itself."

Those who think the little band of rainforest protectors have no chance in the face of super-rich corporations are wrong. Behrend: "In 2006, an alliance of Walhi and groups such as Global 2000 from Aus-

*BOS distributes information material on the conservation of wild animals in even the most remote areas.*

tria, urgewald, Robin Wood and Rettet den Regenwald succeeded in dissuading Deutsche Bank from acting as financial adviser when the cellulose factory Kiani Kertas on Borneo was being bought up by the cellulose corporation United Fiber Systems. UFS has in the past been one of the most unscrupulous destroyers of Indonesia's rainforests. "But that's not all: at the end of 2006 the power giant RWE was forced into submission. Its British subsidiary, npower, rejected the chance of becoming Britain's first energy concern to generate electricity from palm oil, on the grounds that sustainable palm oil production could not be guaranteed. Behrend: "npower had received a lot of protest letters. From our website alone, more than 6,200 people got involved in the campaign in the space of a few weeks."

Conservationists set great hopes on a conference of palm oil producers, investors and customers that took place on 22/23 November

*Apocalypse now. Where over ten thousand species of plants and animals used to grow and flourish, it now looks as if a nuclear war had struck.*

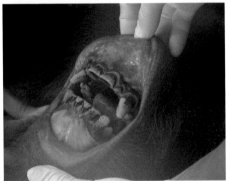

*Cracked lips and worn out teeth—this is the painful consequence for apes when there is no healthy food to eat and they have to feed on bark.*

2005 in Singapore. It is true that the "Round Table on Sustainable Palm Oil" (RSPO) agreed a catalogue of fine-sounding principles for the sustainable cultivation of oil palms; but according to Willie Smits, these are only bluff and deception. Smits: "The palm oil industry only wants to buy time. Despite the resolutions—which are incidentally not binding—they carry on as before!"

This can be seen from the fact, that "of all places, the plantations are planned for the areas where the best kinds of wood are situated," although great parts of these areas are unsuited for the cultivation of oil palms as they are situated too high up or on slopes that are too steep, as has been discovered by satellite technology.

But the oil barons have been looking for the possibility of a three-fold profit: with the felled trunks, with the residual wood which is processed into paper if it is not burned, and finally with the palm fat and the palm-kernel grist.

There are, however, alternatives which would make a devastation of the last lowland rainforests unnecessary: in the Indonesian part of Borneo alone, eight million ha (30,000 square miles) of fallow grassland are situated, in the entire country more than 25 million ha (96,000 square miles) on which oil palms could easily be cultivated—which would be advantageous for the local population. However, this would mean higher costs as, unlike the situation in the rainforest, the outlay could not be offset by the sale of valuable hardwood.

The large-scale destruction of the unique forest wonders is accompanied by a macabre "closing down sale" for animals surviving the chain-saw massacre. They are either immediately huckstered or disposed of on-site to be sold at a loss on the infamous Pramuka bird market in Jakarta or in other "large discount stores" for endangered species which supply the whole of South East Asia with live goods from the Red List. As the *Jakarta Post* reported in March 2003, in the capital alone animals worth about 600 million dollars changed hands in one year.

On the logger "front" in East and Central Kalimantan, we are witnessing an environmental disaster and seeing how orangutans are

*A life-risking job. An unconscious orangutan pasha has not fallen from the tree into the safety net—a situation feared by BOS. In order to save the ape a member of the team has to climb to dizzying heights to lower the sleeping tower of strength down a rope.*

being squandered, tortured, and killed. And repeatedly it becomes apparent that the impoverishment of nature results in the impoverishment of the human beings.

During the journey, I have regretted that supermarket customers in the West cannot see the misery they unwittingly cause with their purchases. If they were just given a five-minute demonstration of the horror which has become an everyday event in wide areas of Borneo and Sumatra, most of them would steer quite clear of tropical wood products and goods made of unsustainably obtained palm oil.

The conservation of orangutans is harrowing work. Impenetrable terrain is one of the easier exercises that BOS staff have to deal with. The daily confrontation with bestial cruelty is far harder to cope with. The orangutan above right was tied to the border post of a plantation as a meat-store. BOS managed to save the emaciated and sunburnt animal.

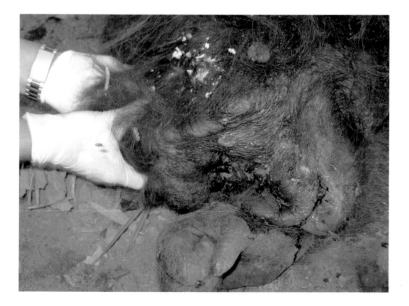

177

# Nightmare and ape apocalypse

## A journey to the logger front in Kalimantan

For hours our cross-country vehicle rumbles, jolts and jumps along a god-forsaken mud slope full of potholes the size of bathtubs, which bears the grandiose name of "Trans-Kalimantan Highway". On both sides, the scenery presents an almost post-nuclear-war appearance, the vestiges of the rainforest of Borneo that formerly teemed with life. The desert of alang-alang grass stretches all the way to the horizon; black and burned giant stubs stand here like a solemn vigil in mourning and a few tousled single trees. They have been left untouched as their latex sap would have adhered to the chain saws. There are no animals any more. Decrepit lorries, completely overloaded with tree trunks toil through the mud by means of snow chains. "Wood thieves!" says Willie Smits. "They are cutting down the very last trees."

The ravaged land is virtually valueless. Smits explains that a great part of the forest was destroyed as a law existed which assigned the ground to the person who cleared it. "One hectare (2.5 acres) would not even cost 50 dollars—if there were customers!" And there are none. The alang-alang grass, the only plant which survives those frequent fires, spreads a green shroud over everything. It dominates the scenery because it sprouts again and again even if only its roots remain unharmed, furthermore, by means of chemical "warfare", it prevents the germination of tree seeds.

Besides the grass desert, the wood thieves and the mud slope, there are only a few scruffy boom towns, clusters of miserable shacks, here and there a filling-station selling petrol in bottles, and brothels in whose windows naked ladies try to stir up trade. In some of these banging shacks, beside 50-cent whores, orangutan females, completely shaven, are to be had. It was in one of these hovels, Smits reported, that BOS confiscated Pony. The ape female, forced to prostitute herself, sometimes decked with jewelry, furnished with an anklet had waited for her punters, drunk beer and operated the CD player of the brothel. Today, she is in the custody of Lone Dröscher-Nielsen in the Nyaru Menteng Rehabilitation Center. Her former owner has tried several times to "liberate" her by force.

In this solitude, Mino has found a job. The 22-year old whose pride and joy is a baseball cap with the inscription "Kellogg's California", sprays the all-out herbicide, Roundup, in an oil palm plantation from morning to night. The weed killer is supposed to kill the alang-alang grass and thus to stop it from suffocating the green fronds of the freshly planted palm trees, which are popping

*Like termites, the small men with the big chainsaws are eating their way through the rainforest. For them, the destruction of the jungle is usually not a profit-making operation. They receive a pauper's wage, get malaria and other tropical diseases, go deaf, and injure themselves on their own saws as they work without protective clothing.*

*Incredibly, the workers are aware that they are sawing the branch they are sitting on when they are carrying out their dirty and dangerous work, and that they are destroying their existence hand in hand with the rainforest. They have no choice if they do not want to starve.*

*The "owner" is angrily pulling the chained little orangutan from the tree. He had been displaying his goods along a lively street when he got an unpleasant visit from BOS (see picture right).*

through between the head-high stumps of the jungle giants. Mino has no shoes, and he has certainly neither protective clothing nor dust mask. His monthly earnings, converted, amount to 22 euros (32 dollars). This is just enough for survival with three rice-meals per day.

Recently, Mino had a chance to eat his fill: they had orangutan. "We discovered the ape mother in the plantation and after a long fight, we killed her with our machetes," he says. "Pity the child got killed with it. We cooked the orangutan in the camp kitchen. It tasted nice—rather like deer."

The dead baby was chopped up in small pieces, which were mixed with the insecticide Dimec and laid out as poisonous bait for wild pigs, which repeatedly attack the oil plantations at night. He knew that it is forbidden to butcher orangutans—"but out here it doesn't matter!"

For the Dayak hunter Sapran, too, nature is a self-service shop. The 53-year old from the boom town of Parengian has shot about 20 orangutan mothers who were on the run with their babies from approaching woodcutter gangs. He gloats over his huntsman's finesse: he did not just fire volleys like the other gun-owners, but he waited—if need be, for hours—until the ape mother he had zeroed in on had climbed down onto a branch situated not quite so high above the ground. It was only then that he pulled the trigger. "If they don't drop down so far, more babies survive." For these he cashes in 100,000 to 150,000 rupiah per baby (ten to 15 euros or 15 to 20 dollars). The corpses of the mothers he left lying there for the wild pigs because he did not want to eat them. "They are too much like humans!"

Two kilometers (1.2 miles) away, still in Parengian, Willie Smits confiscates orangutan baby Nungki in a wooden shack by the river,

which can only be reached via slippery boardwalks after a boat trip. The owner, a man called Rachmat, is not at home. His wife Fahrida tells us that her husband and two friends had recently killed an ape mother with clubs. He had thought the baby would be a good toy for the children.

Rashida and her four children are undernourished. Rachma, the youngest, in whose bed Nungki slept, is badly underdeveloped. She looks eighteen months although she is already three and a half years old. All have dark rings underneath their eyes—according to Willie Smits a sign of an infection with intestinal parasites. He passes the woman some medication. The ape baby is also half starved. Because it has all his teeth already, it must be older than two years, but it looks at most like six or seven months.

The action is attracting dozens of at first curious, then hostile neighbors. There is shouting and scuffle. Willie Smits, who speaks Indonesian like a native, learns in the tumult that two weeks ago and

*Confrontation. Willie Smits has just taken an orangutan baby being offered for sale by a logger in the pay of a palm oil company. The chairman of the German organization "Friends for Nature", Helmut Huber, is watching the dispute.*

a few lanes further an orangutan was executed by his owner, a Hajji Yusup. The crime the animal had committed: it had escaped from its cage in which it had been cooped up for five or six years, and it had bitten a boy during its flight. It was caught, tied to a tree, condemned to death according to Islamic law and garrotted by a rope round the neck.

We are traveling on. On the front passenger's seat, Nungki presses herself against Willie Smits. In the village of Pundu, Hajji Sapran, owner of a humble grocery store, had just got rid of a young orangutan and had cashed in 150,000 rupiah. The ape was meant for Tanjung Puting National Park, the customer had declared. Mecca-pilgrim Sapran laments over the destruction of the forest: "In the past, they had the nicest trees here everywhere but today the lorries have to drive for a whole day and a night to reach the forest. The oil palms are our last hope."

The owner of the shop next door confirms this: the man from Tanjung Puting came by regularly and inquired after orangutans. Some-

Re-education. In a camp in Sampit (Central Kalimantan) loggers are reading brochures that give them advice on how to behave in encounters with orangutans.

times, "the fat woman" would also turn up, likewise a purchaser for the National Park. "In the past, we used to have a little orangutan here on offer every day but now they have become rarer."

Jay Ullal and I are surprised: does the famous National Park acquire ape children and create a market for the hunters this way? What does this have to do with orangutan protection? We asked Willie Smits, but he declined: according to BOS statutes, he is forbidden to comment on the actions of other animal rights activists.

But hardly an hour later we found ourselves talking about the subject of Tanjung Puting again. In a warehouse of the company of Makin near Parengian, manager Said said that he had urgently requested Biruté Galdikas for help four months before. He had written a letter to the world-famous scientist at her residence in the National Park, asking her to catch the orangutans who had intruded in his plantations and to move them away. As the animals were causing a lot of damage, he would have to have them shot otherwise. "But I have not received an answer!" This is why he had turned to BOS. Makin is one of the largest oil palm enterprises of Indonesia.

(On my return, I sent a fax with questions to Mrs Galdikas from the *Stern* editorial department in Hamburg. I asked the scientist among other things for information on the alleged baby purchases, on the reproaches of the plantation manager and on information which had been put into our hands stating that she paid four million rupiah per orangutan infant [which is something around 300 euros or 400 dollars—a small fortune] because she did not

*The burning turf not only increases the emission of greenhouse gases, the people suffer too. Over 30 percent of children in Kalimantan fell ill during the three months in which suffocating smoke emanating from the former forests hid the sun. Instead of going to the root of the problem, the government distributed respiratory masks.*

confiscate any herself but required small apes for the tourists living on the fringes of the National Park in Simba Lodge who bring in the money. The fax left the building but was never answered.)

A few kilometers away from Parengian we visited three woodcutters in their camp, an open shelter roofed with bright blue plastic foil by the side of a drain. Their lot is situated about five hundred meters (one third of a mile) away behind one further ditch. Mosquitoes are zinging. Willie Smits reports that many of the workers here suffer from malaria tropicana, which can be fatal. The little brown men with the gigantic German chainsaws tell us that they received the equivalent of about 40 euros (60 dollars) per cleared hectare, but had to pay the hire charge for their saws, petrol and food as well as transport from this money. It was almost impossible to get by on these wages. They shrugged their shoulders when asked what they intended to do once the rainforest was done with.

"People know they are biting the hand that feeds them," says Willie Smits. "But they have no choice but to destroy the last bit of rainforest for starvation wages. They are exploited, they live from hand to mouth, and they have no money to buy a new pair of trousers or look for a job elsewhere. Nature is destroyed and everybody goes hungry—but in Jakarta or Singapore a handful of gangsters becomes rich."

We take a fast motorboat up the Kapuas to the Dayak village of Mantangai. A special lookout at the bow reports dangerous drifting tree trunks. Mantangai is situated at the confluence of the blackwater river of the same name with the Kapuas, an enormous river—in comparison to which the Rhine is hardly more than a stream. On the banks, a rotting competition of dozens and dozens of abandoned sawmills against massifs of old sawdust is taking place. Those few

*The excavator and the carbon-dioxide catastrophe. After the valuable trees have been felled and removed, the soil of the swamp forest is drained. When oil palms are planted on the meters-thick peat created after deforestation of the swamp, vast amounts of the climate-killer carbon dioxide are released.*

sawmills which are still operating process trunks thick as haunches—matchsticks compared to the jungle giants which once used to be cut here.

"In the seventies we only had to ferry across the river and there was top-class wood galore," complains Hajji Akim Saman, former director of the Mantangai village school. "But since 1990, everything has disappeared."

We also take a voyage up the Black Water River, and suddenly on the riverbank, a gigantic swamp area is looming, overgrown with alang-alang grass. Here, as directed by President Suharto, about one million ha (4,000 square miles) of forest was felled and burned down during the years of 1997 and 1998 in order to make way for a foolish agrarian project, the so-called "Mega Rice Project" which was supposed to make Indonesia independent of rice imports again.

The Food and Agriculture Organization of the United Nations (FAO) had conferred a distinction on Suharto in 1985 because his country had been self-supporting with regard to rice. As in the following years, about one million ha (4,000 square miles) of paddy fields were built on and therefore Indonesia had to import rice, Suharto felt taken up on his promises—and in 1966 seized the idea to have the lost fields spring up like mushrooms again in the jungle of Kalimantan. Willie Smits, at that time adviser of the minister of forestry, Djamaludin Suryohadikusumo, in Jakarta, disapproved of the president's project on the grounds of its unfeasibility.

Suharto, however, wanted to hear no objections. He had the rainforest felled—of course by enterprises inside his own family clique, and had 4,600 kilometers (3,000 miles) of drains cut and houses for 60,000 settlers erected. The smoke from the burning peat bogs in the drained forests got all the way to Africa. This delusional idea cost the lives of approximately 5,000 orangutans and countless other rare animals.

The prediction of tropical rainforest expert Smits was fulfilled: there was too much acid in the soil, the water level of the paddy fields could not be sufficiently regulated, and one epidemic after another haunted the settlers, who in the end lost their heads and fled—or became illegal loggers and poachers.

Suharto paid a flying visit by helicopter and was presented a blooming colony—literally a Potemkin village: fruit-trees in tubs, and paddy fields with rice—also potted. Today, all those hundreds of houses for which the jungle was destroyed are decaying. However, the Mantangai fiasco could not be kept a secret for long; it contributed towards the downfall of the dictator.

As in Parengian, one can see the torment in Smits. During hundreds of confiscations, the BOS chief has put himself into great danger of life and limb and he constantly gets murder threats from the animal mafia over the phone. His family's house was set on fire and his dogs were poisoned. He should by now have become "hardened", should by now have become used to the personal risk he is bearing, to the willful destruction of nature and the cruelties which humans inflict on the red ape.

But he never got into the habit of becoming hardened—the suffering of flora and fauna still touches him deeply as did the death-rattle of the dying ape baby, Uce, which he discovered on a rubbish heap at the end of 1989, and which gave his life a new direction (see page 204).

It is mainly the many tragic fates of the apes which drive Smits from his bed in the early hours of the morning. There are the orangutans whose owners put their eyes out as punishment for the "theft" of a banana or papaya. There is the ape female, Emen, whose Chinese owner chopped off all fingers on one of her hands because she stole two eggs at the toddler's age of three. There is Lilli who during the catastrophic forest fires of 1997 fled from the jungle into a village and hid herself in a garden where a human mob attached her and stabbed her 63 times with knives. There is the baby orangutan Smits found in a Dayak village in a chicken basket of raffia—directly beside the half-eaten corpse of its mother. And there is Lisa who came to the quarantine of Wanariset in November 1992, then a one-year old ape child with a serious case of hepatitis B, still there,

and still contagious despite all the doctors' endeavors.

The orangutans smuggled abroad also rob Smits of his sleep. Although again and again BOS task forces race to Jakarta airport because they have received a hint about an ape sitting in an air freight container, they rarely make a find because the rackets which smuggle the red primates via Jakarta, Bangkok, Singapore, or Kuala Lumpur to all parts of the world—even into the EU—are well-conducted, tightly organized, and secretive. The financial incentive is great: connoisseurs in Europe and Arab countries pay about 50,000 dollars for an ape baby which can be had for ten or 15 euros (15 to 20 dollars) where forests are being cleared.

Insight into the actions of the animal mafia is more than rare. In March 2004, the *Jakarta Post* reported the discovery of 196 young orangutans from Kalimantan in the Thai animal park "Safari World", most of them in bad condition. 40 more red apes were smuggled to Europe and the USA within six months by the Chinese animal trader, Hansen, who has since been sentenced. In 1999, 23 orang-

*Din to avoid death. A team from BOS is teaching workers on a palm oil plantation how to chase orangutans away without hurting them.*

*Wood thieves can often only be found in their remote workplaces by using a motorboat. Here Willie Smits, accompanied by police, is on his way up the River Kapuas to confiscate orangutans.*

utan babies were illegally transported in hand luggage from Bali to Osaka (Japan). Only four of the little apes survived the odyssey and they have since been re-introduced by BOS into the protected area of Meratus.

In the face of this endless suffering, Smits is sometimes seized by a feeling of angry helplessness. "A lot of paper is covered in writing, a lot of learned talk is going on during congresses, and a lot of lamenting is going on about the extermination of the orangutan," he says, "But nobody is doing anything!"

*King in chains. Emaciated and dehydrated this former ape chief is waiting on a street in Parenggean (Central Kalimantan) for a buyer keen on ape-meat. A BOS-worker threw him the banana he is eating.*
*Below: on the way to the orangutan butcher. Tied up and bleeding, this big red ape was to be brought to town. Rescue came just in time.*

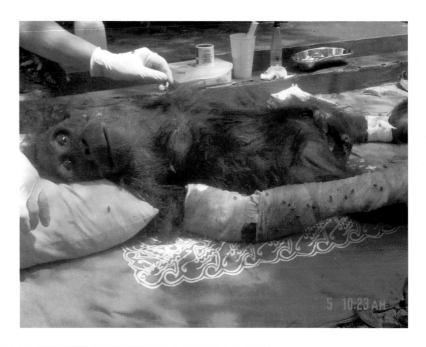

*Gallery of victims. The everyday life of orangutans in the palm oil areas is
so dreadful that even the helpers with the thickest skin are overwhelmed.*

*Stages in a rescue. When the helpless orangutan is found, he is drugged by the "rescue team", caught with a net and brought to the transporting cage on the off-road vehicle.*

*Ape-man. During the transport of the drugged orangutan, rescuer and animal sometimes become one.*

# "Nobody is doing anything!"

## The mournful search for animal-welfare activists who give real support to orangutans

*The loggers earn least from the destruction of the rainforests. They are paid a pittance for their backbreaking work.*

We are perplexed. We have never looked at the problem from this angle. We had of course taken it for granted that at least some of the numerous and quite often well-heeled environmental and animal-welfare organizations were helping the red ape. But were we on the wrong track? Is Queen Victoria's abhorrence still in our brains today?

If it really was the case that animal welfare activists were just looking on while our shaggy cousins are dying out, we must ask ourselves what they are there for, and what is the purpose of their glossy brochures—those with the friendly looking orangutan mother, her nice baby and the bank transfer form for the donation? What are they doing then—those mighty organizations like IUCN, the World Conservation Unit whose main aim is the conservation of biological diversity, or the United Nations Environment Program (UNEP)—an administration with about 800 full-time staff members and an annual budget of well over a hundred million dollars?

Would the apes be in such a deplorable state—we carry on reasoning—if all animal-welfare organizations were fighting for the orangutans? How is it possible that every year 4,000 to 6,000 of the primates die without howls of protest in the media, without public boycott appeals, collections of signatures, demonstrations in front of Indonesian institutions and wood or paper companies—or Greenpeace-style actions against palm oil companies?

Why do we carry on buying the wood and the oil which are responsible for the death of the orangutans? Why do we not find one of the TV consumer reports attending to the subject? Yes, and why do we only find pleasing things (or, at best well-mannered solicitude) in the colorful brochures of the animal-welfare people, and not the brutal truth?

"Because animal-welfare associations cannot collect donations with negative news!" says Swiss wildlife photographer and animal-welfare activist, Karl Ammann. "This is the reason why tough reality has to be camouflaged at all costs, even if the disclosure is a precondition for the solution of the problems and covering up only makes things worse!" Ammann, who has been living in Africa for the past 25 years, is the author of a dozen books. Two of his books are concerned with "bush meat", the massacre of the African gorillas and chimpanzees for the cooking pot, three are concerned with great apes. One of them is *Orangutan Odyssey*, whose co-author is Biruté Galdikas.

In order not to endanger the flow of donations, animal-welfare associations regularly lull their members' consciences with good news, optimistic annual reports and hope-raising visions of the future, feigning an (almost) ideal world of the type in the immaculately beautiful films of *National Geographic*. The good tidings are: "Your donation helps!" This way, every member can get the feeling of being a little bit of a savior of endangered species, a creature of a better world.

This "sense-of-wellbeing nature protection" was so successful for the self-preservation of the animal-welfare associations that all the major non-governmental organizations were financially dependent on it—from Conservation International (CI) all the way to the likewise American and even richer Wildlife Conservation Society (WCS) and the WWF. As real campaigning has become superfluous—the collection box after all rattles just the same and without any kind of activ-

ity just by the "selling" of salved consciences—the idea is to conduct "sticky plaster repair" projects: useless and ineffective alibis and bogus campaigns. At best, they risked a few skirmishes, shouting minimal achievements from the rooftops, losing all the important battles without resistance and losing the war. "The patient has reached the final stage of cancer and is dying," says Ammann allegorically, "but the animal protectors ignore radiation therapy and chemotherapy. Instead, they get out their sticking-plasters."

For Ammann there is "no alternative" to "confronting the public with the harsh reality". If need be, one would have to admit that the war has been lost. This would rob the members of the associations of their beautiful illusions but at least they could not argue they had no knowledge of the dreadful situation of the environment.

"There is not a shadow of a doubt," states the combative photographer, "that careful diplomatic approaches—for nature protection estab-

lishments always ever the line of least resistance—have not only failed but have instead made everything much worse. We have had 30 years of it, and the situation could not be more dramatic."

Tanjung Puting National Park was a prime example for the animal-rights activists who "aspiring to preserve their personal playground and to carry on making money, are sending to their doom the animals that they were meant to protect." The "Orangutan Foundation International" of Biruté Marija Filomena Galdikas sacrificed its principles to the aim of being allowed to continue operations in the national park, and they were consensually risking the consequences of the ravaging of the parks and the deaths of many orangutans. They were fawning on corrupt authorities to ensure their benevolence, and were kidding themselves.

There were two typical incidents which he experienced in the middle of 2002. One day, crowds of illegal loggers, marching into the

*The call of gold. Kalimantan means 'River of diamonds'. However, it is not diamonds but gold in the riverbed that are causing the final destruction of the land. On the hunt for the precious yellow metal, the gold diggers, using massive pumps that sit on rafts, suck thousands of tons of sand and shingle from the river and filter out the gold. They are efficient workers: Hardly a riverbank remains unharmed. What remains is a desert, polluted with mercury. Other than nuggets the adventurers also like to huckster small orangutans, as many eat illegally hunted "bush meat".*

189

*The stolen logs are moved out of the swamp forest with a special train.*

national park, had plundered and destroyed the camp of an American woman who was researching into proboscis monkeys on the River Seycon. The violations were filmed in a TV documentary and the scientist had been asked for an interview. She, however, had refused this. Ammann, sardonically: "The toleration of total lawlessness seems to be precondition for anyone who wants to do research in Indonesia and numerous other corrupt countries!"

Shortly afterwards, Ms. Galdikas in Camp Leakey, the Tanjung Puting research center, had let him know that police boats paid by her had finally driven away the loggers from the vicinity of the camp. "I replied I could show her the trees which had been felled only 50 m [55 yds] away from her boat landing stage. She did not like that," Ammann writes. The loggers had disappeared solely for the reason that there was

not a single ramin tree left in the area to be sawn down. If, by chance, another tree species should come into fashion and carry a yield, they would be back immediately!"

Not only were thousands of wood thieves running amok in Tanjung Puting, also armies of illegal gold-washers were cavorting in the nature reserve, raking up everything and contaminating the rivers of the national park with mercury. In Camp Leakey—with a nearby flourishing gold-digger town—one could hear the permanent screeching of chainsaws.

In 2002, the London Environmental Investigation Agency (EIA) concluded in a study that there a large number of logger camps and illegal sawmills existed in the national park. There are roads especially for the trucks of the wood-thieves and there is even a system of illegal "concessions" within the ecological reservation. Up to 800 ramin trunks per day are floated down the Seycon River—directly past Camp Leakey.

Ammann is particularly resentful of Ms. Galdikas' behavior of not striking back and of not using her international renown in denouncing worldwide the deplorable state of affairs, but instead keeping silent and even paying court to the corrupt authorities. Characteristic is a notice-board which the Canadian scientist had put up on Rimba Lodge at the entrance gate of the national park after a congress of ape researchers. On this, she and all participants of the congress thanked the Indonesian government for their great commitment to animal welfare and nature protection.

The PHVA study also shows a good measure of blindness with regard to the truth. The 260-page omnibus volume, fruit of the Population and Habitat Viability Assessment Workshop at the beginning of 2004, does indeed offer the first comparatively authentic survey of orangutan data and warns that the red apes might be extinct in just a few years, but on the other hand it plays down the brutal reality with an abundance of absurd as well as silly extrapolations.

Although the rainforest is disappearing at record speed (as already mentioned, the study itself cites annual deforestation rates of between ten and 15 percent for six of the seven last orangutan retreats on Suma-

tra), the authors indulge in useless what-if arithmetic: for each of the four dozen of observation areas, they estimate how many of the red apes would remain in the case of annual forest destruction rates of nil, one, two, three, five, ten, 15, and 20 percent—and this in fact in 50, 100, and even in 1,000 years!

An example: an initial stock of 50 apes would—even without any disturbance—thin out within a thousand years in such a way that in AD 3004, only seven animals would remain. In the case of one percent

deforestation, after 100 years, apparently 16 primates would still remain, after a thousand years: none.

The fact that this industrious but uninspired piece of work stands on shaky ground goes without saying: such simulations are speculation rather than science. One single large-scale climatic change or an epidemic amongst the apes would wipe them out. The paper is a document of helplessness and perplexity. It is full of pious wishes remote from reality and as a rule unenforceable, like for example "stop illegal felling

191

*Around 80 percent of the Tanjung Puting national park has been destroyed by palm oil plantations, wood thieves, and gold prospectors. Tourists on the search for paradise are not informed about this. They are shown a small, intact piece of the park, which is presented as a "happy jungle world". The visitors, who are usually seeking contact with orangutans, have infected the red apes with human diseases—a problem with which most of these projects are plagued.*

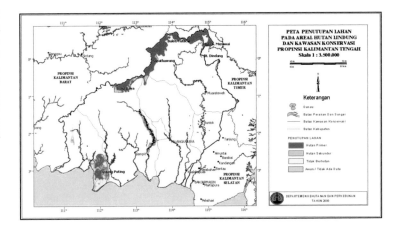

of trees", "protect the region", or "increase the readiness of the enforcement authorities to issue regulations for the protection of nature". There is mathematical pomposity and off-the-peg academic rigmarole galore. What is missing is an uncompromising accusation of those guilty of murdering the apes and of the massacre's billionaires.

Ammann classes the PHVA conferences as "band-aid projects": they were popular because the participating scientists received remuneration for their journey and their accommodation in a five-star hotel, they could cultivate old friendships and feel important. "There is much back-patting but no-one ever checks whether the conference has ever saved even one single animal!"

*When animals turn into exhibits. Direct contact between orangutans and tourists is not only illegal, but also against the rules of a serious release into the wild venture. Here a few examples from the Tanjung Puting national park.*

*Other places also break the rules on a routine basis. From above left to below right: Pattaya beach in Thailand, Bohorok in northern Sumatra, Taman Safari in Bogor (Java) and Sepilok in Sabah (Malaysia).*

*The basic prerequisite for a successful rehabilitation program for orangutans is the conservation of the forest. However, this is disappearing like snow in the sun.*

# Grand words and nothing behind them

## How UNEP helps orangutans

*Over ten orangutans had to die every day in 2006 because unscrupulous profiteers were clearing the rainforest to make room of for oil palms. In 2007 nothing changed. The surviving babies are in demand as child-ersatz or commodity; the grown-up animals are slaughtered or burnt alive, such as this big male ape in a palm oil plantation belonging to the Makin Group in Parenggean.*

**W**ith open eyes into species extinction—this is also the motto of the Great Ape Survival Project (GrASP), founded by UNEP chief Klaus Töpfer in May 2001. Having ignored the theatrical performance and PR spectacle like the multitude of "ape ambassadors", "special advisers", "technical relief organizations", and the "GrASP partner organizations", very little remains of the project.

The aims of the organization contrived by the former German minister of the environment are also of a modest kind: in studies, the "historical, recent, and current" presence of the apes should be clarified, likewise the main reasons for their extinction, and the actions "necessary for stopping the species loss of the great apes".

While they are miserly with pertinent aims—the main reasons for the extinction of the red apes are widely known (as they already were in May 2001)—there is lavish self-praise. GrASP were a "dynamic" and "truly international alliance", playing a "unique role at the highest political level", and evolving a "maximum of effectiveness" in the endeavor "to stop the decline of great ape populations".

From 5–9 September 2005, about 500 delegates met in the Kinshasa Grand Hotel for the "first inter-governmental meeting on great apes and the project for the survival of the great apes (GrASP) and the first meeting of the GrASP council". At the end of the conference, the participants signed the "Kinshasa Declaration" in which they were "for the first time in the history of the great ape, manifesting political will at the highest level", amongst other things "securing the future of all species and subspecies of the great apes until 2015".

If you wish to make your flesh creep, carry on reading on the web page of the UNEP.

Töpfer took his leave after eight years as UNEP executive director in the middle of 2006, leaving his seat warm for another sedate environmental bureaucrat, Achim Steiner, until then head of IUCN, to replace him.

Why all this useless juggling with words, all those unctuous declarations of intent which will never have any effect? Why this cynical stage production by Töpfer, who has always preferred show to genuine protection and who on 14 September 1988, as West German minister of the environment, preferred to swim across the completely contaminated river Rhine rather than trying to do something concrete to clean it up? How was it possible for four and a half years to elapse between the foundation of the organization and the first council meeting, during which time probably more than 20,000 orangutans died? And why is the year 2015 taken as a deadline for "salvation" although everybody knows that many of the acutely threatened populations will be long extinct by that time?

"Quite easy," says Karl Ammann. "GrASP is a creation of politically correct diplomats who are not willing or not in a position to call a spade a spade and who endeavor to avoid a confrontation at

*The longer the chainsaws are screeching in the rainforests, the more the centers of rehabilitation of BOS are filling up with uprooted orangutans. In May 2007 the organization cared for around 900 animals in their centers—a sad record. Here, at the station Wanariset, a dozen four-year-old orphans are waiting expectantly for BOS director Willie Smits.*

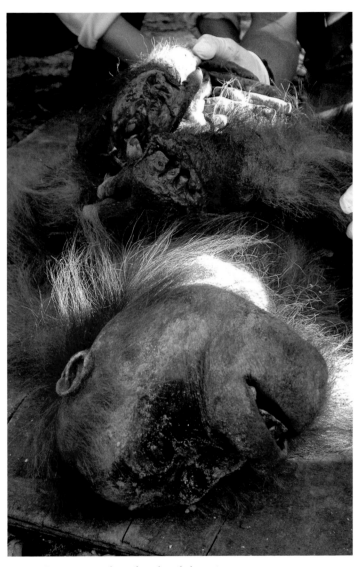

*Once again workers of a palm oil plantation in Central Kalimantan have slaughtered orangutans with their machetes. When this picture was taken the corpse was about to be taken to the local orangutan butcher. The butcher flogs the meat of around eleven apes per month.*

any price. They neither can nor may admit that UNEP and all the major nature protection organizations have miserably failed for thirty years, nor can they name the reasons for this. And this is why they do what masters of their trade do: sell nature protection, organize workshops and study problems."

And flatter the killers of primates. "One of the first smaller GrASP meetings in Kinshasa was opened by the Congolese minister, Salomon Banamuhere Baliene, who was responsible for the Department of Land, Environment, Tourism, Nature, Fishery, and Forestry", says Ammann. "Shortly before his opening speech, Banamuhere had signed new acts liberalizing the catching and shooting of internationally strictly protected animals like mountain gorillas, bonobos, chimpanzees, okapis, and white rhinos for an appropriate fee."

Anybody with the desire to kill one of the last 600 or so mountain gorillas had to pay 500 dollars; anyone wanting to catch the animal alive had to pay 1,000 dollars. If a customer intended to make a primate suffer lifelong confinement, Ammann continued, he had to fork out 3,000 dollars. Ape protector Töpfer obviously found no grounds to criticize the actions of his colleague. In 2006, Banamuhere became Minister for Energy, apparently during the course of a national anti-corruption campaign.

But also those politicians who have proved to be open to confrontation only let out hot air when it comes to the rescue of the orangutans. Thus, President George W. Bush announced with a voice full of conviction on 14 February 2002, that he had "instructed his Secretary

of State to create a new initiative for helping the developing countries to stop illegal felling of trees which destroys the diversity of species and releases millions of tons of greenhouse gas into the atmosphere". The "initiative" has not saved a single leaf in the rainforest.

One could continue ad infinitum with this listing but the frustration created by this would be unbearable. A revision of the achievements of the individual animal-welfare organizations and nature-protection authorities in their respective protection areas (according to the PHVA study, in the Indonesian part of Borneo alone at least 27 groups are active) would also unearth only very little to reassure us. Why else are the orangutans doing so badly? While a small number of groups, like for example BOS, are doing good work and do not shy away from confrontation, others—like WWF or Traffic, the species protection program of IUCN and WWF—prefer to work at their desks compiling reports which may be of some use, but very many others have got on the gravy train or act as free riders.

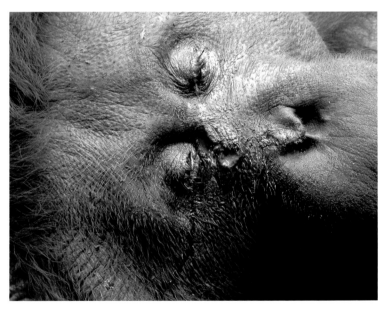

*This large dominant male orangutan from the district Sampit in the province of Central Kalimantan was hit between the eyes. The bullet came from a hand-made gun.*

A very particular role is played by the researchers. A number of them—van Schaik, Rijksen, Russon—had tried in their books to bring the unknown creatures, *Pongo pygmaeus* and *Pongo abelii,* closer to their readers and to arouse respect for the fellow-creature. However, did those scientists who reached worldwide fame with their preoccupation with orangutans and who were offered chairs at top universities also lobby for the apes?

Karl Amman does not believe they did and points out the example of the world-famous chimpanzee researcher, Jane Goodall, a figurehead of primatology, alongside gorilla protectrix Dian Fossey and Biruté Galdikas. "In her research station in Gombe in Tanzania, Ms Goodall looked on for thirty years while the forest was being felled," he said. "Now it is just a small island of forest with two groups of chimpanzees."

Although the professor had performed scientific pioneer work, she only promoted completely unsuitable action to combat the destruction of the rainforest and, like Galdikas, lacked courage in standing up for nature. In October 2001, for example, during the celebration of the 50th anniversary of the "Association Technique International des Bois Tropicaux" (ATIBT) in Rome, she delivered a commemorative speech in front of the league of the destroyers of the tropical forest who—as the photographer stated—were celebrating half a century of non-sustainable jungle utilization and gloated over an annual turnover of 800 million dollars.

Later, Ms Goodall explained her appearance in front of the tropical wood mafia in an interview with a Canadian magazine as follows: as one cannot see the timber companies disappearing from the jungles in the foreseeable future, they will have to be included in the solution. Whilst others tried to maneuver industry into better environmental practice by "embarrassment", she preferred a different strategy: "I think it bet-ter to bring about change by praise rather than by criticism."

Now what would the Indonesian journalist and protector of the rainforest, Abi Kusno Nachran, have thought of those pious words? Near his home village in West Borneo, shortly after Dr Goodall's speech, Nachran was attacked by about twenty machete-swinging bum-bailiffs on 28 November 2001. For minutes, the killers, probably sent by mafia godfather Rasyid, lashed out at the then 60-year-old moped rider. Considered dead, he was thrown onto a pick-up truck. Only when one of the carriers realized that Nachran was moving a foot, was he taken to hospital.

There, more than 200 injuries had to be given emergency treatment. According to the statements of Hamburg doctors who treated him several times in 2002, the reporter suffered several potentially fatal injuries, amongst them a grave wound to his head and a gaping cut across his spine. His right arm had been raised in self-protection, and it was almost cut through in several places. As the bones were already so very much fragmented that their remains could not grow together again, the activist had several bone implants in Hamburg. Abi's left hand was chopped off in the middle so that only the thumb remained, and a fist-sized piece was missing in his left shoulder.

The journalist had incurred the wrath of Rasyid because 18 days prior to the assassination attempt, he had three freighters of the timber baron, loaded with stolen Meranti trunks, arrested at sea and

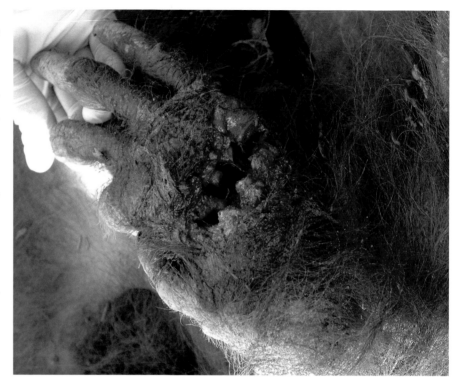

*In deadly terror this orangutan has tried to defend himself with his hands from the machetes. One of his hands was nearly severed in this action. The overworked BOS vets were forced to amputate a finger.*

*A landscape of scars. Abi Kusno is showing some of his healed wounds.*

*This illustrious panel of orangutan scientists carried out the PHVA study in 2004. There is no indication that the thick document has saved even one orangutan.*

van Schaik. "But we have a responsibility with regard to the tax-payer because most of the time we teach and guide students." Not all scientists were effective protectors of nature—this probably required other abilities.

Moreover, the question was raised whether primatologists and anthropologists are not, first and foremost, effective by furnishing full-time conservationists with data on orangutans and their living space. In any case, however, "We educate a lot of students who might later become nature protectors!"

"Obviously, there is no longer such a fear of being deported from Indonesia when branding the grievances there," the head of the Zurich institute explained. "In the past we had to be silent or otherwise our residence permits were countermanded!" Between 1999 and 2001, there had been several interviews with very clear statements in Indonesian papers, "and my students are still not allowed to enter the country."

For Anne Russon, harsh criticism of government and authorities is not the tool of choice. Most of the time, reproaches were counterproductive as Asians showed a "non-positive" reaction to slanderous remarks. As far as she knew, "most of the orangutan researchers were spending a good part of their time convincing authorities and local populations that apes should be better protected." She knew no scientist who was indifferent with regard to the fate of the apes. Her colleagues and she were standing up for the red apes in interviews, popular scientific articles, tales, documentary films, and books.

had them chained up in Jakarta, where, however, they "disappeared" (including their precious freight). In July 2006, Nachran lost his life in a traffic accident.

I asked Carel van Schaik and Anne Russon to answer my question whether it was true that those scientists keeping quiet in the face of the ecological disaster become accomplices of the rainforest destroyers, and whether they should—or rather must—leave their ivory towers and intervene in favor of the apes. "If society gave scientists the chance, they would rather leave their ivory towers," answered

Because the spreading of knowledge was decisive: "If we do not manage to make people understand how wonderful orangutans are and what an important role they play in biology and in our understanding of ourselves then there is no hope for them!"

Apart from that she and her colleagues tried with words and deeds "to prevent the worst of all the nonsense which is taking place in the name of orangutan protection". There were "nightmare projects" of overzealous animal lovers with such a gross deficiency in knowledge that it was harming the apes.

Perhaps one cannot expect real involvement on the part of the majority of the scientists for the survival of their research objects. And probably no real mourning of their destiny but rather a brief and professionally controlled emotion similar to that of a doctor in hospital in the face of the death of a patient on whom he had operated. Like for example John MacKinnon who—after eight years of absence from Sumatra—just found it "strange" to walk on wood-cutter paths through a region "which I had once known as untouched forest".

The result is clear: the orangutans are dying out because there is no lobby for them. Greenpeace is only fighting for one animal species—for whales, which are probably better milch cows for donations

*Lots of expense, no result. Again and again the cream of orangutan experts meets to talk eruditely about the plight of the apes. Meanwhile the bullets of the poachers continue to fly.*

*Ideal world and reality.*

*The remains of the haul of the loggers who fell trees in the rainforest in the area Kuala Kapua (Central Kalimantan) for a megalomaniacally insane project doomed to failure—one million hectares (1,455 square miles) of rice fields were to be wrested from this area. The so-called bush meat trade is more widespread in Indonesia than is known in the West.*

than great apes are. WWF is just as large and rich as it is sedate but it does manage to record the decline of *Pongo pygmaeus* and *Pongo abelii* in studies. Many other conservation groups use the orangutan in name or as an emblem but are engaged in saving their own skins. UNEP practices mercy killing.

Researchers write books, give talks and interviews—composed, factual, and most of the time, ineffectual. Desperate calls for help like those by Michelle Merrill, a Ph.D. student of van Schaik's, in the light of the increasing destruction of her research area of Suaq Balimbing on Sumatra, published in June 1999 by the news agency Agence France Press (afp), are rare, really passionate appeals even rarer. Most scientists just pack their things and go when it becomes uncomfortable.

Or they throw in the towel. "The orangutan populations are disappearing at breakneck speed," writes Carel, who left Suaq

Balimbing in 1999 on the occasion of the symposium, "Orangutans Compared". "At some research sites we can only rescue relevant information before the researchers or their data have disappeared... Up till now our influence on bringing about a change in the complex processes which have been elicited by the mindless destruction of orangutan living space has been frustratingly limited. But we owe it to the animals who have given us the most precious experiences of our life to give the world an impression of what it is about to lose."

Besides an ecological sense of responsibility which is still comparatively wide-spread amongst scientists, rescuers of the red apes need courage and love of the animals. Although the latter is frowned upon by many scientists as an unscientific disturbing factor, the real helpers of the orangutans will require this to an extent which might even endanger academic career, marriage, and health.

Willie Smits too is a graduate scientist. However, he was unable to overlook or turn a deaf ear to the groaning of a discarded orangutan baby in its death-throes. And this changed his life—and gives the red apes a little bit of hope for the future. The BOS chief has freed hundreds of them from their cages, he carries the responsibility for almost 1,100 animals in various stages of their rehabilitation and re-introduction into nature, and he works towards the realization of a great dream: a secure, untouchable, last resort for orangutans.

*His posture, the position of his arms, the rigor of his limbs and the hacked off right hand tell the tragic story of this orangutan who suffered over 30 cuts and blows. He was buried alive by the workers on the plantation after they had chopped his hand off. The men who work for famine wages supplement their salary with the murder of apes, as many plantation companies pay a premium equivalent to 17 dollars per animal. The right hand of the ape is used as proof of the killing.*

# From Meranti proliferator to orangutan protector

## Willie Smits' journey to the apes

*Primates amongst themselves. The orangutan female Laura, who was confiscated by BOS in the oil town Bontang is cuddling her savior, BOS founder Willie Smits.*

**S**mits was born on 22 February 1957 in Weurt near Nijmegen in the Netherlands. He studied forestry management and soil sciences at the Faculty of Agriculture of the Agricultural University of Wageningen. After his exams in 1981, he traveled to the rainforests of the Meratus mountains in the Indonesian province of East Kalimantan on Borneo. "I wanted to go to places where nobody had been before me!"

In 1985, Smits, who had returned to the Netherlands, went back to Indonesia. By 1987, he had built up the Wanariset Forestry Research Station in East Kalimantan. "When I arrived there on 1 September 1985, there was—instead of a research station—just a red earth hill with two wooden huts and a greenhouse on top of it," he remembers. "There was no electricity, no telephone, and no water—nothing!"

Smits whipped the place back into shape, created a tree-nursery and a herbarium. After just six months he had encouraged the growth of more than 20,000 young trees of the valuable Meranti wood. For this, he was aided by the knowledge that the propagation by scion cuttings only functions in the presence of the species-specific endophytic fungus which lives in symbiosis with the Meranti. Without the right mycelium the little trees would die. "The trees are so extremely adapted to the conditions of the rainforest that they cannot bear any distur-

bances by humans!" He examined the biocenosis in the Meranti roots and passed his knowledge on to Indonesian scientists.

At the end of 1989, Smits visited a vegetable market in the coast town of Balikpapan. On this occasion, a sick orangutan baby crouching in a cage caught his eye. When Smits returned later in the evening he saw the little ape lying on a rubbish heap, its breathing rattling. The trader had thrown his "perished goods" away.

Smits was shocked and fascinated at the same time: "I had never seen an orangutan baby before. Her eyes went right to the heart. She seemed to be patiently waiting for death." He took the badly dehydrated animal home with him, forced it into drinking diluted milk, massaged the baby's tummy all night and warmed it with his body. "In

the morning, its breathing was back to normal again." He called the little ape Uce after the sound of its stertorous breathing.

Two weeks later, a second orangutan baby was entrusted to his care: Dodoy. "At first I wanted to send the little one to Tanjung Puting, to the famous Ms Galdikas," relates Smits. "But I wanted to know beforehand how the little apes would be cared for

*Uce one year after her rescue, in the house of Willie Smits.*

*The bite-test. One of the higher "baptisms" in the relationship between man and orangutan is the friendship verification with teeth: With one "bite" the ape is trying to find out to what degree the human trusts him. Who flinches, fails.*

there, and I read about orangutan rehabilitation. And a few things went against the grain for me: something was not quite right about Ms Galdikas' projects."

In those days, the doyen of the nascent rehabilitation movement was the Dutch scientist, Herman Rijksen, who worked in Ketambe in the Leuser National Park of North Sumatra. Rijksen had, after a few years, given up his endeavors for re-introduction into nature which he had started in 1971. One of the reasons for this was the pressure of infections to which the orangutans were exposed in stations operated by human beings. When he had a cold or even only conjunctivitis, the ape babies picked it up quickly—and a short time later so would the wild orangutans in the rainforest. The contact at the feeding place was enough to pass on the pathogens. Rijksen examined the red primates with regard to the highly contagious inflammation of the liver, hepatitis, and this led to his discovery.

The other reason was the meager supply of nutrients in the rainforest. Rijksen concluded that only a certain—low—number of orangutans per square kilometer (250 acres) of rainforest found enough to eat—and that a release of additional apes would enormously disturb this sensitive balance between supply and demand and would bring hunger and stress upon all the apes.

Willie Smits asked himself why, in the face of such research results, the other orangutan rescuers carried on as before. Biruté Galdikas, for example, released orangutans, which had been freed from human hands and which had often not been examined for infectious diseases, by helicopter into areas inhabited by wild conspecifics. "This is a disaster for the released animals!" said Smits. "They end up in an area where the entire territory is already shared out amongst the territory bosses and where there is no home for them." The scientist also cut costs in the training of the apes and hoped that the animals would teach themselves those skills which were needed for life in the forest.

She considered the danger of infection for free-living populations to be negligible. She told the *International Wildlife Magazine* at the end of 1996 that to her knowledge there had been no epidemics among

*Medical control. Every orangutan that arrives in the BOS center is first of all tested for about five dozen diseases. This picture shows Lone Dröscher-Nielsen and her vets during the examination of a totally relaxed orangutan.*

*Dr. Nuning Lestari, the Muslim vet of the BOS station Nyaru Menteng, is affectionately auscultating an orangutan. The patient is fascinated by her headscarf.*

*Happy to see you again. On one of his rare visits to Nyaru Menteng*
*Willie Smits is energetically greeted by three of his little charges.*

*Primate's picnic. Lone Dröscher-Nielsen and Willie Smits in sociable communion with orangutans in Nyaru Menteng.*

the orangutans, and no wild red apes had "dropped dead" yet. It goes without saying that infected animals do not die all of a sudden, but only after months or years of lingering illness. They would simply disappear in the rainforest without scientists or animal protectors getting wind of it.

Quite considerably more concern for the animal was expressed in the re-introduction guidelines which Rijksen finally published: after confiscation, the orangutans first had to undergo quarantine and subsequent socialization. Then they had to learn to be an ape. Their "timetable" included climbing, orientation in the forest, and instruction regarding edible plants. Fourthly, they were not allowed to be released in forest areas inhabited by wild orangutans.

Willie Smits decided that under these circumstances he could not deliver his fosterlings to the trust of Ms Galdikas. He reported Uce and Dodoy to the forestry ministry and tried as well as he could to look after them alongside his work as a researcher. Financial support from the International School in Balikpapan, which collected 10,000 dollars for the emergent orangutan project, allowed him in 1991 to found the Wanariset Orangutan Rehabilitation Center. "It started with that donation," says Smits. Until 1993, the contribution from the school made up the lion's share of his revenues.

As events came to pass, he was positively overrun by homeless orangutans. In the shortest space of time, his premises in Wanariset were crowded with 23 animals. Smits was welding new cages as fast as he could. "There was no way back anymore!"

He got into the headlines for the first time when the Indonesian government delivered seven of the famous "Taiwan Ten" orangutans to his trust in Wanariset—the remaining three of the ten animals, repatriated from the Far East in a great media sensation, were suffering from hepatitis or tuberculosis and had to go into quarantine. The apes returned by Ms Galdikas had spent one year in a kind of garage in Jakarta's Ragunan Zoo as a result of various quarrels between her and the authorities…

In 1992, Willie Smits founded the "Balikpapan Orangutan Society" (BOS) which was later renamed "Balikpapan Orangutan Survival Foundation" and in then in 2005 "Borneo Orangutan Survival

*Above: An orangutan baby that is not yet a year old is pulling himself up with a strong grip on Willie Smits' hair.*
*Right: A gripping hand for each finger. Hanging head-down this orangutan baby is laughing at Willie Smits. In contrast to humans, the red apes in this position have no problems with perception and orientation.*

*Rapid diagnosis in the rainforest. An orangutan in Halfway House (see diagram page 218) has got a thorn in its finger and is seeking help from Willie Smits. One of its friends is watching the operation.*

Foundation". Soon, BOS was acknowledged by the government as an orangutan rehabilitation project—and received subsidies from Jakarta. The official blessing was favored by the fact that Smits was adviser to the forestry ministry in Jakarta.

In this capacity, he also managed to get Act 280 through parliament on 5 September 1995. It prohibited the re-introduction of orangutans into areas in which wild red apes already lived. The importance of this was proved by laboratory tests in the veterinary hospital at Wanariset: about 70 percent of the first 114 orangutans which were examined there proved to be carriers of contagious afflictions at the time of admittance. They were suffering from parasites, hepatitis or tuberculosis.

Willie Smits' hope that the number of the "admitted" orangutans would gradually fall after the great fires of 1993 was shattered. The catastrophic fires in the rainforest led to the accommodation of about 200 animals "at one fell swoop" in 1997 and 1998. As the enclosure in Wanariset was bursting at the seams, Smits had no choice but to build a second animal shelter unit. The Nyaru Menteng Orangutan Reintroduction Project came into being in 1999 on premises of the forestry ministry near Palangkaraya, the capital of Central Kalimantan, about 500 kilometers (300 miles) away from Wanariset.

The oil palm boom meant that the second station was also quickly filled up to capacity limit with ape orphans. The flood of motherless little apes is no reason for joy for Willie Smits, but a sign of defeat in the struggle against the destruction of the rainforest. In March 2006, BOS attended to 200 orangutans in Wanariset and 440 in Nyaru Menteng. All in all, 450 red apes have been released into freedom. BOS was represented in 14 countries and had about 20,000 members worldwide. The foundation was directly employing 340 members of staff and indirectly provided income and sustenance to about 1,500 families with about 6,000 people.

In Nyaru Menteng, a dozen plastic washing-baskets are standing under a shady bamboo roof. In them, orangutan babies are sleeping, dozing, or tumbling about, some of them in diapers. It is surprisingly quiet because little apes do not cry like human infants. At most, they cheep like chicks—and throw us heart-rending glances with their great and earnest saucer eyes. Young Indonesian nurses warm-heartedly attend to the little ones.

Each of the babies—there were 118 ape infants of under three years of age in Nyaru Menteng in March, 2006—has witnessed how its mother was either shot by humans, or hacked up by machetes, slain with clubs, or burned. Most of them were extremely undernourished, completely dehydrated, and badly traumatized when they arrived here. Like little Bali, they had bullets or lead shot in their bodies, were suffering from burns because men with machetes had driven their mother into a fire while they were clinging to her fur, or were suffering from inflammations of the lungs, typhoid, or other infectious diseases.

In the case of some little apes, their trauma has caused states of fear or hospitalism. They manically jerk backwards and forwards, and twine their little arms—seeking help—around their own bodies. Their surrogate mothers have to give them their bottles, give them a bath as if they were human babies, swaddle them, and sing them to sleep.

The slightly older little apes from the "kindergarten" are teeming and bustling about, self-absorbedly handling a piece of cardboard or a drinking-straw, playing hide-and-seek with each other, or placing themselves in front of us and stretching out their long and thin arms.

If we lift them up as they want, they cling to us and look at us with their great, serious and sad eyes.

Lone Dröscher-Nielsen clothes part of their feelings in words which go right through you when you hold the little survivors on your arm: "The trust these poor victims place in us makes you ashamed."

The care of the little primates is optimal, and their medical provision is exemplary: at the time of their admittance, each animal is, during one to two weeks' quarantine, thoroughly checked for parasites and various infections like TB and hepatitis A, B, and C. Daily, blood samples are sent to Jakarta. Loads of gigabytes of patient data—blood counts, behavior data, complete patient histories—fill the computer disks of the hospitals of Wanariset and Nyaru Menteng.

*Often Willie Smits risks life and limb when he is freeing orangutans. He can relax with female ape Uce, with whom it all began. She passes Willie her first son, Bintang (above left) and enjoys her freedom.*

*When illegally kept apes are confiscated, the Dayak are mostly more understanding and easy-going than rich Indonesians. With the latter, Willie Smits frequently has to rely on his bodyguards as resistance is common.*

*Visiting time. The apes that are still in captivity in Wanariset congregate eagerly when the founder of BOS comes by for a visit.*

213

# Human beings as climbing teachers and jungle trainers for orangutans

## An almost impossible task

*Foster mothers as role model. In Nyaru Menteng, the 60 Dayak women who care for hundreds of ape orphans every day have to live by example. If they stay on the ground their little charges are scared to climb.*

Love and health care are, however, not everything. The carers have to attempt the impossible, namely to administer basic knowledge for a life in the rainforest to their little wards, who would (without the interference by poachers or loggers) otherwise have enjoyed many years of training by their mother. It is roughly as if a mole were teaching a young swallow to fly.

As there is no alternative, people do everything conceivable: the Indonesian "surrogate mothers" help even the tiniest ones with their first climbing and nesting attempts and show them which fruit they can eat and how fruit can be prepared for consumption. In the kindergarten, which is attended by little apes up to the age of about two and a half years, training is continued in the nearby forest and extends to nine hours daily. After the little ones have learned to hold their own in a group, the best of the class move over into "Halfway House".

This forest area of about ten hectares (25 acres), enclosed by a painted wall is a kind of "high school" in which the young orangutans (aged two and a half to five years) are put through their paces and where they have to pass a kind of school-leaving exam. In order to qualify for the next stage of their rehabilitation, they have to fulfill all the following criteria:

▶ to be at least 4 and a half years old
▶ to have six good "friends"
▶ to weigh at least 14.5 kg (32 lbs)
▶ to know at least 100 different fruits
▶ to be able to build a sleeping nest and
▶ to climb, and swing about well
▶ to care for themselves, and
▶ to find their way around in the rainforest.

The stage of education of each individual candidate for freedom is subject to constant assessment.

Graduates of the "Halfway House" as well as of the "socialization cages"—where orangutans who have arrived at BOS at the age of four or more years are given their "social polish"—are released on one of the three untouched river islands in the region that Willie

*Restaurant in the treetops. In the wild it is potentially lethal to eat on the ground; so, in Halfway House this dangerous habit is eliminated. BOS staff train their "students" to eat high above the ground, where there are no crocodiles or big cats.*

214

*Nervous before the first time. Shaking and whimpering, the newly arrived babies are looking around the still totally alien forest. The adoptive mothers have to do all they can to calm the small apes.*

Smits purchased from the Dayaks after months of negotiations and after ceremonies lasting for days on end. The "islanders" do receive their food but are also able to prepare themselves on the islands under practically natural conditions for their final reintroduction. Even if they scorn the fruit which is delivered daily by canoe, they do not have to suffer from hunger: botanical studies showed that 70 to 80 percent of the islands' vegetation is edible for the apes.

Much to the enjoyment of the BOS observers, many of the apes first released on the 158 ha (390 acres) of Kaja Island learned quickly how to harvest wild honey with little sticks or how palm hearts are broken out of the trunks. Each night, they built their sleeping nests and it was not long before the first pairs of lovers emerged.

By the aid of a four-step education program (nursery school, kindergarten, Halfway House, and island training), BOS has managed to turn traumatized, sick, and injured orphans into orangutans, which get as close to being "genuine" kings of the jungle as possible. There are, on and off, apes that prefer to stay in the "safe" proxim-

*Enjoy the meal! At lunchtime the smallest ones get a snack, as all the climbing is exhausting for the little apes. Their nurse, like many Indonesian women, protects her face with a layer of rice flour. She is trying to prevent getting any more bronzed.*

216

ity of human beings rather than risk venturing into the wilderness, but the method practiced in Nyaru Menteng and Wanariset makes the release efforts of other ape protectors appear amateurish. On the other hand, the BOS method is also more expensive. 3,500 dollars per orangutan is the estimate, which is more than twice that of other centers.

We fly with Willie Smits in the seaplane of a missionary from Balikpapan to Palangkaraya: two hours over endless plains of desolated forest. The territory is blotchy like the back of a person inflicted with an acute attack of neurodermitis—dark remnants of forest on the crests of hills in between, as far as the eye can see, light-green oil palm plantations. "The whole forest down there was illegally destroyed!" laments the BOS chief.

Then his face is transfigured: we are flying over the high point of his life's work, a secure place of refuge for the last orangutans. Repeatedly his face lights up because he has seen a reddish-brown spot deep down there, in the branches of a jungle giant—a wild king of the jungle. Smits must have eyes like a hawk—we see nothing.

*Above: Help, a photographer! Frightened, these little ones are clinging on to the leg of their foster mother. The photographer is a stranger to them and he has come too close.*
*Right: Small, but strong. This orangutan, which is not yet a year old, is already a real bundle of strength. Effortlessly it hangs from a branch with just a few fingers.*

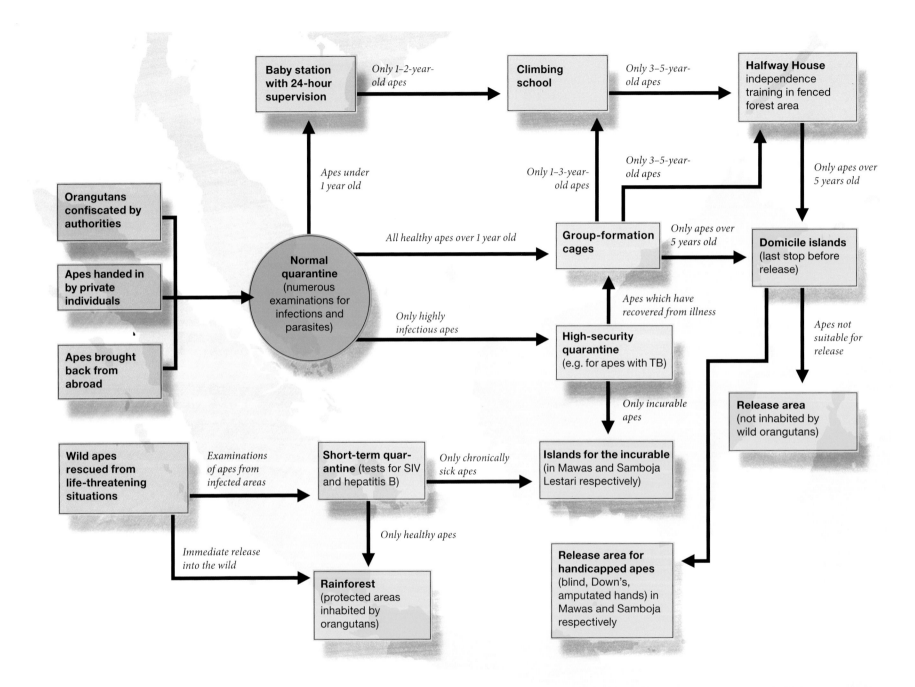

*The babies in the center Nyaru Menteng are often badly
traumatized and require round-the-clock care.*

*Mornings are very busy in the BOS centers. The smallest ones are carried to climbing school, the older ones are taken to the forest, and a group of five-year-olds are being driven into the countryside in a pick-up (one ape is looking at the unfamiliar passenger, Jay Ullal, with distrust). Really lazy orangutans let themselves be carried along on the legs of humans.*

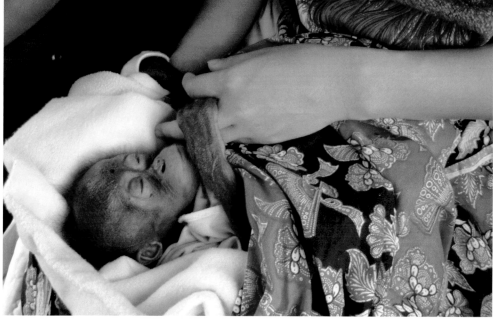

*Fun in the forest. Whilst the babies are napping, the little rascals are tearing around with their nannies or are playing with a ball.*

*Ballet in the branches.
A three-year old "forest
student" flies through
the branches like a
hairy ballerina.*

*igestive siesta. After*
*e ample lunch the*
*ndergarten group,*
*ll up with delicious*
*opical fruit, fall into*
*wholesome sleep.*

*Sucking the third thumb.*
*Even though this little*
*one is already four*
*years old and a fairly*
*experienced climber he*
*finds comfort with his*
*"pacifier"—however, he is*
*not using his thumb but*
*his thumb-like big toe.*

*Fits of vertigo. In Nyaru Menteng an orangutan baby that has spent a long time with humans has to relearn the basics of climbing. Apes find things difficult at first, too!*

*Advanced exercises. This two-year-old is a little overexcited. Carelessly he is exposing himself to risk by swinging with one hand. Immediately his friends follow his bad example.*

*A happy family. A small group of the Dayak women who selflessly and round the clock care for the orphaned orangutans are posing for a photograph. BOS supports the livelihoods of around a thousand Dayaks.*
*Right: This totally exhausted baby cannot wait for the gathering on the lawn and has decided to be carried home.*

*Nightcap. In Nyaru Menteng, before the little climbers go to sleep at the end of a strenuous day, they get together on the "orangutan lawn" for a sip of milk.*

# Mawas, the last refuge for the orangutans

## Why ape protection is also protection for human beings

*Swamp forest as far as the eye can see. Large areas of the Mawas area, which covers 377,000 hectares (1,455 square miles), are still totally unexplored. BOS has so far fought off all attempts by palm oil companies to set up their destructive plantations even here.*

The retreat of the red apes—that is 364,000 ha (1,405 square miles) of nearly untouched swamp and peat swamp rainforest between the rivers Barito and Kapuas. Here, largely undisturbed, approximately 4,000 orangutans are living. Smits will see to it that it remains this way. The area designated as release area is situated to the west of the Barito and is sealed off from the living space of "native" apes by river courses. Here, the orangutans of Kaja, of the other islands, and of the other BOS re-introduction areas are to find a home where they can live as their ancestors did before human beings arrived.

The new national park is to be financed by a "debt-for-nature-swap" (see chart). The principle is as follows: Indonesia preserves her nature and is "paid" for this by the remission of her foreign debts. The running costs of the reservation are to be met by a fund which is fed by money from emissions trading—not within the framework of the Kyoto Protocol but via VERs—voluntary emission rights—which is to secure the population of the park "for good". Shell Canada, subsidary of the international petroleum giant and one of the most important financial backers, has already made a promise of several million dollars—providing BOS succeeds in enforcing the remission of the debt and in turning Mawas into a national park.

They are all to profit from the preservation of the species-rich swamp forests of Mawas: the financially bankrupt country of Indonesia, which gets rid of foreign debts and in return has only to declare the Mawas territory national park; the orangutans and the entire flora and fauna of the territory which now get a chance to survive. The local population, which thanks to the forest and its myriad plants and animals also keep their local climate, their water and pure air, which

*The mighty River Kapuas forms the westerly border of the Mawas area. It meanders through one million hectares (4,000 square miles) of swamp rainforest in which the world's most important orangutan population lives.*

234

*The canals at the southern borders of Mawas are the sad legacy of an insane project. President Suharto wanted to squeeze one million hectares (1,455 square miles) of rice fields out of the rainforest here. The plan failed miserably. BOS is using dams to stop the destructive draining of the marshlands.*

remains untroubled by floods, soil erosion and epidemics, and which is able to make use of BOS' health and education programs. Furthermore, many new jobs will be created—for example by sugar palms, rattan, and fish farming.

And finally the whole world will profit, too.

That is to say that the fate of peat bog forests like those of Mawas is a decisive factor for the destiny of our planet. The destruction of the forest involves the release of gigantic amounts of the greenhouse gas carbon dioxide ($CO_2$), which further accelerate the warming of the earth.

Suharto's nonsensical project alone led to the release of approximately one billion tons of $CO_2$ in 1997 and 1998. (For comparison only: the Kyoto Protocol which came into effect in 2005 obliges Germany to reduce her annual emissions per year of the Kyoto period [2008–2012] by 256 million tons of $CO_2$ equivalent. In order to reach this aim, industry is investing billions of euros.)

A few million euros put into the Mawas project, says Willie Smits, will do disproportionately more for climate protection. By protecting the swamp forests against unscrupulous racketeers, who would love to turn them into dollars, we could help save the globe (which is already getting more and more to a stage where it is beginning to simmer) tremendous amounts of $CO_2$, and this for a give-away price. At the same time, we would gain a continuing $CO_2$-sequestra-

tion system where the greenhouse gas is embedded in peat and thus withdrawn from circulation.

Smits provides a calculation whose enormous figures are just as baffling as its simplicity: in many thousands of years, peat layers with a thickness of up to 18 meters (20 yards) have formed in the 500,000 hectares (2,000 square miles) of Mawas territory. So much carbon dioxide is stored here that the combustion of the peat would release about 3.5 billion tons of the gas into the atmosphere. In total, one third of the carbon dioxide resources of the earth are bound in peat bogs, of which about half are to be found in Indonesia.

Each year one to two mm is added to the peat layer in the forests by leaves falling to the ground and by other organic material. If one assumes one millimeter as a basic value, this means all-in-all 10 m³ (350 cubic feet) of peat per year and per hectare (2.5 acres). As peat consists of about 90 percent water, ten percent of organic material remains, half of which is carbon. This equals half a cubic meter (18 cubic feet) of carbon or 1.84 tons of $CO_2$ per hectare (2.5 acres) per year.

If this is rounded up—which is legitimate in view of a peat formation rate with thicknesses frequently more than one millimeter (0.04 inches)—each hectare (2.5 acres) of peat swamp forest forms two tons of $CO_2$ per year. Applied to the entire Mawas territory of 500,000 ha (about half of it growing peat), this results in an annual storage of one million tons of $CO_2$. Extrapolated to the province of Central Kalimantan with about 12 million hectares (46,000 square miles) of peat bog, this would "save" 24 million tons of $CO_2$ in a natural way and without involving any costs.

However, what if one does not maintain this 12 million ha (46,000 square mile) peat bog as a carbon store but transforms it into oil palm plantations instead? "Because in these plantations about 12 cm (5 inches) of peat per year are degraded and converted into $CO_2$, about 84 billion tons of greenhouse gas frizzle away into the atmosphere," says Willie Smits. "A catastrophe."

*Airborne eco-detectives. With the help of SarVision, BOS can pinpoint any destruction in the rainforest. A comparison of old and new satellite images indisputably documents even small changes in the vegetation cover (see images below). If the organization finds that trees are missing, it sends out its ultralight surveillance planes. As here in the Sebangau National Park, the pilots often catch the wood thieves red-handed. They look for gigantic wood rafts and smoke billowing from peat fires.*

Dieter Teufel, head of the Heidelberg Environmental Prognosis Institute (UPI) agrees with that. The expert has studied Smits' calculation and regards it as being "absolutely accurate." 84 billion tons of $CO_2$ equals one hundred times the yearly emissions of the Federal Republic of Germany, 25 times the emissions of all of Europe, and three times the $CO_2$ emission rate for the whole world in 2004 (28.2 billion tons). The 17,600 wind generators which existed in Germany at the end of 2005 would have to run for 3,400 years in order to save that amount of $CO_2$.

Teufel also backs Smits' assessment that these figures show the EU projects (which are promoted as apparently environmentally beneficial) to be sheer madness: for example the "biodiesel" fuel which contains more and more palm oil from non-sustainable Indonesian production and the use of which is supposed to reduce $CO_2$ emissions, and also the erection of "green" palm oil refineries and co-generation plants, as planned in several EU countries. Palm oil, obtained illegally in Indonesia, does not reduce the $CO_2$ discharge but vastly increases it.

The result is clear. If we save the orangutans and their habitat, we are also saving ourselves. If we—despite all warnings—look on while our red cousins are being murdered and while their wonderful forests are being destroyed, we have not proved ourselves fit for survival. And then there's no reason to waste any tears on us.

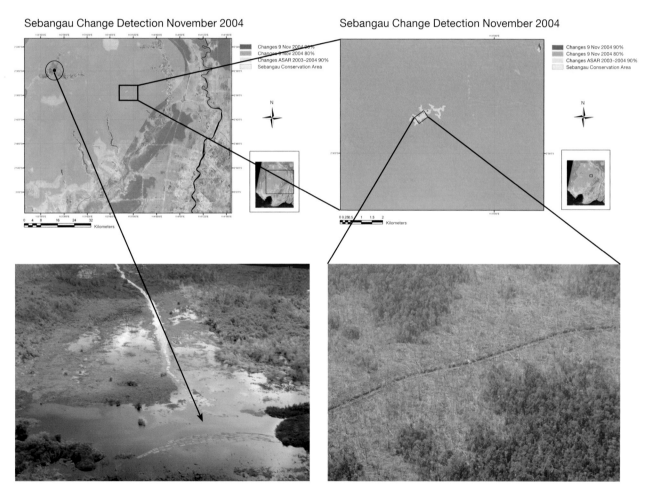

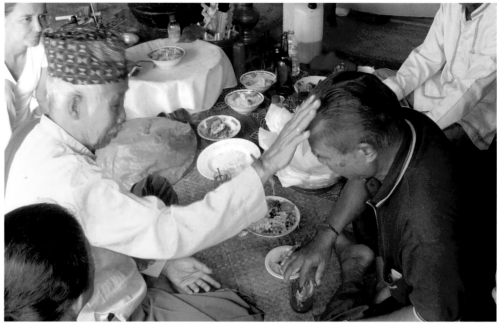

238

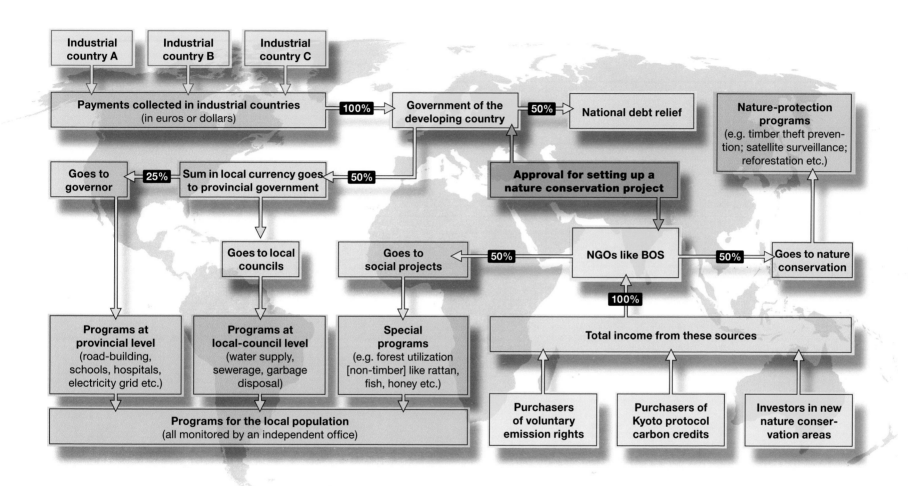

Industrial country A → Industrial country B → Industrial country C

Payments collected in industrial countries (in euros or dollars) — **100%** → Government of the developing country — **50%** → National debt relief

Nature-protection programs (e.g. timber theft prevention; satellite surveillance; reforestation etc.)

**50%** → Sum in local currency goes to provincial government — **25%** → Goes to governor

Approval for setting up a nature conservation project

Goes to local councils

Goes to social projects ← **50%** ← NGOs like BOS — **50%** → Goes to nature conservation

Programs at provincial level (road-building, schools, hospitals, electricity grid etc.)

Programs at local-council level (water supply, sewerage, garbage disposal)

Special programs (e.g. forest utilization [non-timber] like rattan, fish, honey etc.)

**100%** → Total income from these sources

Programs for the local population (all monitored by an independent office)

Purchasers of voluntary emission rights

Purchasers of Kyoto protocol carbon credits

Investors in new nature conservation areas

*Above: Wise suggestion. If common sense played a role in politics, this method of financing nature conservation would be reality by now.*
*Opposite page: Technology is not everything. The conservation of the rainforest depends just as much on gaining the hearts of the native population. For example, in order to purchase the Mawas area from the Dayak people, BOS founder Smits had to endure ceremonies that lasted for days—called Manyanggar—and cut the throat of a pig.*

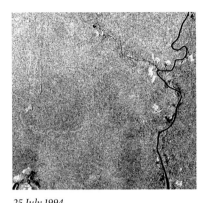 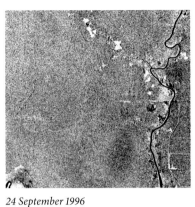 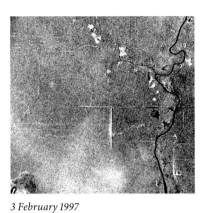 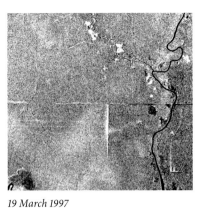 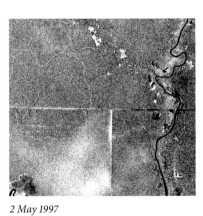

*25 July 1994*      *24 September 1996*      *3 February 1997*      *19 March 1997*      *2 May 1997*

*Chronology of a catastrophe. Using satellite images one can follow how a virgin area of rainforest is first crisscrossed by canals and then drained and partially burnt. The consequences are also documented: vast amounts of former bog turns to peat and burns off or is turned into carbon dioxide by micro-*

*organisms. A huge "peat-dome" collapses and turns into a lake of water, soured by peat acids. According to the calculations of forest ecologist Willie Smits, more than 100 million tons of carbon dioxide have been released into the atmosphere during this process.*

*The end of a "peat dome". The drainage channel is finished and the water is pouring out of the dome—a huge sponge. The drained dome has collapsed (left). The young oil palms, the cause of this evil, drown. What remains is a barren waste (right).*

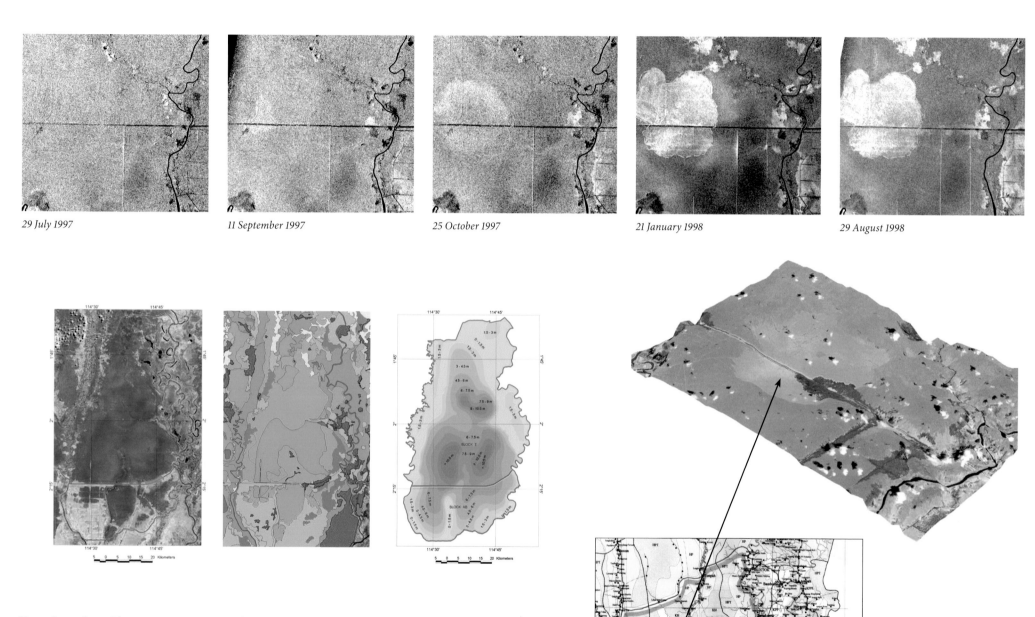

*29 July 1997*

*11 September 1997*

*25 October 1997*

*21 January 1998*

*29 August 1998*

*X-ray of a rainforest. Three pictures, one message. The Landsat image (left) shows the intact Mawas rainforest with three large "peat domes" (dark green patches). The vegetation map of BOS-protected areas (middle) proves that these hills have their own unique flora. The map on the right documents the thickness of the peat. Smits: "By saving Mawas we are preventing around three billion tons of greenhouses gases from being released into the atmosphere. Therefore the conservation of the orangutans means conserving the climate and safeguarding humanity!"*

241

*Subterranean inferno. The evil starts with a drainage canal. The peat dries (above left). When the forest burns the peat eventually goes up in flames, too. No flames can be seen even though the thick layer of peat keeps smoking long after the last tree has gone (above right). The smoldering fire deep in the soil can go on for months. When all organic matter has been burnt a sandy desert remains (below left).*

*Rescuing rattan—and the rainforest. With the help of the German embassy in Jakarta, BOS has established a nursery for rattan south of Buntok along the mighty River Barito. This is of more benefit to the Dayak than if they exported the raw materials. The intention of BOS: if you protect rattan you automatically protect the forest.*

*A swamp rainforest with a natural black water river. Untouched by humans, this is a stable system that produces oxygen and stores carbon dioxide—the best remedy against global warming.*

# So similar and yet so different

## The species and subspecies of the orangutan—
## from *Pongo abelii* to *Pongo pygmaeus pygmaeus*

*The black male Bento in the Meratus forest. The Black Orangutan (Pongo pygmaeus morio) has a comparatively oval face, leathery skin and prominent jaw muscles that are fixed to a bony ridge on the top of the skull.*

The urangutans of Borneo and Sumatra are distinguishable from each other by the color of their hair, by the length and density of their shaggy fur, by their physique, shape of face, character, sociability, culture, menu, reproduction rate, pitch of the voice, sound expressions, sexual habits, and a lot more—in other words, by almost everything.

Therefore, it is no surprise that science has recognized two independent species. But—stop—it is not quite that easy. "Both species, *Pongo abelii* (Sumatra) and *Pongo pygmaeus* (Borneo) were for a long time regarded as being two subspecies called *Pongo pygmaeus abelii* and *Pongo pygmaeus pygmaeus*," explains Anne Russon of York University in Toronto. "But today some of the leading taxonomists regard them as different species."

Although in general, this opinion seems to be gaining acceptance, it does not necessarily have to be "true" or "right" because: "Who knows what people will be thinking in a few years, and whether by that time orangutans will still exist at all?"

Only too true. The interesting profiles of the individual species and subspecies of orangutans seem doomed to perish in the academic quicksand of scientists' squabbles, lack of knowledge, and lack of interest as well as in the apocalyptic maelstrom of extinction. Even now, it is extremely difficult to work out.

It is characteristic that—looking for "Black Orangutan" on the web, otherwise an inexhaustible cornucopia of knowledge—one only finds a cocktail (of vodka, orange-lemonade powder and Coke!) under the catchword but not *Pongo pygmaeus morio*, a threatened subspecies which I had the chance to observe at close range in the Meratus mountains of Central Kalimantan.

The classification is also rendered more difficult by the fact there are even great differences within the subspecies. For instance: some orangutans on West Borneo are of a punky bright orange while on Sumatra—considered to be the domain of russet apes—dark brown furs can be found as well.

Nevertheless, we must attempt to assemble the characteristics known.

*A portly pasha. Dominant Black Orangutan males stand out with their fat, relatively irregular cheek-pads.*
*Right: After a male and a pasha, now a female. One immediately notices the oval face, the dark eyes and the straight maroon hair.*

*Left: Golden Eye. The 'golden' eyes and flowing soft red hair are characteristic for this young Sumatran Orangutan.*
*Above: Red to yellow-red fur, a blond goatee, blond hairs on the slim, evenly shaped, nearly round cheek-pads, amber eyes, white spots on the eyelids—this is the Sumatran Orangutan Pongo abelii. Pictured is Sumo, a 26-year-old male from Jakarta Zoo.*

247

*Chalk and cheese. A Black Orangutan (left) and a Sumatran Orangutan (right) sitting on a bench in Ragunan Zoo. It does not take an expert to see the big difference in the texture of the fur (left: thicker, stiffer hair; right: soft, silky, curly hair that blows in the wind).*

*A bearded lady. The female Sumatran Orangutans, too, sport a lush blond 'male adornment'. Yellowish facial hair is one of the most important features of the Sumatran Orangutan.*

*Broad mouth, curly red hair, comparatively fair facial skin and bright eye rings—this the orangutan from Central Borneo,* Pongo pygmaeus wurmbii.

The Sumatran Orangutan *(Pongo abelii)* as a rule has much more intensively red-colored fur than the Borneo variety. It is considered to be more sociable—which, however, as previously mentioned, seems to be the consequence of a more varied diet, and is to be found (probably for the same reason) at still greater heights than its relatives from the neighboring island. It not only consumes more fruit but obviously also enriches its diet with more insects.

"The coat of the Sumatran Orangutans is lighter, thicker, and longer," explains Canadian psychology professor Anne Russon. "Their faces are paler and narrower, and all in all they are more gracile, rather more graceful than robust." Their beards are more pronounced and they spend more time in trees than their counterparts from Borneo—probably because there are still tigers on Sumatra, which do not exist on Borneo any more.

For Willie Smits just one glance at the face is enough to identify the species: "The eyes are golden brown, yellow hairs grow on their faces and pashas tend to have heart-shaped cheek-pads."

An especially important distinguishing factor is the birth frequency: on Sumatra (according to anthropologist Carel van Schaik), the ape females on average give birth to one child about every nine years as against every six years on Borneo. The figure for West Borneo "lay somewhere in between the two". According to Smits' experience with wild and re-introduced Black Orangutans, the inter-birth interval (IBI) on East Borneo is just four years.

The reason for the shorter IBI on East Borneo according to Schaik is probably "a slightly higher adult mortality rate" due to tougher climatic conditions and a different diet. The apes there had less fruit at their disposal and had to feed on leaves for longer periods of time, which brings about a greater risk of poisoning.

Even with regard to ape love there are very significant differences between the two islands: while on Sumatra about half of the babies are sired "consensually" by dominant territory-owners with ape females who go on a pilgrimage to see them, about 90 percent of the Borneo births are traceable to rapes of itinerant single females by "young adult" males without pasha status (see page 86). According to statements of Honolulu Zoo, the ape females often get injured by brutal bites in the process. In cases of "consensual" matings, the Sumatran Orangutans took several weeks for their liaison whereas on Borneo the few non-violent affairs ended most of the time after just a few days.

The Bornean Orangutan *(Pongo pygmaeus)* has to struggle with far more extreme fluctuations in his food supply and—especially on the east coast—atmospheric conditions than his cousin on Sumatra because on Borneo long drought periods and meager fruit yields occur much more frequently. The meager times in which mainly leaves and bark dominate the menu are, however, now and then sweetened by

*The Central Bornean Orangutan also comes in lighter shades.*

*A splendid pasha specimen. The Central Bornean Orangutan (Pongo pygmaeus wurmbii) resembles his cousin from Sumatra in some respects; however, his beard is smaller and the blond facial hairs are absent. Furthermore the eye color is darker and the cheek-pads are more irregular and rougher.*

*A kind of 'hybrid' between the black and the Central Bornean Orangutan is the Northwest Bornean Orangutan (Pongo pygmaeus pygmaeus).*
*On this rare picture of a confiscated animal in West Kalimantan it can be seen that his hair is straight and his jaw unusually broad.*

One of the ways to differentiate between the two orangutan species is their fingerprints. This may also be the case with the subspecies. The research is in full swing at BOS in Wanariset. The scientists make use of fingerprint sheets from the Dutch police and identification software from Interpol. The data gathered are used within the framework of an official collaboration between BOS and Interpol to identify confiscated animals.

253

what are known as "mast" years. At such times, many trees of the same kind are all heavily laden with fruit, and the apes can practice gluttony for weeks.

Anne Russon traces back the differences in the fertility of the two islands—beside climatic differences—to their geology: Borneo lies mainly on sedimentary rock whereas Sumatra is of volcanic origin.

Because on Borneo—apart from a mountain range bisecting the island from southwest to northeast—there are many large rivers like the Kapuas, Barito, and Makaham, forming insurmountable barriers, "two to four" subspecies had formed in the areas isolated from rivers from each other. Three are currently distinguished by zoologists: the Central Bornean Orangutan *(Pongo pygmaeus wurmbii),* the Northeast Bornean Orangutan *(Pongo pygmaeus morio)* and the Northwest Bornean Orangutan *(Pongo pygmaeus pygmaeus).*

The Central Bornean Orangutan, represented by about 38,000 animals (as of 2002) is the most frequent subspecies of the island. It is mainly to be found in Southwest Kalimantan, south of the Kapuas, and west of the Barito, and its considerable, though increasingly fragmented, habitat is situated in swamp and lowland winged-fruit forests (see page 147) of Central Kalimantan. Respectable populations also exist in Tanjung Puting National Park, in the Sebangau and Mawas territory of Central Kalimantan, in Gulung-Palung National Park of West Kalimantan, and in the forests along the borderline between Central and West Kalimantan.

Information on the physiological particularities of the subspecies is unfortunately scanty: Anne Russon merely noted that the Central Bornean Orangutans were "much redder" than the other varieties on the island.

With approximately 14,000 animals (as of 2002), the Northeast Bornean Orangutan represents the second-commonest subspecies. The fragmented remnant populations of the Black Orangutan are mainly to be found in the Malaysian province of Sabah, in Gunung Gajah, and in the Berau region of East Kalimantan south of the Makaham, where about 11,000 animals survive. More than half of the

Sabah population (according to the PHVA study) live in the plantations around the Danum Valley nature reserve. Although investigations by WWF and of the Hutan Organization show that orangutans obviously seem to be able to adapt to life in the affected forests if there is no poaching or large-scale forest destruction, the prognosis for the Northeast Bornean Orangutan is nevertheless negative as there is no money for effective protective measures.

Thanks to its blackish-brown to black coloration, *Pongo pygmaeus morio* has without any doubt the most eye-catching appearance of all the Borneo subspecies. This seemed to have prompted primatologists to give them attention they had previously denied both other subspecies.

According to Willie Smits the orangutan—surely the animal best adapted to living conditions on the island—has a more oval-shaped, slimmer and less angular face, smaller jaws with larger eye-teeth, a pronounced cranial bone forming a base for its extremely strong chewing musculature and eyes of a deep blackish-brown to black. It has glossy, less wavy, dark brown to black fur, stiffer and rounder cheek-pads, a higher pitch of voice, and a shorter "long call" (see pages 76 and 82). The black ape—experts call the color of its hair "maroon"—lives almost entirely on leaves and bark, has longer forearms (rather than upper arms) than the majority of the orangutans—BOS measurement data are being currently evaluated—and, according to Smits, gives off a very particular smell of tea and sweat.

Its comparatively very short IBI, which according to Willie Smits ranges between three and four years, is noticeable.

Even within the subspecies, there are significant differences in appearance: right in the central zone of *Pongo pygmaeus morio,* variations can be seen in the shape of the skull and the color of the fur. Smits: "In the southern part, all orangutans are totally black, in the north; the hair under their arms is slightly paler. There is still a lot of research to be done!"

The Northwest Bornean Orangutan, the poor cousin of the three subspecies, only appears in Northwest Kalimantan, north of the

Kapuas, and in the border area between Malaysian Sarawak and West Kalimantan. Its total population is estimated at only 3,000 animals, and it is acutely threatened by extinction. Significant populations still only exist in the Batang-Ai/Lanjak-Entimau reserve complex in the south of Sarawak, in the southwest part of the Betung-Kerihun National Park, and in the Danau Sentarum National Park (both in West Kalimantan).

According to the PHVA study, this last "stronghold" of the subspecies is strongly affected by the felling of trees and by hunting. The sole hope of the 1,500 or so apes surviving in the national park was that the Betung Kerihun reserve with its lowland rainforest areas could be extended to the south and could be connected with the reserve

in Sarawak—probably a great dream. Little hope is raised by the fact that the study underlines "the necessity of obtaining well-founded information on Betung Kerihun or at least properly analyzing and publishing the available information". There seem to be quite a few problems here.

This is also what Anne Russon's answer to the question regarding the characteristics of the animal suggests. "Not much is known about *Pongo pygmaeus pygmaeus*," said the professor. "There hasn't been a lot of research done on this."

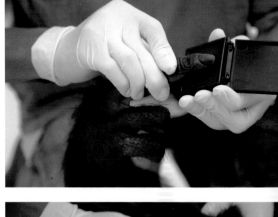

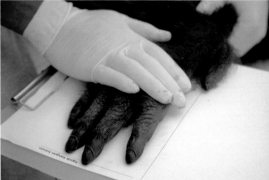

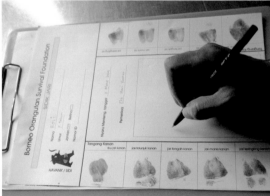

*Black hand on the 'criminal record. Highly interested in the procedure, this orangutan has his prints taken by the Dutch police specialists Jan Geerdink and Cees Bosveld in Samboja Lestari. More 'volunteers' are waiting.*

255

# The *Pongo pygmaeus* polaroids

## How ape female Uce got photos for her "family album"

*'Look, this is us!' Enthusiastically, Uce and her baby Matahari look at their images on Jay Ullal's Polaroids.*

What can an ape in the middle of the jungle do with photographs? Does it understand what they are? Does it recognize itself on the pictures? Does it enjoy those photos? Does it have the wish to collect its snapshots? You think not? In that case, there is a surprise waiting for you…

The unbelievable thing with Uce and the polaroids would have never happened without a series of coincidences. It all started in the spring of 2003 when I was assigned to write a big story about great apes in general and orangutans in particular for *Stern*. To start with, my research was entirely concentrated on the work of Canadian scientist Biruté Galdikas, because she was the superstar of the orangutan scene and her name loomed large. All paths led to her.

I read anything I could lay my hands on about her in order to be prepared for my planned visit to her in Indonesia. However, the more I read, the greater my uneasiness became: Tanjung Puting on Borneo where the scientist is working and holding court was for the most part in the hands of illegal loggers who are increasingly cutting it to shreds, and only a few kilometers away from Camp Leakey, the center of field research in the reserve, thousands of gold-diggers were churning up the earth and polluting the rivers with mercury—but nobody seemed to mind, least of all Ms Galdikas. What was happening there?

For the sake of clarity, I visited Ashley Leiman, the London aide-de-camp of Galdikas' Orangutan Foundation International (OFI). Unfortunately, my reservations were not resolved but were instead confirmed: instead of showing decided initiative and energy for the saving of the orangutans that—according to OFI warnings—were just given a reprieve of just a few years, Ms Leiman was pinning her hopes totally on careful use of tactics and polite pussyfooting when dealing with the corrupt Indonesian authorities and military.

The thought of a story in *Stern* gave her no pleasure but headaches instead—despite the desperate situation of the national park and its orangutans which she seemed to shut out. If the story turned out to be too tough, she said, it could endanger the relationship with the Indonesian authorities which she would have to carry on treating with "kid gloves". This is why she did not want to be seen with me under any circumstances by showing me the gold-diggers' town near Camp Leakey. This I had to find on my own.

It was clear to me that I did not wish to collaborate with these people. I wanted facts and clear statements and not faith-healing or dithering. However, which expert would then be able to present me a picture of the situation? I needed someone who really wanted to save the red apes.

*'Willie, look over here!' Proudly Uce shows her savior Willie Smits the new portrait photographs. In the meantime Matahari is taking refreshment from Uce's breast.*

*'How am I supposed to climb now?' Uce discovers that she has a transport problem. With child and Polaroids even an orangutan does not have enough hands to grip. Her solution: she leaves the photos in the safekeeping of ranger Misry and comes to look at them once in a while.*

I was frustrated when poring over my folder of press clippings. Galdikas everywhere. Then I came across two articles in American magazines, which were concerned with Willie Smits, obviously a man of action. I "X-rayed" him and came to the conclusion that here was a person who did not present an animal welfare show but who really lobbied for our shaggy cousins, no matter how dangerous it became and how many tropical diseases he picked up.

*Stern* photographer Jay Ullal and I took a plane to Indonesia and, together with Smits, visited all the important arenas in and around Jakarta and on Borneo. When we heard that, without the female ape Uce, BOS—the most active orangutan protection organization in the world—would never have materialized (see page 204), we pressed Smits to have his photo taken with her. The animal-rights activist and the female ape who set the ball rolling—that was not just one of those photos typical of *Stern* reports; it was a must.

Willie Smits, who was very busy, was reluctant at first, but then agreed. A few days later, he told us he had told a gamekeeper in Sungai Wain, the territory where Uce had been re-introduced, to inform her that we would come to visit her. This seemed a rather a strange piece of information to us. We asked ourselves: how does one convey such a message to a wild-living orangutan in a jungle area of more than ten thousand hectares (40 square miles)? And how does the ape understand the message?

When the Uce photos were due to be taken, we took a plane to Balikpapan, drove to the forest area, wandered for a while over a mile-long wooden footbridge through the swamp rainforest and then fought our way through the thicket. I learned that "rattan" is by no means a harmless fiber from which perfect seating furniture can be woven, but that rattan in its original state is a twine covered with minute black thorns which one can hardly make out in the shady jungle and which clings to the face like a kind of biological barbed wire. In the evening, I counted 23 thorns in my right hand.

Uce had really and truly waited for us. But she did not like Jay Ullal or me at all. The large female ape, whose seven-month-old baby Matahari was shyly peering out of her long fur, stretched out her endlessly long right arm in defense. Her lips became tight and hard, the hairs on her cheeks stood up, her eyebrows slid down and became thick, and her eyes seemed to assume an even darker brown. She further alternated angry bass grunting sounds with penetrating kiss-smacking—a sign of strong aversion.

Willie Smits explained to us that orangutan mothers were very suspicious, extremely strong and had no sense of humor. He would calm Uce down and we should withdraw until then. So we took ourselves to the BOS ranger station in the vicinity with its 65-meter (70-yard) fire-watch tower and drank some water. Then from a distance of about 20 meters (around 20 yards) we watched Willie Smits talking to Uce in a very familiar way, stroking her and clearly congratulating her on Matahari, her second child. Despite all this, she did not stop throwing angry glances at us. Jay took a few telephoto pictures.

After more than an hour, Smits signaled that we could separately come closer. I let Jay go first because we mainly wanted the picture of the founder of the BOS and his first female ape. When he had taken

*"Can one see into this marvel?" Uce, who has never seen a photo before, explores all dimensions of the portrait. She inspects the front and back of the photo and even tries to look into the picture.*

*'Thanks and good-bye'.
Uce bids farewell to
Willie Smits and sends
a thankful smile to
photographer Jay Ullal.*

But what was Jay doing now? I held my breath. He flashed into Uce's face with the SX-70 although a moment before Smits had forbidden this categorically: Uce would be scared and could become aggressive. However, Smits did not scold us, and the orangutan female was by no means angry; on the contrary: she seemed very interested. As the first picture shot out of the camera with a loud burr, she demanded it immediately with her long arm, and Jay handed it over to her.

The ape turned the photo about in her hands, only threw a tenth-of-a-second glance at the black reverse side, and noticed immediately that a photo was starting to emerge on the other side and was delighted to recognize Matahari and herself. She showed the plastic square to her child, who likewise started to beam, happily pressed the photo against her forehead, kissed and hugged it—and wiped it clean on her "sleeve"!

Two minutes later, Uce held three instant pictures in her extra-long hairy hand. She placed the photos consecutively, like playing cards, looked at them one after the other, showed them again to her child and to Willie. Then Uce looked at Jay—glowing with happiness, her mouth round, her eyes glittering like stars. The aversion was gone with the wind!

After half an hour, she wanted to return to the forest—and realized that the Polaroids in her hand made climbing difficult. She considered this for a moment—and then delivered her photos in trust. However, not to Willie Smits, whom she knew would only visit her every few years, but to Misry, the gamekeeper and ranger who lived in the little ranger house. At his place, she would be able to look at the photos every now and then.

Unbelievable? Willie Smits has asked Misry. Uce had asked to have her photos shown to her six times during the past two and a half years.

several photos, Jay retreated and I took his place. I looked at Smits, Uce and the baby from a distance of about three meters (around three yards), suspiciously eyed by Uce, took my notes and withdrew again.

Jay carried on taking picture after picture with his Canons but suddenly he bent down, rummaged around in his 40-kg (90-pound) photo-bag and got hold of his Polaroid camera. I could not believe my eyes because the foldable SX-70 normally only came into operation when Jay wanted to gain the favors of grumpy doormen or bad-tempered cross-grained government officials by giving them a photo present—a rare treasure in many Asian countries (the ploy was successful most of the time). It always used to amuse me when Indians, Nepalese and Indonesians—for whom polaroids certainly presented a complete novelty—as a rule first stared at the black reverse side of the plastic picture while their outlines slowly appeared on the other side.

*'I will miss you.' Uces parting look goes straight to Willie's heart because he can see her gratitude and deep affection. Willie: 'This is my favorite picture!'*

# Psychograph of a primate

## Experiences with a thousand orangutans

*Tenderness amongst primates. The six-year-old ape boy hugs Willie Smits, full of joy at seeing him again. Smits rescued him two years ago from a cage in Balikpapan. Shortly after the picture was taken the orangutan was released into the wild.*

One would like to believe that orangutans are too good for this world. They are quite different from chimpanzees, which are loud, hectic and often aggressive, or from gorillas, which appear slow, anxious and often a little dull. The red great apes of Borneo and Sumatra are, as a rule, extraordinarily smart, thoughtful, gentle and kind-hearted. Their altruism and their lack of vengefulness constantly baffle scientists. Willie Smits is trying to put their nature into words.

Some time ago, I went with a group of orangutan babies and their nurses into the newly planted forest of Samboja Lestari near Wanariset. Here in East Kalimantan on Borneo I wanted to watch how the two-to-four-year-old orphan apes learned to climb and how they tried to find a first few delicacies on their own. The BOS coordinator, Jo-lan van Leeuwen, accompanied me because she wanted to take a few photos.

It did not take long before she drew the attention of Yunus, the roughneck of the group, who liked nothing better than terrorizing his human custodians and his little companions in misfortune. Yunus, hardly weighing eight kilos (18 pounds) and only half a meter (1ft 8in) tall, pushed Jo-lan about, bit and scratched and did everything in his power to get on her nerves.

While Jo-lan was mobilizing all her strength to fight against the little scallywag, it came to my mind what a big exception Yunus was. I know far more than a thousand orangutans personally, so to speak, and I can nevertheless count the louts amongst them on the fingers of one hand. For example Kai of Ragunan

Zoo in Jakarta or Ancha from Wanariset whom we had to put into a group of elder orangutans because the babysitters were unable to cope with him any more—and who was made considerably more peaceful by the educational influence of his stronger fellow apes.

I looked at Yunus and reflected how peaceful the "normal" orangutans are, how friendly and gentle their behavior was when one was able to read their eyes and lips as well as their body language and when one approached them when properly informed about this.

*Vise-like grip. This ape is holding on to BOS staffer Jo-lan van Leeuwen with both hands in the rehabilitation center at Nyaru Menteng. The ape wants to prevent the visitor from leaving as she brings a welcome distraction to the monotony in the quarantine section.*

*Excitement before the day in the woods. The little climbing students can hardly wait to swing into the trees. Sumi (far left in white overall) shares their happiness.*

*The boss distributes the treats. Even though the young pleading ape has put himself into a submissive position, the orangutan male from the BOS island Kaja lets him wait whilst he provides access to food for the higher ranking female with baby.*

As these thoughts went through my head, something happened which showed how incredibly altruistic they can also be.

Jo-lan had tried everything to get Yunus to stop but he would not let go and obviously seemed already too strong for her although he had to be classified at least twenty wrestling-weight classes lower. Therefore, I decided to interfere and I just managed to loosen the little ape from Jo-lan's leg. I held the little one in a wrestler's grip and carried him away.

Of course, I could have rebuked Yunus through my eyes or body language without touching him but this would not have been helpful for Jo-lan and the other little orangutans in the long run. Therefore, I wanted to teach him a lesson—certainly one that would not hurt him. All he was supposed to get was to be taken down a peg or two, just a little lesson taught, similar to those given to little rainforest orangutans by their moms when they are misbehaving.

When I plucked Yunus off from Jo-lan's leg, he must have become a bit panicky because he realized that he had no chance against my physical strength (in younger years, I was a heavyweight wrestler; I am 1.87 m (6ft 2in) tall and I tip the scales at about 105 kg (230 pounds). He was obviously scared and was shaking, not knowing what was

going to happen to him now and what kind of punishment was awaiting him. Like all orangutans, Yunus knew perfectly well that he had misbehaved in the case of Jo-lan—and he shouted something to the other 14 babies and toddlers.

As an answer to this call, suddenly almost all of the little ones—the same ones he normally used to jostle and thump about—came to his aid. They tried to bite me in the leg, tugged at me and quite obviously wanted to stop from carrying Yunus away. Of course, the little ones in their diapers could not do me any harm, and they seemed to be aware of this because they did not bite me properly and merely plucked at my clothes instead of seriously tearing or ripping. It was rather an attempt to propitiate me because they begged me with little cheeps to let go of Yunus.

When I put the little rascal on the ground a few meters away from Jo-lan and gave him a clear rebuke with my wagging finger, they stopped immediately and resumed their game of climbing as if nothing had happened. A few other little apes came to me and wanted to be cuddled or to play with me, just as if they were trying to make up for Yunus' naughtiness (he was now sitting in a tree with a face as long as a fiddle).

This was not the only incident of this kind. On the lawn of the BOS centre in Nyaru Menteng in Central Kalimantan, where the babies gather in the evenings after a strenuous day of climbing in the nearby forest, Dancow (named after the brand of milk powder which he is so fond of) wanted to find out how far he could go with his biting. When I finally held his arm in a grip of iron, he also let out a cry of alarm—just like Yunus—and the other little ones came forward to his rescue! So, even orangutan babies are already programmed to help each other.

## Experiences with fellow creatures— not data from animal experiments

I am not writing this as a primatologist or as an ape-research academic because this is not my field. My training is that of a rainforest ecologist and if I write about orangutans then this is not about my research but about my experiences and emotions, my attempts to understand them "instinctively". However, when I do this, I often use anthropomorphisms (a serious mistake of primatologists) when describing certain behavior patterns which I have observed with them.

So I certainly do not insist that I draw the proper conclusions from what I have observed; I would quite simply like to share my experiences of orangutans with you. Some observations are second-hand, by far the largest part, often repeated, my own.

So I am not ladling out pure science to you. But maybe one has to be an amateur, a scientific outsider, to be able to write on such a pretentious subject. Let me then fall deliberately into the "trap" of anthropomorphism, the "humanization" of animals. And don't say you haven't been warned!

As I live a fairly dangerous life I thought it would be better to start early enough putting down on paper my very special experiences with orangutans. Let us then speak about friendship between orangutans and humans, about altruism, about attempts to explore the mind of a furry counterpart, let us "read" his emotions, let us feel and communicate.

Altruism—unselfishness and mildness—is very rarely observed in nature as it seems to contradict the iron law of survival of the fittest. In the case of ants, however, altruism seems to be programmed in the genes, and bloodsucking bats filled up with the blood of cattle share their spoils with others that had no luck during their nocturnal hunt. Here, altruism is a means of conservation of the species.

Although there are other examples, we human beings often regard altruism and empathy as purely human traits. Compassion and the ability to recognize and to interpret the emotions of the others mean not only a tremendous progress, going beyond the sheer delight in imitation which is anchored deeply in us and in many other living creatures; a number of scientists regard them as the origin of language.

Altruism, however, can only work if it is based on mutuality. Not only in a small group of bloodsucking vampire bats. But how about the orangutans? How altruistic are they? And how does it show?

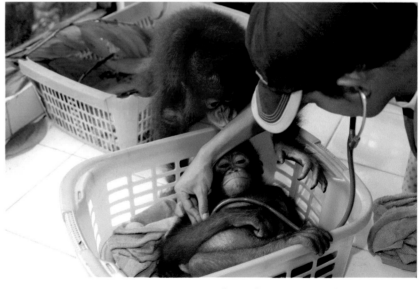

*Consultation for orangutans. Calmly the orangutan (top) allows an examination by a vet. Below, a friend of the patient is 'supervising' every move of the vet.*

*It is far too boring in this joint, let me out!*

*I wonder if I can manage to open this darned lock? The humans manage it in the blink of an eye…*

*Let's give the lock a lick. A kiss might work wonders…*

*Groan! Another failed attempt! The accursed thing cannot be opened…*

Let us start with empathy. It is based on compassion. It was absolutely clear to the little apes who rushed to Yunus' support that he was in danger and it is for this reason that they dared to take me on—me, a 1.87 m giant who had got hold of the strongest member of their group—although it was certain they were very frightened.

The only other logical explanation for their behavior would be that they followed a verbal command of Yunus. But this is rather unlikely. Something went through the minds and the hearts of the group, moved creatures who are still dubbed "loners" by so many people who cannot understand that one does not necessarily have to be antisocial if one spends a lot of time on one's own. There is a tremendous difference whether one is alone because one shies away from the company of others or because the scanty supply of food and other circumstances force you to live that way.

Compassion does not require language. In the old silent movies, the faces and body language of the actors were enough to move an audience to tears or to make them laugh.

Are orangutans also able to read their feelings—and your feelings, too—from faces? Even much less intelligent macaque apes have shown various strong reactions under trial conditions, depending whether they were presented with pictures of angry or uninterested conspecifics.

Orangutans are vastly better readers of facial expressions than macaques are. They are able to recognize changes which are a thousand times more subtle than the raised hackles of an angry dog or the bared teeth of an aggressive ape. They are able to discern such minute, almost imperceptible differences in a physiognomy and to evaluate them so precisely that you would probably feel quite uncomfortable if you knew how far this ability has developed.

There is every indication that they can read our faces like an open book. This is especially the case with orangutans who know "their" human beings better and over a lengthy period of time. Uce, my very first orangutan, whom I encountered for the first time as a dying

baby and who is now something like a female friend (see page 204), is one such.

But Nian also achieved something quite amazing: endlessly, he had to spend long periods of time alone in a cage of one of our isolation wards in quarantine as a result of his active hepatitis B. But the little fellow did not lose heart. When I visited him—for which he was more than grateful—he at first pretended lack of interest and a preference for playing just to show how much of a survivor he was and that he needed nobody. But then he stretched hand and arm through the bars and allowed me to stroke him.

He always knew exactly when the time came for me to go. Even if I had not risen but only intended going, he started to ask for a bit

*Mother's kiss. The nanny, who is from the Dayak tribe, cuddles and kisses her little charge as if he were her own child. Until the ape babies are about two years old they are spoiled with affection by their surrogate mothers, who talk to them in their Dayak dialect. When they get older the contact becomes more distant and the language will be Indonesian.*

more tenderness and concern. When it became time for me to say good-bye, Nian did everything to arouse my interest in him and to occupy my attention in order to make me stay.

As his apprehension of the time of my departure had occupied my mind for some time, I performed a little experiment: I sat by his cage, stroked him—and then made the decision to get up and go in ten seconds. While doing this, I concentrated with all my might on not giving myself away by facial expression or body language. However, it was of no avail: at the moment I decided to leave him, Nian knew, and fear of loss took possession of him. I believe for sure that tiniest changes of my eye area or other signs must have given me away because he must have seen something which told him: Willie wants to leave!

Now some people will say: no, the orangutan has read your thoughts! But even if Nian's achievement seems impossible and reminds one of telepathy: it has nothing to do with extrasensory perception, rather with intuition, with subconscious—or as in this case quite conscious—reading of the most subtle of physical indications.

It is completely clear to me that these are not the sober statements of a scientist. However, as I have already mentioned, this is not important for me. If you think I am writing nonsense then simply stop reading. If you do however think that such exchange of emotions and matters between non-human primates and us humans is within the range of our possibilities, please, do carry on reading.

That is to say: the differences between humans and orangutans could be far smaller than commonly thought. The experiences I had with orangutans have time and again given me goose-pimples, have brought tears into my eyes—and have brought anger into my heart and made me fly into a passion against those who kill these unique beings for a few dollars or keep them for years, suffering in small cages.

In former times, when I still selected the primate keepers in the BOS centers myself, I often subjected the candidates to a "screening test" which was regarded as extremely unfair by them: after they had spent a few weeks with their group of orangutans, had fed them, had cleaned their cages and done other tasks, I joined them and sat by a cage. Doing this, I pretended that all this was none of my business at all: I nibbled at a blade of grass or scribbled in my notebook.

I acted as if I were not there so that the orangutans' interest in me ebbed and they were able to concentrate on other things and would not take any more notice of me. However, this is easier said than done: they can watch us out of the corners of their eyes, and it seems as if their attention never fades. By the way: in cases like this, one is well advised to settle at such distance from the cages that their inmates will not be able to piddle or spit at you, and that one is beyond the range of branches, fruit leftovers and excrement. It takes a while, but the time comes when one knows the tricks orangutans use for trying to draw the attention of human visitors.

Once I have managed to become uninteresting for the orangutans, the time for the little test is ripe. The new keeper is doing his work and I observe—no, not him—the eyes of the apes. If they lower their heads just a little bit, when their eyes throw a certain direct glance at the keeper and when their lips tauten just a tiny bit, then I know…

## Reading orangutan eyes

And you too? Is the orangutan interested? Is he happy? Or upset? No, none of this! The glance means: "Oh, there he is again, this boring and impersonal distributor of food. Nothing doing with him at all!" If the majority of the red giants just have this sort of glance for the

*Silent happiness in mother's lap. This two-and-a-half year old orangutan is fully relaxed as he puts his head on the knees of his human guardian and calmly looks at her.*

keeper, I have to start working on them, not the animals, of course, but with the humans.

If, however, the orangutans turn away when their keeper appears, and if they sound their aggressive and smacking kissing or if they start to piddle, then I know that something unpleasant must have happened and that I have to take a tougher line.

Of course, I do not only observe the eyes of the great ape but those of the human being, too. They tell me quite a lot about the opinion they have of the orangutans, whether they are no more than any animal for them or whether they have taken them into their hearts, or if they are just doing their job.

If I suspect that something is wrong between the orangutans and the new keeper I take him or her aside and relate some of the things about the red kings of the jungle which I am putting down on paper in this little story. After that, there is hardly ever one of them who would remain cold-hearted in dealing with orangutans.

Sometimes I can recognize even more in the eyes of the orangutans. At one time, I stood beside Bonzo's cage and asked a keeper whether he had problems with this difficult orangutan male. He vehemently denied this—a little bit too vehemently, it seemed to me. Therefore, I positioned my self close to Bonzo and asked the keeper to come closer. And there—there was vengefulness glowing in Bonzo's eyes!

I asked the young man again, but he carried on denying it. Then I said: "Just put your arm through the bars—just as I do—and ruffle his chin!" It was then that he broke down and started to cry; then that he told me what had happened. When he was hosing the cages distractedly at one time, Bonzo had snatched the hose and

*Certainly not an advert for Colgate. The laughing orangutan has lived with humans until recently and has been fed with sweets; hence his teeth are partly ruined and not as white as they would be naturally.*

had given him a thorough shower. When he had tried to wrest the rubber pipe away from the ape male, Bonzo had hit him with the hose. He had taken his revenge by hitting Bonzo on his arm with a stick.

I did not throw the young man out because I knew that he was a good worker to whom the orangutans meant something; what had taken place was one of those things which simply happen. Some time later, the same keeper showed me full of pride that he and Bonzo had become firm friends.

I have had hundreds of similar experiences with orangutans, quite frequently with animals I had never known before. The example of the difficult and really dicey confiscation of Candy and Friska comes to my mind here. Both rainforest dwellers had spent more than ten years locked inside a tiny house by the side of a noisy through road, polluted by exhaust gas clouds, in the south of Jakarta. During their imprisonment, they had become chain-smokers and so fat that their legs could not carry them any more. Friska, the female ape, weighed about 130 kg (290 pounds), more than three times her normal weight, and Candy, her male fellow-sufferer, was a little heavier still.

Several attempts to free Candy and Friska had already failed and it looked to us that they would fail again this time. The "owners" threatened to "pull strings" and fought viciously against the confiscation of their shaggy home-companions. As usual, they flew off the handle. In all probability, they had already ordered a gang of thugs for reinforcement and we had to hurry.

The two wobbly orangutans with their thick fat-bulges were rolling about like balls inside the tiny room and we had to assume that they too could become dangerous for us. It was clear to me that we only had one chance and this only if we could make the animals cooperate with us. (By the way, we had hardly evacuated both heavyweights after the arrival of a police-unit when a truck with very unfriendly, much tattooed gentlemen stopped outside the house. The rearguard of the police was given a heavy beating!)

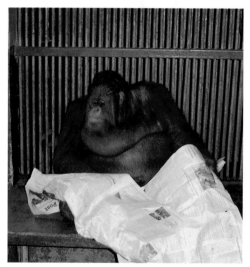

*Two ape dumplings. Friska (top) and Candy (below) lived with a family in Jakarta for around ten years. Both of them were given Coke and beer, were chain smokers and weighed 130 kg (290 pounds). Shortly after their rescue they died of hepatitis and lung cancer.*

*Bruno's 'coin'. Bruno, a large ape male from Los Angeles zoo, gave Willie Smits, on his second visit to the zoo, a 'dollar': The ape's present is made from chewed orange peel and jute fiber.*

While the squad leaders of the forest police were—as was customary—obligingly conversing with the owners of the orangutans instead of taking drastic measures, I sat down on the ground by the side of Candy. At first, he pulled and tugged at me in order to test my strength and to see whether I was frightened and how decided I was.

I must have impressed him because suddenly he took a deep look into my eyes. I suppose that he must have recognized that I was none of the usual visitors who would normally shake with laughter when he lit a cigarette or got himself drunk and was staggering about. I felt burning compassion with this gentle giant with his fat bulges around his tummy and the thick double chin who had started to grow cheek-pads—the marks of dominant kings of the jungle in the freedom of their rainforests—inside this dump by the side of the stinking main road.

All of a sudden, Candy showed me his right foot. I saw a nasty open gangrenous wound and asked him: "Kenapa ada luka?" (Where did you get this wound?) Immediately he looked at the hot-water bottle which was lying on a cupboard. (Orangutans who have spent a long time with humans understand several hundred words of the language of their hosts. And any animal keeper in a zoo knows that one must never use terms like "jab" or "tranquilizer" when an orangutan is within hearing distance.)

I then asked him: "Siapa yang bikin?" (Who has done this?), and with a quick turn of his head, Candy looked at a skinny chap in a dirty sleeveless shirt who stood in the corner. I immediately accused him of having tortured Candy and he admitted it. There was no other way of keeping these huge apes at bay, he said, than by inflicting pain on them. Yes, and he had scalded Candy with boiling water.

However, that was not all: Candy, who held my hand, drew my attention to a small bottle with eucalyptus oil. As it turned out the "animal lovers" of this house used to spray the essential oil (which burned like hell's fire on the mucous membranes) into their eyes to make them docile, or they threatened to do it! Each member of the extended family always had a pocket flask of eucalyptus oil within easy reach!

It is remarkable how fast Candy decided that he could trust me and tell me his story. It was almost as if he had known I would be coming to get him out of his misery. So much sadder for me that he died only a month later. He suffered from hepatitis, and TB and cancer were destroying his lungs, which had turned pitch-black from the tar of the cigarette smoke. What an endless pity that he was never again able to see the rainforest to which we would have loved to bring him back. Unfortunately, Friska also died a few months after this.

Something incredible also happened with Bruno. The big orangutan male from Los Angeles zoo surprised me with a present although he hardly knew me; I had seen him two years before for the first time and had only visited him for about ten minutes. But he recognized me immediately and spat something into my palm. It was a "coin", a round "dime" of chewed-up and then dried orange peel which Bruno had carefully wrapped with jute fibers which he had pulled from a sack.

Maybe the orangutan had watched people handing out coins and thereby recognized that these flat round things were of a particular value. Because he wanted to give me something valuable, he had made his own coin!

I tried to give the present back to Bruno but he pressed it again into my hand, closed my hand into a fist, turned round and left. It was clear to me what he wanted to express by this: This is for you! Keep it!

While it is difficult even for adepts to interpret the facial expression of orangutans, they however can read our faces like an open

272

book, as I have already mentioned. I do not wish to offend any of the scientists who have made so many efforts to decipher the communication with the red jungle giant with the aid of statistics and charts, but I am fairly sure that facial expression plays an extremely important role in this. The language of the face is complex as well as rich in expression and it makes physical contact, loud noises and agitated features completely dispensable. Because they possibly do not understand this, many scientists wrongly consider orangutans to be uninterested in contacts, antisocial, and introvert.

Another important factor is the role played by communication by means of facial expression—depending on the kind of decision-making process of the orangutans—which works with the speed of lightning, being done in fractions of seconds, usually while the scientist, sweating in the rainforest at a level 50m (55 yards) below, is still in the process of adjusting the focus of his binoculars. The red primates are simply too fast and too subtle for us.

One further reason for the absolutely wrong estimation of the animals lies in the fact that the speed of their decisions and judgements is in sharp contrast with their slow and sometimes grave climbing movements and many observers believe that a slow climber must also be a slow thinker.

## Personality test, orangutan-style

Orangutans are able to appraise humans so well that one could use their abilities as the base of a personality test. Of course, not all animals have identical abilities in this domain but their power of observation, their cleverness and their sharp eye baffle us and the results are consistent.

My friend Jan Geerdink for example takes the hearts of all orangutans by storm. He, a police officer, normally concerned with the taking of crooks' fingerprints, was a perfect ape novice when he came to Indonesia, but it "clicked" immediately: the orangutans loved him

because he loved them. They read his sympathy in his nice open face with the friendliest eyes in the world which, appeal to all humans, too, and they gave him their trust.

The "emotion radar" of the orangutans can however not be deceived by outward features like friendly blue eyes—it easily penetrates any façade. The apes know exactly when I am sad or distressed or in pain and they react accordingly. There is, however, one important limitation: when they are bored or hungry and if I have something with me which they fancy, their attention is completely concentrated on this and they don't give a damn about my emotional state. They can be bribed with delicacies as easy as anything!

But—and the difference is significant—it is, as I have said, just bribery, "ape feeding", no communication, no real contact. The animals put on a few tricks, but their respect cannot be gained this way. I am sorry to say this but all these photo sessions with orangutans hanging around the neck, all these "breakfasts" with the jungle dwellers offered by zoos and amusement parks mainly in Asia have much more to do with hypocrisy, lies, and deceit than with affection. It is nothing other than the exploitation of wonderful creatures and has nothing at all to do with conversation, let alone with conservation—namely nature protection.

It might well be that one visitor or another enjoys having his photo taken with an orangutan. However, this is pure show and it would be a thousand times better for the animals to let them freely swing from branch to branch in their fascinating jungle than grinning for a silly Polaroid photo on a fairground.

*The 'bite test'. Before an orangutan 'opens up' to a human he carries out a proof of trustworthiness with his teeth. If the human 'testee' flinches he has failed the exam.*

If the spark is to jump across, one has to meet an orangutan without food and without things which might distract him. This is why I never feed the apes and why I never carry objects with me which I know they would love to pinch from me. I encounter orangutans with open heart and mind and with the respect they deserve—and they are aware of this immediately.

When I started to write these lines, I had intended to gather information for interested readers and to contribute towards a book just as this is usually done, with an introduction, body and end. I also wanted to make full use of the time I normally spend in traffic jams, airports, and on planes, which I almost permanently use for my travels (I got to as many as 385 flights in 2004!). It was supposed to become a well-structured contribution on altruism, on selflessness, mildness, and on the so very little grudge-bearing nature of the orangutans. However, I did not keep to the planned structure; I have simply written down everything which came to mind and I have also laid out in front of you some quite personal thoughts and experiences.

Maybe I did it out of a guilty conscience because I have written so very little during the past two years. But times were not easy. I had health problems and I had a few narrow escapes from death. In addition, I was terrorized for five months for my convictions and for my standing up for nature. I had a great need to catch up with things.

Also, please allow me to let my thoughts wander a bit and let us see where they are going to lead us.

During the past twelve or thirteen years, I have pulled hundreds of orangutans from little wooden crates or rusty wire and iron cages

*Bet on the wrong horse. Exasperated and acutely frustrated this group of orangutans on Kaja island discover that the supply boat with its cargo of tasty fruits is not landing where they are waiting today, but at the alternative feeding site a mile away. Instead of getting the richest pickings, they will now have to make do with left-overs.*

*Correct bet. These three apes are overjoyed as they greet the supply boat that lands right in front of them. They bet on the long odds and won.*

with my own hands and I have looked into their eyes full of fear. And I have tried to imagine how they, the animals, have experienced this dramatic moment of the first encounter.

It cannot be that they experience this moment as a start to freedom, they must experience this like a nightmare: suddenly this stranger appears from nowhere and starts making direct contact with them! He looks completely different from everything the orangutans have seen until now, and furthermore: he is dangerously tall and strong.

The former "owners" (this is in fact a word which is completely wrong because these people who have captured or bought little orangutans can never be their legal owners) vehemently vent their anger on me and let off their concentrated hate. They scream, spit, and hit at me. Cage locks, closed for years, are cut open with steel saws, which

we always carry with us for this purpose, or are knocked off with hammers. Everything is exciting and unaccustomed, and then this terrible noise!

And how would you feel? What would you do if you had the choice? Would you want to stay with those humans who have now and then brought you food, or would you put your trust in the awesome tall strangers? Probably, I reckon, you would cling to your cage in mortal fear in order not to be confronted with this new and uncertain experience.

And this is exactly what most orangutans do. They squeak, piddle, make themselves look tiny, and crouch in the farthest corner of their small prison.

As their savior, you are now in a predicament: how do I help the poor creatures, you ask yourself, considering how very little time is at hand. During confiscations, it is more or less normal for many curious onlookers to gather, for neighbors to interfere, and quite often heat up the anger and frustration of the owners. Quite frequently, unpleasant and dangerous situations arise.

With all the bickering and screaming taking place and numerous onlookers flocking together, you have to rely completely on your own people. You have to be sure that they will give you rear cover, and then you just concentrate completely on the small frightened being in the cage in front of you, on the little ape that will have to trust you to make the hectic situation a bit more bearable. You have to focus your attention completely on the orangutan and must not allow the smallest distraction because the little one would not trust you, would not put his arms around your neck unless he realizes that you are one hundred percent keeping to the point.

*Pony was held captive for years with her whole body shaved (see page 178, picture page 152). Now her hair has grown back she is just like a normal orangutan again.*

*Faced with brutality every day. On a palm oil plantation near Parenggean a BOS staffer comes across a sick and badly-neglected orangutan which has been kept in the hot sun for a long time, and is suffering from scabies.*

## Three years of solitary confinement in burning heat—orangutans in the hands of humans

An example from 1998. We had driven to a small place near the village of Muara Ancalong because we had heard that an orangutan was being held there. As usual, nobody who was questioned by the forest police knew anything about an ape. However when I was chatting with a few children who had come running close to our boat, I got to know immediately where the animal was captive. In such situations, children always are the best source of information.

We moved straight on to the house they had named, crossed through and came to a wooden terrace where an ironwood box was standing. It was about 70 cm (28 inches) wide, of a similar depth and about one meter (one yard) high, and its walls were so smooth and gapless that it almost looked as if it were air-tight.

278

It had a hole of about twenty by seven centimeters (eight by three inches) through which two huge and very unhappy eyes were peering. There was no flap and no lock—the hole with the sad eyes was the only opening!

The "owner", a man of the Dayak tribe, explained he had swapped the orangutan for a carpenter's tool and was keeping it as a pet. He said that he did not know whether it was male or female because he took a quick look when he locked up the animal in the box three years ago.

Three years! Inconceivable. Three years of solitary confinement in a glowing hot wooden prisoner's cell on these naked planks right in the middle of the glowing tropical sun, without any cooling, and with just this tiny hole for letting in the air. Thirty-six endless months with nothing to look at than planks and a timber fence! How was it possible that anything had survived in the box—and had remained mentally stable?

I broke the boards out of the box, one after another, until the opening was large enough. In a cloud of terrible stench, a very pale and already fairly big orangutan was squatting on a huge lump of excrement, which was alive with ants, ticks, fleas and other vermin. There he sat in a dungeon of the size of less than half a cubic meter (18 cubic feet) in which he had been imprisoned for three years, and he was blinking into the harsh sunlight!

I spoke to this poor orphan with my voice and my eyes, and he understood. I stretched my arms out to him and he rose, wrapped his arms—sticky with dirt around my neck, pulled himself up and flung his arms round me. Truly—he embraced me and pressed me against himself!

Can you imagine this? Can you imagine an orangutan, a thinking and feeling being trusting me in such a way after three years of indescribable torture? Or do you think he had given up and believed it was all the same to him and he might just as well come to me?

However, in a case like that, would he not have rather remained squatting in his corner, waiting until someone got him out? Why did he not try to escape to the nearest tree? Why did he not look out for a possibility to escape but instead only look into my eyes? And why did he press and hug me like this? How was this possible after three years of martyrdom, hunger and thirst, loneliness and boredom, fear and horror?

Another example, which took place about three years earlier near Bontang, a boom town of the Indonesian oil industry. After hours of driving along the customary pot-holed roads, we reached a small village. At the side of a house, a cube-shaped box of only about 50 cm (20 inches) on each side was hanging. A little ape, about one and a half years old, was peeping through the gaps. I had hardly broken open the box, the ape—a little orangutan girl—jumped out, threw her arms around me and covered my face with kisses. Therefore, I named her after my wife, Syennie…

How is it possible that these poor maltreated creatures can trust an absolute stranger so quickly and set their heart on him?

*Life in a box. This ape had to endure three years in this tiny cage (see text left).*

Maybe because they do not regard us as strangers at all because we, the strangers, have something in our eyes, in our nature, which they recognize.

An indication of the truth of this is that the orangutans which we rescue normally show such confidence only to very few people and certainly do not throw their arms around everybody. A study has shown that they give their affection with caution. During the annual performance evaluation of the entire staff of the BOS centers, they all have to answer the question: "Which member of the team is liked best by the orangutans?" And there you are: more than 90 percent of our staff named Sumi first—Sumi, the babysitter with the nicest and most innocent and open smile in the world who is so tiny and tender that it is hard to believe at first how many little apes she is able to carry, and that she dares to get close to them at all. None of the orangutans has ever hurt her because they knew that Sumi loved them.

It was similar with Udin, who has been with me from the time of my very first three orangutans onwards and who has the same ability. He can look into the minds of the red primates and they all trust him. Even humans, I think, could see in the faces of Sumi, Udin and Jan Geerdink, the police officer, what wonderful people they are.

So there cannot be any doubt that orangutans can read in our faces and that they can discern our emotions in our features. This ability is to my mind rooted in the fact that reading in the eyes of others plays such key role in their own communication.

*It seems incredible, but emaciated, sick, and traumatized bundles of fur can become happy little apes again if they are given good treatment and loving care.*

## How to introduce oneself to an orangutan

If you sit or stand eye to eye with a captive orangutan who is not frustrated, he will first of all, for about seven seconds, look straight into your eyes and start his analysis. After the pupils he will evaluate the area around your eyes, he will all the time fix his glance at you, and then—with the speed of lightning—he will come to a decision! He decides whether you are boring or interesting, whether one can trust you or whatever.

If he classes you as one of the normal people he sees every day his attention will wander to outward things—a nice ring or an eye-catching pen. However if he considers you to be particularly interesting, he will try to touch your nose or your hair. Finally, he will kiss your nose and he will want to look into your mouth, and he will make the tiniest skin injuries or blemishes which you have most probably not even noticed the subjects of a very thorough inspection. In the case of small wounds he will be very careful not to hurt you when he looks at these.

*Bite test number two. Only the more 'cheeky' orangutans dare put a human to a test like that.*

Orangutans are always very interested in my warts and in the small white blotches on my hands. They feel them carefully and then look at me questioningly to make sure that this touch is all right and that they have not hurt me. They are so loving and caring!

This applies first of all to the little orangutans with which I started this story. Grown-up apes behave in a slightly different way: it may be that the initial contact has broken the ice but has not been enough to gain their respect, and then things can become a bit unpleasant because they might decide to let the visual inspection be followed by a kind of body search. They could try to inspect your pockets, to smell them out properly or to bite them.

This sounds worse than it is because the kings of the jungle will not overdo it although they could bite off your finger without any problems. It is in fact nothing but a test.

I have to point out here that orangutans are extremely strong animals and that they can despite all their inherent good nature become nervous or irritated—for whatever reason. Of course, there are also neurotic animals, damaged during captivity. I strongly advise humans who have never had anything to do with the red ape against becoming the subject of an orangutan inspection. Do regard the following hints as theoretical hints and only put them into practice after explicit permission and in the company of a declared expert.

So when the orangutan becomes active, do not withdraw your hand, do not look frightened or scared, no, do not even think a disheartened thought. You have to be absolutely convinced that the animal will not harm you, and your eyes have to mirror that! Therefore, do not act the big guy under any circumstances when in fact your heart is in your boots!

Should the orangutan you are dealing with decide on administering a test-bite, he will immediately afterwards look at you to note your reaction. Usually, he finishes then; in rare cases, however, he will bite once more, this time a little bit firmer. Now you are allowed to say "Ouch" and to grimace a bit. However, do not withdraw your hand, do not hit the orangutan or display any other reaction: you have just passed your entrance examination into the category of "interesting human".

I had never planned to write the manual, "How to make friends with orangutans", although it might well be an interesting thing to do. It is important that you enable the animals to read in your eyes and to test you—and maybe to test you again. Even if you are possibly not aware of it: here, a very conscious and deliberate evaluation process is running whose subject you are—and your innermost being.

But let us again talk about the altruism of the orangutans—about kindness of heart, the willingness to share, generosity and helpfulness, even at the risk of their own health. I am thinking of so many amazing examples that I do not know which ones to choose. Sorry for the rather basic joke, but I feel just like a gnat in a nudist camp.

## Ape altruism—is that possible?

It is best if I just start. Near Buntok, a small town in Central Kalimantan on Borneo, Becak, a rickshaw driver, told us the following story, which was also printed in a local paper: his nephew worked as a wood-cutter for an oil palm plantation. With his chainsaw of German origin, he felled giant tree after giant tree. Finally, he came to the last tree of a plot, to the top of which a large orangutan had fled. The trunk crashed to the ground and with it the red ape. He was stuck underneath a thick branch, and the wood-cutter attacked the helpless animal with his machete, hacking furiously away on it.

Other wood-cutters came running with their machetes to finish off the bleeding ape. Suddenly, a large male orangutan disengaged himself from a nearby group of trees and came to help his fellow-ape. He pounced on to Becak's completely surprised nephew, grabbed hold of one of his thighs with his huge grasping hands and broke it with a brief movement of his wrists.

With great efforts, the other wood-cutters freed their injured mate from the grip of the ape and hacked to pieces the orangutan who had broken his legs.

Why did the large ape leave his hiding place and make the suicidal attempt to save the smaller fellow ape from the humans? Was he the father? This is improbable because dominant orangutans sire children from lots of females and wander through such huge rainforest territories that with all probability they do not know their offspring (as is supposed in the case of chimpanzees).

The fact remains: this large orangutan—with his thick cheek bulges seemingly a typical loner—came to the help of fellow orangutan, just as a human would behave who—running into a burning house with unknown occupants—saves them from the flames. Or like people who jump into rapid streams at the peril of their lives to pull drowning people out of the water. Altruism, that's what it is.

Or was the great ape thinking of revenge? Did he want to pay back the humans who were destroying his rainforest more and more to the extent that it was becoming increasingly difficult to find food and shelter? Did he recognize that his survival would be impossible without trees, anyway, and had he decided to balance accounts with one of the humans?

But if it really had something to do with revenge, then the action of the old orangutan was unconsidered, well, even fairly stupid—which surprises us especially when it comes to the red giants for they are patient planners and they have prepared actions thoroughly and for a long time before they start putting them into practice.

The dominant ape male could have remained hidden near the wood-cutters' camp and he could have waited until one of the humans had gone alone to the river to bathe. Then he could have attacked—and this way could have immobilized one after the other. However, what he did was sheer madness. Unless, of course, it was—altruism.

How unusual the suicidal attack of the orangutan was becomes clear if one knows what tremendous role caution, consideration, and—

*A robber's kiss. What looks like love and affection is in fact a mugging. The orangutan on the left is forcing the ape on the right to pass over the contents of his mouth.*

*Robber repulsed. The owner of a coconut is fending off a 'bandit' who had an eye on his booty. Whilst fighting for his possession he is holding the heavy nut with his teeth, as if it were nothing. The aggressor who got kicked in the face is peeing with fear.*

as already mentioned—patient planning play in the life of the kings of the jungle. A grown-up orangutan has learnt over many years how to avoid all the dangers in the rainforest—snakes, wild bees, humans.

Living several dozen meters above the forest floor, caution plays a decisive role. When he is swinging from one jungle giant to another, an orangutan always has to know exactly in what kind of tree he is right at the moment, onto which kind he wants to be flung, whether the branch on which he is sitting and the one on which he wants to land can bear the strain, and how far he can use the tree or large branch which he wants to use as a "catapult" can swing without breaking. Orangutans are after all the largest and heaviest tree-living animals in the world.

Planning is of vital importance for orangutans because they have to lay out their climbing tours through the foliage roof of the rainforest in such a way that they can reach their scarce food-supply with the lowest possible input of strength and energy, that is: choosing the shortest and least strenuous way.

The lack of edible matter, by the way, is the reason why the animals live alone. This has undeservedly given them the reputation of being "loners". It is in fact true that always during simultaneous rip-ening periods of a large number of trees in the rainforest, or if a huge old fig tree grants rich harvest, several orangutans can be observed in harmonious co-existence.

If therefore consideration and planning play such an important role in the life of the red ape, it is more than improbable that—but for altruism—an orangutan would do what the huge territory-owner with the cheek-bulges did: come to help a fellow orangutan completely unselfishly, one he did not know and to whom he was not tied by any bonds.

Quite similar—and yet completely different—is what happened to the Indonesian scientist Dr Suce Utami, who works for BOS. Because the incident is embarrassing for her, maybe also for religious reasons, she does not like talking about it and has until now hesitated to publish it or to talk about it in great detail. It is, however, too important to be covered up.

Suci Utami was doing field research for her dissertation on Sumatra Orangutans in Katambe (North Sumatra). For about six months, she had been observing a large ape male with cheek-bulges. Quite on her own, she followed the red ape on the ground during his wanderings through the rainforest and recorded his behavior when two illegal loggers attacked her, wanting to rape her.

But then—incredible but true—the wild orangutan, who, during his "observation" had ignored the scientist as completely as possible, climbed down from his jungle giant. With aggressive kiss-smackings and throwing thick branches which he had torn off with one hand, he marched right forward towards the wood-thieves and put them to flight! After that was done, he waited patiently close to Suci until she had gained her composure –only then did he climb back into the safety of his treetop.

This raises the question: why did the huge orangutan risk his life to come to the assistance of the young woman he had until that moment so completely "overlooked"?

For me the situation is clear as daylight. The red ape knew what Suci was doing—that she wanted to understand his life and that she therefore followed him day after day at a respectful distance without acting improperly and without disturbing him. Maybe her attention even flattered him a bit; maybe he liked the human female. In any case: he knew that the two men were up to something evil and he drove them away.

One really has to make an effort if one wants to regard the deed of the red ape as other than species-crossing altruism. One would otherwise have to assume that the territory-boss was helping the scientist selfishly—maybe because he wanted her to report about him and to make him "famous" amongst humans!

But this is much too far-fetched. I am sure it was a demonstration of flawless altruism, an absolutely selfless deed, helping another being.

The story of Buddha and Romanis also reveals much about the character of the orangutans. Both animals were sent back from Taiwan (to where they had been taken away) to Borneo in 1990 and they were among the first group of apes who had been released in the forest of Sungai Wain in East Kalimantan.

They were obviously friends and I can well remember how I was filming them high up in the trees. At that time, Buddha was making a nest. It was a particularly large one and it looked as if he was building it for Romanis, too, whom I had never even once observed at nest-building. And in fact the two young males were huddling together in the sleeping place!

Whenever we checked up on the situation of the released primates, the records of the observers showed that Buddha and Romanis were swinging through the trees together. When one saw Buddha, one could be sure that Romanis was not far either, but had gone into hiding because he loathed the presence of humans.

Three to four months after the release, Zainal Arifin, one of our observers, entered into his recordings that Romanis was sitting at a height of about 5 meters (5 yards), close to the path leading to the cage out of which he and Buddha had been released together, and that he was squeaking and crying. Zainal believed Romanis was hungry. He

fetched some fruits, showed them to the animal and put them just a few metres away from Romanis on the roof of the wooden release-cage. There we usually made a feed depot for the freshly released apes in case they still had difficulties in finding sufficient food in the rainforest by themselves.

On the way back from the cage, Zainal saw that Romanis had paid no attention to the food at all. He sat on the same spot as before, crying. Because this behavior was quite unusual Zainal put it down in his records.

On the following day, the keeper again brought fruit to the feeding-place. He noticed that Romanis was not sitting in his tree anymore—and then he noticed the smell of death. He left the path and only a few meters away came upon Buddha who was dead. His shoulder was fractured and maybe his spinal column was broken, too, although this injury might have been caused after his death—by a wild pig which had slit open his abdomen and eaten his entrails. Traces in the soil seemed to give evidence that Buddha had dragged himself to Romanis' tree.

This is an unhappy story but it teaches us a lot about the nature of the orangutans. What explanation exists for the fact that Romanis—so afraid of humans—was sitting so close to the path but this one, namely that he wanted to get help for Buddha? And why did he cry if not to draw Arifin's attention to him and getting him to help his dying friend who was lying at the foot of the tree? And is it not probable that Buddha had dragged himself there because he expected altruism—and help—from the human beings?

We never saw Romanis again.

## Made's visit to the vet

Luckily, there is also good news from the group which had been released together with Buddha and Romanis in Sundai Wain. For example Made. He was suddenly sitting on the top of his release cage one day, waiting for help. Sri, his girlfriend, was crouching on

*Solitary confinement. Orangutans are often kept in appalling conditions in small, disgustingly dirty boxes or cages in the blazing sun. Often they have lost the will to live and a lot of love is needed to rehabilitate the traumatized animals.*

*Oh, I am so tired. This climbing business is hard work. I think I need to build a sleep nest.*

*Good grief! Someone has been watching me and even taken photos.*

*This is embarrassing! One should really hold one's hand in front of one's mouth whilst yawning...*

*Who knows who gets to see these photos? My reputation is ruined!*

287

*Gluttony. This orangutan has narrowly escaped starvation. As a result of the trauma he has lost his sense of proportion and has been eating at the BOS center at Nyaru Menteng until he has become a round blob. Even though he can hardly manage any more food, he is intent on keeping his hoard from other apes.*

a nearby tree. Made had a large and deep wound on the inside of his right thigh. Obviously, he had slipped somewhere and a pointed branch had injured him.

Although Made, released for more than a year at that time, was a royal male with the strength of an ox, one must not forget that he was an orphan and that he was lacking many years of climbing training (just like Buddha) which he would have had if his mother had not been shot by humans who had incarcerated him in a tiny cage. The kind of climbing training which we humans can offer is only a very inadequate substitute.

When the keepers saw Made sitting there and realized the degree of his injuries, they called the station and two hours later, Joko the vet turned up with his emergency bag. The vet knew Made from his rehabilitation in Wanariset as a difficult patient who hated having blood-samples taken and who only reluctantly allowed himself to be measured and weighed—and who loathed vets in general and Joko in particular with all his heart!

Because Made had become so big and strong and because he had not taken enough anaesthetic for the orangutan with him, we had to do a lot of convincing before Joko was prepared to approach the ape. Made, however, made no aggressive kissing noises and did not stare at the vet either, but instead pointed at his injured thigh. While Joko examined the wound, Made did not stir one finger!

On the roof of the cage our vet gave Made a series of little injections with a local anaesthetic around the wound, cleaned the fissure, and finally stitched it up, tissue-layer after tissue-layer. Made only sat there and looked on. Nobody held him or encouraged him. Only his girlfriend who had come with him sat in the trees and observed everything.

When Joko had finished the operation, we asked the ape to climb into the cage and Made obeyed as if this were the most matter-of-course thing in the world. During the following week, Made obediently put his arm through the iron bars every day for the administration of his antibiotics jab. Then he was released. Sri climbed down from her tree to greet him, thoroughly inspected the inside of his thigh, carefully plugged off a few stitches which had already come loose from the healing wound—and off they went, on their way back into their jungle!

Is this friendship, this trust and understanding not simply wonderful?

It is almost normal that injured or sick orangutans seek the help of humans. Dutch animal protector Edwin Wiek, who lives in Thailand, even reported to me about a gibbon who had taken upon himself a long and exhausting journey to his house in Thailand so that Wiek could treat his wounds. Jimmy, a Black Orangutan who was confiscated by us at the end of 1994 from a colonel in Samarinda, and who was released by us in the Meratus Mountains on Borneo in the spring of 2003, came to me and asked me to remove a thorn from his foot. It was there, too, that the female, Maja, asked for help. She turned up from the wilds with a fracture of her left arm and waited patiently until her plaster cast was removed.

Many other red apes equaled her at this. They know that we can help them, and although humans had killed their mothers, their logic and common sense commanded them to turn to us despite it all. They know that they are ill and their survival is more important to them than fear or hate.

Of course, it is clear to the orangutans which were in our care that not only poachers exist but kind people, too, and therefore they wait for support from us because they would also help their conspecifics, just as Romanis had tried to save the injured Buddha, and like Sri who waited for a week for the recuperation of Made. Once more, this is not primatology, but seems beyond all measure clear and logical.

Even more astonishing is a case which is not concerned with orangutans who know us humans, or who have experienced poachers, keepers, or vets but which concerns "wild" animals who were seeking help and rescue from humans, although they did not know them. Their insight, understanding and logic must be evaluated so much higher. The story I would like to tell now is so moving that my

eyes still start to get moist when I remember it.

In the beginning of 1998, a thick cloud of suffocating yellowish-gray smoke from burning forests lay over the whole of Kalimantan. The smoke from the peat and forest fires turned day into night in such a way that the automatic illumination of a mine about a hundred kilometers (60 miles) away from the coast never switched itself off for three complete months. Most trees had cast off their foliage and the water level of all the rivers was as low as never before. Even the normally enormous inflows of the Makaham River had dried out into small rivulets.

The rice harvest had not taken place and people had to eat up next year's seeds to prevent starvation. They were dangling over a precipice because they had neither clean air for breathing nor rice, nor did means of transport exist any more. They were starving. Just a little bit of rice could be cultivated directly on the banks of the rivers because

*An interested patient. This four-year-old red ape is curious, not frightened, while having his anti-worm injection.*

twice a day a bit of water was pressed up into the river courses by the tide, and there were also miserable, barely two-meter (two-yard) wide, stretches of fields. Kalimantan's inhabitants were suffering. They were unable to understand what the destruction and the change of climate had to do with their misery.

289

While I am writing this, I can feel the permanent headache again, the burning and the throat—as dry as a bone—and I can also smell the biting smoke which even forced its way through the tiniest gaps in the walls of the houses.

We had to fight forest fires day and night. Because of the drought, we were forced to drill for water; but the first mud had hardly oozed out from the hole, when wild pigs came running, half-crazy with thirst, and chased us away.

It was dreadful: deer with burned legs everywhere, unable to run or even walk, birds with no strength to fly. Innumerable animals died. Today, six years later, there are still no leeches, insects are decimated by eighty percent, and the small remaining stocks have lost their genetic diversity once and for all. One ought to write a book about this terrible catastrophe, but to what purpose? The disaster will return, probably even worse than before!

The orangutans were not one bit better off then the humans were. It was a bad omen that all of a sudden it was teeming with orangutan babies. They seemed to be everywhere and we were on our feet day and night confiscating them, saving primates stranded on lonely trees and looking after apes with bad burns.

We were standing on the road from Sebulu—a small village on the Makaham, about 80 kilometers (50 miles) away from the coast—to SP1 (an immigrants' village further towards the interior of the island) and we were just loading cages with confiscated babies on the roof of our 4WD vehicle when a truck stopped beside us and its driver jumped down from his cabin. "Hey," he said in South Sulawesi dialect, "do you buy orangutans? I've got one for you—how much do you pay?"

*Natural pacifier. This two-year-old ape baby is in his own little world whilst he is sucking his thumb. Is he day-dreaming about his dead mother?*

## Ape love—a mother gives up her baby to save it

I could not get a word out because of the audacity of it! But I managed nevertheless to ask him to show me the ape. I had no idea whether—or where—he had hidden it on the truck. It might well be that he as acting only as a go-between. Captured orangutans are still something quite normal for far too many people in Indonesia—goods which one flogs and which also mean profit for those who act as intermediaries of the deal.

But no! To my surprise, the man reached behind him in the cabin and pressed the almost lifeless little body of a completely dehydrated and starved orangutan baby into my hand. The tiny baby whose arms and legs were hanging down like petals from a dead flower was nothing but skin and bones and—despite her age of two which I could recognize from her well-developed teeth—weighed hardly two kilos (five pounds). This is about their weight at birth!

The eyes of the poor creature, which hung lifelessly on my left lower arm, were so deeply sunken into their hollows that they had almost disappeared inside them, and the skin was ash-gray, dusty and brittle like dried-up parchment. Occasional painful breathing was the only sign of life which could be discerned. The tiny ribs, which were protruding like the teeth of a rake, were moving, maybe twice a minute, then silence again.

Nobody would buy the dirty and lifeless bunch of misery, which was lacking everything which on the infamous Pramuka bird market of Jakarta, where animals of all kinds are offered for sale, would encourage a buyer to reach spontaneously for his wallet.

The cunning dealers there know exactly what they have to do to make orangutan babies attractive or even irresistible for prosperous-looking passers-by: while in the case of other little apes they mostly only dye and brush their fur, they use psychological refinement in the case of orangutans. These little consumer items are washed and kept hungry. If then a well-to-do potential buyer passes by in the middle of the chaotic market bustle, he can give the baby a piece of banana—and

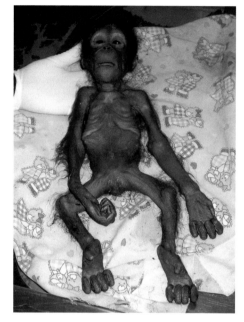

*As if freed from a concentration camp. Again and again BOS staff save totally emaciated orangutans from palm oil plantations. Even if the lives of the starvation victims can be saved, they are plagued with mental problems.*

*Above: Fun in the jungle. In 'Halfway House' Lone Dröscher-Nielsen is spraying three roughly six-year-old orangutans with brown swamp water, which is leading to heightened levels of amusement. Even though the mouths of the hairy primates are wide open, their laughter is hardly audible. One can only hear gentle gasping. Right: Tots in the tree. The first climbing lessons demand a lot of courage from the novices, who are still in diapers. But unity is strength. The unity can be very close; there are three orangutans in the picture, not two, as one would think.*

294

it touches his heart to see how much attention the funny fur bundle pays to him and how much it likes him—or his banana.

And then the last trick: the dealer gives the little ape a pinch just at the right moment, and of course, without the potential buyer knowing about it, and the crying baby flings his arms around the neck of the person who had given him the banana. This makes the deal well-nigh perfect. The interested party wants to save the poor baby, wants to feed and protect it, and wants to take it away from this dreadful place with all its noise and crowds.

Although these huge, so very human-looking eyes might possibly arouse altruistic feelings in the customer, hardly any of the visitors of the market is aware of the cruelty and of the outrage committed against the species, which is daily routine here. For them, Pramuka is a place of inexpensive entertainment, and they do not think anything when they look at all those many animals in their tiny cages. To most of them, the kind of grief I experience is totally alien to them.

But let us go back to the truck-driver and the half-dead baby: there I stood in the ghostly silence, which, together with the smoke, had spread over the land, at the road to the godforsaken place, Sebulu. The driver and his young assistant were much less crafty than the pushers of animals on Pramuka were. Full of expectation, they stood in front of me and looked up at the strange foreigner who spoke Indonesian so well. They had not the faintest knowledge of orangutans and their value, and they certainly did not know either how they were sold. The little ape was simply something interesting which they had given to me and they hoped to make a bit of money out of it.

My anger left me, and I asked them where they had the baby from. "We found it three kilometers (2 miles) from here, in the middle of the road," they said. As we had passed this spot hardly an hour ago without noticing an orangutan, I asked them to tell me in more detail

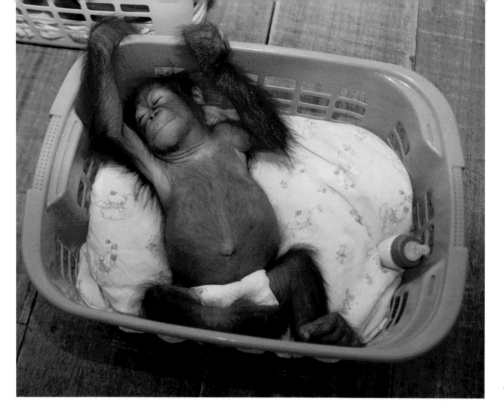

*The reflex to hold on is found equally amongst large and small orangutans.*

*Safety anchor. Even in deepest sleep orangutans hold on with at least one gripping hand or foot. This is obviously genetically programmed.*

*Peekaboo! From his lookout in the tree the orangutan is watching the scientists on the ground with curiosity. Whilst he has a clear view of the primatologists, he is nearly invisible to them. This picture shows the difficulty that field researchers face when they are surveying orangutans.*

a large orangutan who was sitting motionlessly 10 meters (10 yards) away at the side of the road, and both had realized at the same time that the brown something was a baby ape. Quickly, the co-driver had fled back into the truck. Both men had waited for a while but nothing had happened. The baby was lying on the road, and the adult ape—probably the mother—was squatting on the side.

Finally, the driver had moved his truck closer to the little ape and—when the mother showed no further reaction and when it was only a few meters to go—the co-driver had jumped out of the cabin, had grabbed the baby and had rushed back into the safety of his cabin. But the mother had not moved even now. Only when she saw that her child was in the hands of the humans, had she got up, turned round and had clumsily gone back into the smoke of the burning forests.

Immediately, I recalled a story from the Old Testament: the mother had relinquished her child to prevent him being severed into two—as Solomon the Wise had ordered. She rather endured her child living with the woman who had stolen him than risk harm being inflicted on him. As she loved her child and wanted to save it, she renounced him. Just like the orangutan female did.

Please do not think now that apes are unable to estimate their situation realistically because that would be completely wrong. Animals stricken by such catastrophe know exactly that their world is disintegrating and that there is no more chance for them.

Just like the large orangutan male who in 1998 was sitting on a very high tree in the middle of the inferno during the fires that raged for months at Muara Wahan, completely closed in by an ocean of flames. He climbed up to the top, and then he screamed. It was not the familiar "long call" which territory bosses use for attracting females or for driving away rivals, it was a completely different, strange cry which

*Heartfelt love. The caring manner in which the director of the BOS center Nyaru Menteng is holding the ape baby needs no further comment.*

how they had got hold of the animal. And this they did, loudly and with many gestures, as if it were clear to them that this story would hardly be believed, anyway.

They had slowly and carefully driven through the thick smoke along the winding road to Sebulu when they had seen something brown lying on the tarmac. The co-driver had jumped out to inspect the object from a closer distance, but then both of them had noticed

made my hair stand on edge. And when the flames finally blazed up to him, he jumped.

I am perfectly sure that the ape-mother by the side of the road was able to judge the situation correctly: she knew that the baby was dying. But how could she put her child into the hands of humans who had let her world go up in flames, who pursued and killed her? Who had repeatedly driven her away from the stretch of land along the river, which held the only little water, and where trees with green leaves stood—food! On the dried-up hills around, the green foliage had long ceased to exist.

Many half-starved orangutans paid with their lives in the attempt to reach these trees to peel the bark off and to eat the green leaves. I want to spare you the dreadful details, but I witnessed how many of the red apes were slaughtered by the poor farmers who were hardly in a better situation and who wanted to prevent the last of the living trees from being destroyed by the "monsters" of the jungle.

The mother with the sick baby knew that humans were still in possession of green trees. It might well be possible that she had also seen how they were eating and drinking. Therefore, she did the incomprehensible: she gave her baby to the enemy to give it a chance of survival. If she had to die, her child should survive if possible. What sacrifice, what altruism! And what wisdom!

I could fill a whole volume with incredible incidents in which orangutans are the heroes. As a rule, they are involuntary heroes because they frequently only react to human brutality—like the ape mother who was shot and wounded up high in the branches of a jungle giant. It was often reported to me that they climbed down to the ground with the last ounce of their strength to save their baby from the lethal drop from a height of 30 or 40 meters (33 or 44 yards).

At one time, a Dayak shot at an orangutan mother with her child using a home-made Winchester gun. Although she was hit, she quickly climbed down from the tree and approached the poacher. Then he got frightened because reloading was a tricky thing. However, the orangutan female did not attack him: she put her baby down on the ground in front of the rifleman—and dropped down dead. She knew she had to die but she wanted her baby to survive.

Unyil, too, was a victim. At the age of about two, the female ape was bought from a colonel of the Indonesian army in a round cage, which was just large enough for her. Unyil grew larger but they kept her in her child-sized cage, which was fastened to a fig tree with a chain of a length of about three meters (three yards). Her arms and legs grew through the bars and she always had to keep her head (which was stuck in her prison together with her rump) deeply bent down.

The buddies of her keeper gave her alcohol, brayed with laughter when she was drunk and rolling through her excrement in the cage, which was corroding more and more, and they put out cigarettes on her chest. She got TB. She endured the torture for ten years.

For many months, we searched for the animal of which we had heard, but we did not find her. One day, the colonel called us up and told us to pick up Unyil. He must have thought she was dying, as she was completely lethargic and coughing blood.

Udin set out immediately with the steel-saw to sever the bars of cage. When this was done, the ape female stood up—both halves of the cage still around her upper and lower body, stretched herself, stretched out her arms to the sky and, crying, embraced her rescuers.

*Text by Willie Smits*

*Refuge with 'mother'. Unintentionally Jay Ullal has upset a few babies again.*

*Help, a strange man! Whilst the nannies are still wondering what has scared their charges, the latter are nervously fixing their sights on photographer Jay Ullal, who is approaching them with 'dangerous' camera eyes.*

# The fairy tale of Samboja Lestari

## A dream comes true

*Rainforests that were cut and burnt down by humans are irrecoverably lost. Forest scientists and ecologists considered this an irrefutable fact—until BOS proved the opposite.*

O nce upon a time…": this is how fairy tales begin. The sad fate of the little town of Samboja on Borneo is typical of the ecological decline of many places in Indonesia: in the beginning, it was situated in the middle of rainforest, bursting with life, then, suddenly, it found itself back in the wasteland of a gigantic clearing. However, in the case of Samboja, the misery was only of comparatively short duration. There was a turn for the better, which nobody could have expected, and the place became the scene of an ecological miracle, a fairy tale come true. Let me tell you the story.

There once was the small town of Samboja on the east coast of Borneo. Approximately 200 kilometers (120 miles) south of the equator, it was founded about a century ago because oil had been found in the area. Over the years, about three hundred Dutch people settled in Samboja. Most of them were in the pay of the oil company Bataafsche Petroleum Maatschappij (BPM) whose activities were later taken over by the Shell concern, and which later still was swallowed up by the national Indonesian oil company, Pertamina. The Dutch people found the best living conditions in Samboja. There were villas by the beach, which, despite their proximity to the ocean, had their own swimming pools. There was a cozy club, there was nature in abundance, and life was good.

In the 1950s, BPM started to cut wood near Samboja. This was done selectively and only few of the best and most expensive high-grade woods were removed from the dense rainforest.

The construction of the so-called "Russian Road" was the beginning of the end. It led to the north, to Samarinda, the capital of the province of East Kalimantan, and it followed the outline of the coast across the rainforest about 20 kilometers (12 miles) inland. As a result, the old coast road to Samboja lost its significance, and consequently the little town was lost, too.

While Samboja fell into a deep sleep, a small migration wave to Balikpapan, the booming oil town nearby, set in. People came from all parts of Indonesia and started out from the old coast road as well as from the new stretch of the road to clear the forest and to burn it down. They fell over the jungle like locusts, and soon there was nothing left but a sparse patchwork carpet of miserable secondary forest islands. Samboja became a poorhouse, the Dutch left, and their colonial club deteriorated.

All those who had thought it could not get any worse were to be disappointed: during a heavy drought-period due to a particularly

*Before. Where once a majestic rainforest swept across the area, there is now a sprawling wasteland—the area of Samboja Lestari before the project began.*

*After. From desolation luxurious life has sprung. The renaissance of the rainforest has created an island of ecological diversity in Samboja Lestari. The project was considered a scientific impossibility before it began.*

*Before. The project started with a lonely cabin in the middle of a hot biological desert that was lifeless apart from swarms of flies.*

pronounced El Niño in 1982 and 1983, in the worst firestorm then known in a tropical rainforest, the last green islands burned down. Even virgin jungle went up in flames, an occurrence unheard of before!

Between the charred stumps of the jungle giants, alang-alang grass spread out. This plant with the botanical name of *Imperata cylindrica* carries out a kind of chemical warfare with hydrocyanic acid, which prevents the germination of tree-seeds buried underneath it. Once an area previously covered with forest is overgrown with this grass, this usually means the end because the grassy desert is regularly stricken by fires, which ruin what has escaped the grip of the natural herbicides. Once alang-alang desert—always a desert.

Now, Samboja was lying in a moonscape. No screams of parrots, no butterfly flapping its wings, no bird singing, no lizard flitting across the path. The handsome colonial town had turned into a ghost town, a place of the hopeless. Its inhabitants were destitute and desperate, crime was flourishing, and the unemployment rate of 50 percent was only slightly above the sick-rate.

People were suffering from hunger, lack of hygiene, malaria, typhoid, and other infectious diseases. Drinking water, which had before bubbled in abundance out of the ground and had streamed by in brooks, had to be bought at high prices—in plastic bottles. On average, people spent about a fifth of their income on it.

During 1997 and 1998, the years of the fire, the horror reached its absolute climax: everything was wrapped in thick, biting smoke. Airports had to be closed, and the traffic on the roads and on the waterways also collapsed because visibility was too bad for traveling and because the rivers did not contain enough water. People died, and there were no harvests because rainfall avoided the area of the inferno. Although nominally tropical rainforest climate prevails, marked by permanent rainfall and the non-existence of a real drought period, not a single drop of rain fell during the first 81 days

of 1998, and over a period of six months, it was more arid than in the Sahel belt south of the Sahara!

When the misery had become completely unbearable, the miracle happened. Today, young rainforest high in biodiversity is growing on the area of almost 2,000 ha (5,000 acres) of the former alang-alang desert; there are 12 percent more clouds from which 20 percent more rain is falling. The average temperature has sunk by about 5 °C (9 °F), poverty has given way to modest prosperity, and sickness and crime have also come to an end.

The miracle started quite modestly: in 2001, the Borneo Orangutan Survival Foundation (BOS) started to buy land near Samboja. Two ideas contributed to this: Peter Hos of BOS/Netherlands had suggested purchasing ground in this area because—according to his plausible reasoning—the Dutch would donate especially sustainably for the purchase of Borneo soil on which an orangutan protection territory was to be established if the

*Now. Where the cabin once stood there is now a complex of buildings that house one of the world's two satellite transponders as well as the administrative center of BOS and SarVision. Several visiting researchers are at work here.*

302

# Samboja Lestari

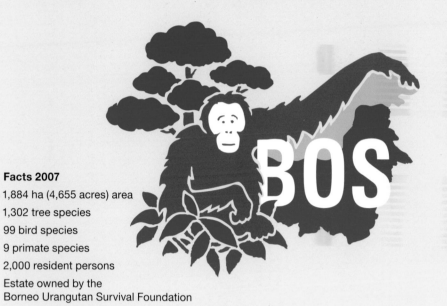

## "Living in Harmony"

**Facts 2007**

1,884 ha (4,655 acres) area

1,302 tree species

99 bird species

9 primate species

2,000 resident persons

Estate owned by the
Borneo Urangutan Survival Foundation

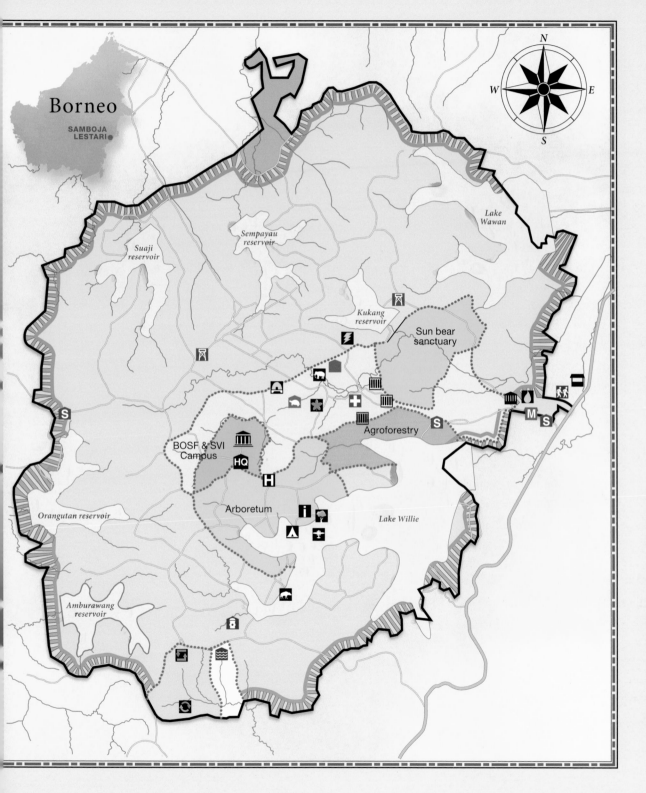

Borneo

SAMBOJA LESTARI

Suaji reservoir

Sempayau reservoir

Lake Wawan

Kukang reservoir

Sun bear sanctuary

BOSF & SVI Campus

Agroforestry

Arboretum

Lake Willie

Orangutan reservoir

Amburawang reservoir

| Symbol | Description | Symbol | Description |
|---|---|---|---|
| ▦ | Group-formation cages | ✚ | Floatplane landing area |
| ▦ | Quarantine station for sun bears | HQ | Offices of BOS and StarVision |
| ▦ | Base of the sun bear protection zone | ▥ | Balai President |
| ✳ | Bio-garden | ≈ | Waterworks |
| i | Information center | C | Composting works |
| H | Helipad | ♺ | Recycling complex |
| ⚡ | Generator (wood-gas driven) | ⛏ | Firewatch tower |
| ▲ | Camping ground | 🚰 | Pumping station |
| 🐢 | Tortoise center | ✚ | Veterinary clinic |
| 🐘 | Elephant enclosure | ⚘ | Tree nursery |
| ▭ | Shop for local crafts | ▨ | Eco guesthouse |
| ▨ | Beehives | ▨ | Eco garbage dump |
| 🏃 | Sports facilities | ◊ | Petroleum museum |
| 🐾 | Animal Island | ▥ | Agricultural academy |
| S | Security guards | | |

*Original condition. After the inferno a layer of alang-alang grass spreads over the former areas of jungle. The grass is like a shroud—it prevents the sprouting of bushes and trees.*

area was one which was known from colonial memories.

And there was Suwaji, then accountant in the forest research object of Tropenbos which was under my management. When he went home from the office, he was a passionate farmer. He pottered about in his vegetable garden, was always planting trees and was always full of new ideas. His pet idea was to induce the local population to reforest the devastated land around Samboja—no matter how great the risk of failure. From the ideas of both of them, I worked out the concept of Samboja Lestari, the translation of which means roughly "Samboja forever and ever". The name says it all.

Three things were of particular importance for me: first of all, the purchase of each individual plot had to be in accordance with the regulations and beyond any doubt documented by letter, official seal, and security copy. And secondly, the BOS land had to be guaranteed and to be absolutely free from any foreign influence, and its protected status had to be secured for all time.

After all, I had had to look on when the research station of Wanariset near Samboja where I had worked as a young scientist for so many years had gone down the drain due to mismanagement and bureaucracy, and when the likewise nearby Kutai National Park was destroyed by deliberate and shortsighted official alterations to its protective status. Thirdly, the project could and should only prosper with the help and sympathy of local people—and never against their resistance. During my time in the Wanariset research station, I had learned a lot to that effect.

As far as the soil was concerned, the conditions for our project, which was supposed to survive eternity, were anything but favorable: infertile and extremely low-nutrient clay soil prevailed, being inter-

spersed with plinthite clods, hard as steel. Due to this, the meager soil was not only very much prone to erosion but often more or less impenetrable for plant roots.

To crown it all, burning coal seams were situated not far below the paradise we planned to create. During each drought period, when the soil is burst open, air rich in oxygen gets through the cracks to the

*The first step forward. This nursery is the cradle of the new rainforest. Over a thousand tree species have been grown here. Pineapple, amongst many other plants, prepares the ground for the seedlings by suppressing the growth of grass.*

*School 1. In the BOS school the farmers' children are taught the basics of ecology. Amongst other things they learn how important the forest and the orangutans are for humans.*

smoldering coal layers, and they flame up, the reason for the constant grass and bush-fires during the dry period.

How in the world were we to recreate the majestic rainforest which stood here just a few decades ago—with its sky-raking jungle giants, its myriads of plants and animals and its closed nutrient cycles? How was it humanly feasible to influence the complicated climatic feedbacks between cloud density, heat radiation and water circulation in the "proper" way to get them going again?

And anyway: what size would the new forest have to be to improve the local climate, to promote rainfall—and to serve as a last refuge of 1,000 orangutans if in fact all other rescue projects should fail? (If orangutans are to be granted long-term survival with some certainty without being decimated by inbreeding, the starting population according to the 2004 PHVA study should be one of at least 1,000 animals.)

We racked our brains: in a "positive" rainforest in East Kalimantan, three to five of the great tree apes per 100 hectares (250 acres)

could find enough to eat. Therefore, we would have had to buy about 20,000 hectares (nearly 80 square miles)—which was an illusion. The booming oil-town of Balikpapan and its access roads were too close and land prices were rising too fast.

Therefore, we considered whether the necessary area could be reduced by a forester's trick. One possibility was to raise the proportion of forage plants as opposed to natural rainforest by a factor of about 25, mainly by the planting of various kinds of wild fig-trees. Their fruit could provide nutrition throughout the year for the red giants, which are often dependent on a diet of leaves and bark on Borneo, while there is more fruit on Sumatra. The expert climbers happen to one of the few animal species which can also metabolize unripe figs.

If that were possible, we thought that about 1,000 ha (2,500 acres) might be enough because it is not the space which limits the number of orangutans per square kilometer (250 acres) but only the food supply.

The forestry experts laughed at our project. They were unanimously of the opinion that we were attempting the impossible. The axiom was unambiguous: once the rainforest was cut and burned down, it would never return under any circumstances—or only after a "short eternity". The scientists were even more convinced that it would be an impossibility to create a jungle more or less synthetically, as an artificial man-made product. A complex biotope such as a rainforest—this was crystal-clear—could not be planted!

*School 2. The parents have to learn, too. The courses cover organic fertilizers, crop rotation and mixed crops.*

We were of a different opinion. In the May of 2003, we bought 1,200 ha (3,000 acres), most of them with credits from the Gibbon foundation, which is also under my management. In a tree-nursery of three hectares (7.5 acres), 250,000 small trees of about 400 species were waiting to be planted out in wild confusion as befits a natural rainforest habitat—Bangkirai next to mango and ironwood next to figs.

Later, we wanted to raise 1,762 tree species in the tree-nursery or buy them from local suppliers, amongst them about 500 trees alone whose fruit is especially appreciated by orangutans and whose seeds we had often obtained from the feces of wild red apes in all parts of Borneo. (For comparison: there are 66 tree species in Germany).

The compost which lined the planting holes as fertilizer and water storage was produced in enormous quantities in our own compost plant from organic waste of all kinds, from sawdust all the way to fruit remnants from the ape cages as well as from beef cattle and chicken manure. A special bacterial promoter meant it only took three weeks to mature in our humid climate.

It was and is important that the well-being and the protection of the orangutans (no matter whether we give a home in Samboja Lestari to incurably sick animals, mutilated by humans or handicapped [our shaggy relatives from the rainforest also suffer from cataracts and Down's syndrome] or to the last orangutan population there) go hand-in-hand with the well-being of the local human population. And it will be for this reason that the local people take a genuine interest in protecting the territory because without their involvement there will be no future for the primates.

So we created involvement: at first we bought land at a good price, land which was in principle of no value to them, and which would at best yield a few miserable Cassava shrubs. We paid such good prices per ha of alang-alang desert that some sellers believed we were looking for oil or wanted to mine coal.

We further gave priority to employing local men and women: in the tree-nursery, the compost plant, as grass removers and planters—

*Prosperity. The land is healthier—and so are the farmers. The revenue from vegetables and fruits even pays for houses and motorbikes.*

*Growth. After just eighteen months a small forest has emerged from the desert. The fast-growing trees in the background have a two-fold use: they give shade to the sprouting rainforest saplings and bring profit when they are felled.*

after all, between 1,000 and 1,300 young trees have to be planted every day—as construction workers, fire-watchers and fire-fighters, surveyors, road-construction workers, dam constructors, and a lot else. All in all, we employ about 200 Indonesians.

But not only that: we encouraged the local population to utilize the soil between the young trees which we have planted about 5–10 m apart, making use of our compost for the cultivation of fruit and vegetables. By cultivating watermelons, beans, pineapple, papayas, chilies and bananas, tomatoes, corn and a lot more, we kill three birds with one stone: first of all, we keep the farmers happy by offering

them rent-free land, secondly by buying their produce which was grown on BOS ground—the orangutans of our Wanariset station alone eat a ton of fruit and greens a day!—and at the same time we promote the growth of trees. Not only the fruits of the field profit from plentiful supply of manure of the farmers but also our future jungle giants!

It has not taken long for modest prosperity to start to develop in the Samboja area. The previously destitute farmers have bought houses, mopeds, even tractors! And by the end of 2004 already the supply and quality of water had considerable improved. The newly planted trees and the climatic changes they have brought about have made the groundwater level rise and have prevented the brooks from drying out again.

It goes without saying that the air is no longer being poisoned by the thick smoke of burning forests. The floods, too, which had cut off the village five to six times every year, have—except for one brief one of two hours' duration—failed to appear.

The welfare of the population is no short-term streak of luck to be followed by a rude awakening: measures have been taken to ensure that the blessing is of a long-term nature. When the crowns of the trees have become too dense and the farmers are unable to produce melons or pineapple on the space between them, they are each allocated 3,000 square-meter (32,000 square-foot) plots with sugar palms, which are laid out in a unbroken ring around the core area of Samboja Lestari.

Each family receives the tools required for the tapping of the palms, and they can sell the palm sugar to a sugar factory which BOS is going to build, sustainably guaranteeing them three times the usual average income. Under consideration is the construction of a power-station which could be fired with alcohol gained from the sugar. Of course, the cables of the supply-grid will be laid underground for aesthetic reasons. Underneath the palm-trees, the tappers of the sugar-sap can cultivate shade-tolerant and flame-resistant crops like ginger.

*Wilderness. It borders on a miracle how quickly plants and animals return to the new rainforest without human help. Six years after planting the first seedlings nearly a thousand kancil (dwarf deer the size of a cat) live in the area.*

The plots, 30 m wide and 100 m long (100 by 320 feet), are little fortresses for securing the orangutan district in the center from which they are separated by a firm ring of thorny Salak palms, whose delicious Salak fruits are to be harvested by humans on the outer side and by the apes on the inside. The width of the plots is chosen in such a way that it is easy for family-members to keep a watch on their plot and that nobody—neither poacher nor forest fires—can approach the Samboja Lestari sanctum without being seen.

Those who stick to the few rules, tap their palms each morning and afternoon, help to reduce the danger of fire, break no laws and do not become violent, can furthermore profit from a fund which not only finances schools and community buildings but also prom-

*Fire. Surrounding the BOS paradise barbarity and wickedness continue to celebrate their happy resurrection. Land speculators torch the trees and bushes again and again. They have learnt nothing.*

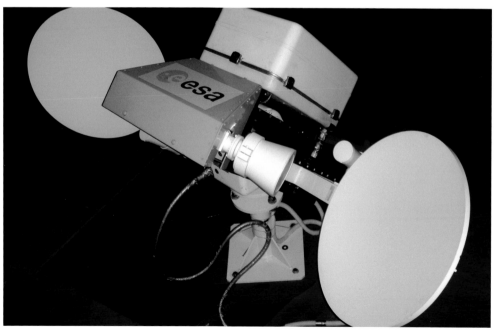

*Protection against fire. BOS tries everything to protect the new-born jungle against approaching walls of flame. Watchtowers, fire extinguishers, ultralight reconnaissance aircraft, and satellite locating are used to help protect Samboja Lestari.*

*The watchtower grows in the empty landscape.*

ises its shareholders a small monthly dividend. Fund membership is renewed each year.

So we have made sure that Samboja Lestari is not seen by the local people as a forest for orangutans but as a forest for the people of Samboja! A farmers' school with a comprehensive teaching program—ranging all the way from humane slaughtering to organic cultivation and the construction of fish-ponds—sportsgrounds, and a community center with a shop are going to tie the Samboja natives closer to the project of "their" forest.

Should there be an outrage in the sanctum, should orangutans be stolen or killed, the payment for all families will be cancelled for that month. This might not be "just" because innocents are punished, but this way one can be sure that the guilty party will be very quickly found thanks to the great social pressure.

However, the sugar-palm plots not only serve for providing the opportunity for a livelihood for the local people and for establishing a security service with many eyes: they are also important for fire protection. Fire is a great danger—not only because of the subterranean flamethrowers. In particular during the first five years, a project like Samboja Lestari has been especially prone to fires coming from outside.

Sugar palms are an excellent natural fire protection because—unlike the easily inflammable eucalyptus and many local conifer species, which are of course a taboo in Samboja Lestari—they offer little food for flames. Further, the tenants of the plots are required to clear the ground of their territory from inflammable alang-alang, thicket, undergrowth or organic waste. While we advise the people on the utilization of energy-efficient wood-burning ovens for cooking, and make fire-wood available for them, care is also taken that in

*The forest grows. The tower is finished and around it a new forest now thrives.*

future the dry leaf sheaths of the sugar palms do not lie about but are burned instead.

There will be plenty of firewood when the first generation of the shade-providing and soil-forming "pioneer trees" has to be felled in order to make room for the future jungle giants. As "pioneers" we planted primarily the drought-resistant Sungkai *(Peronema canesceus)* and legumes like the robust and undemanding *Acacia mangium,* which enriches the soil with nitrogen through its tubers.

When the sugar-palm plots are handed over to their users, it is time to harvest the acacias. Although this wood is not of a particularly high value owing to its susceptibility to fungi and insects (although it can be made durable in the smoke of burnished bamboo bark, an old Japanese temple technique), it is valuable construction material from which the sugar-palm farmers can build their houses.

Together with the circular road around the core area of the project, which not only serves as firebreak but also as an access route for the fire-brigades, sugar palms are the outward defense-line against approaching fires. If enough money is available, we want to erect water-tanks for fire-fighting at regular distances along the road.

*The water arrives. Where there was drought lively brooks flow with crystal clear water.*

Of course, we have planned for people to be able to take water from them for their personal requirements. The small lakes planned in the center will serve the same purpose: they not only represent interesting wet biotopes, but are also water reservoirs. If—as planned and already observed—rainfalls increase with the growth of the forest, the ponds should always be well-filled. Then the settlers will be able to fill up their rice-paddies with this water.

311

*All the birds are back... over a thousand species of bird have returned to the young forest. Here we see a bee-eater during his morning song.*

It goes without saying that—beside state-of-the-art monitoring technology with infrared cameras and satellite monitoring—we have also thought of firewatch towers, and of all kinds of small vehicles suitable for off-road driving able to rush teams to the location of the fire. Neither were a helipad for a fire-fighting helicopter nor an airport with an associated workshop for ultralights for the surveillance of the forests of Samboja and also of Sungai Wain and Meratus left out of our planning.

The technological core of the project is situated on the highest hill, in its center: the headquarters of SarVision with the satellite ground station by the aid of which the high-tech earth satellites racing past in orbit can calibrate their instruments and adjust their cameras. Here, their pictures are received, recorded, processed, and transferred. Keen young Indonesian radar technicians and electronics experts with environmental protection at heart sit in front of their PC monitors. They work on behalf of BOS together with the American space authority NASA, its European counterpart ESA, the Japanese JAXA and the German DASA.

The work of the "green" electronics specialists sounds like science fiction: from space, they not only monitor the growth of the sprouting new rainforest of Samboja Lestari but also keep an eye on the other forests of Indonesia. With the aid of new algorithms developed by SarVision for the evaluation of the satellite photos, it is possible to discern individual trees on the photos, to identify these and to document their growth—and their disappearance.

Together with countless digital photos from the human perspective, the satellite pictures allow a precision and richness of the documentation which has never before existed. Virtually each millimeter of wood, each kilogram of biomass, which comes into being in our forests, is digitally recorded in all stages of development. One day,

*And from the forest rises the magical white mist... every morning the woodlands are steaming. The water cycle has been regenerated.*

when our shoots have become jungle giants, we shall be able to look at their "baby photos"!

But the potential of satellite monitoring goes far beyond digital writing of history for Samboja Lestari, far beyond the prosecution of offenders against the forest laws and the gathering of data for exciting research projects of all kinds: the technology which is currently being perfected by SarVision and BOS could be the key for future agreements within the framework of trade with waste-emissions certificates and debt-for-nature swaps: because this "exchange" of environmental protection in developing countries for debts amounting to millions from development aid, which the Third World countries have been remitted by the donor countries, has a crucial Achilles' heel: to date, there has been no verification process worth mentioning.

This, however, becomes possible by biomass monitoring from space: by the aid of this, it can be ascertained whether Country A—as a service rendered in return for remission of debts by Country B—does in fact protect its forests or not.

If I walk through the new forest these days, I can often hardly believe that this was grass-desert a few years ago: although we have not even finished planting half of the area, rain has returned—just as we expected. Rivers and brooks are bubbling, and in the mornings, a thick layer of mist is draped over the valleys.

By the end of 2005, when we had planted more than 800,000 trees on about 740 of the 1,750 ha (1,800 of 4,300 acres) acquired until then—about 690 ha (1,700 acres) with fruit and wood-trees, about 50 ha (125 acres) with boundary and cordon trees—, the fastest-growing of the shoots planted in 2001 (*Acacia magnum*) were already 17 m (56 feet) high. Temperature had gone down by a few degrees, the new prosperity was obvious, and the police as well as the hospital were almost out of work. Floods after downpours of rain—normal in former days—are a thing of the past, and the concert of songbirds and cicadas has replaced the ghostly silence of the grass-desert.

Not only the orangutans and the Malayan bears and tortoises reintroduced into protection areas by BOS but also the animals from the breeding program for species conservation are living in the jungle, which has experienced a renaissance through human aid: several animals—about 70 bird species and seven primate species, many mammals and reptiles—have returned to their lost paradise. Together with them, in the form of seeds inside feces and in other ways, plants have also come back. We observe with great excitement the new interrelations and flora/fauna communities that are beginning to form, and how the "artificial" forest is changing into a "natural" one.

In the spring of 2006, one of my greatest triumphs was the completion of the contract for the delivery of 10 million cubic meters (2.6 billion gallons) of water to Balikpapan—water of a value of more than half a million euros (733,000 dollars) for the drought-tortured oil town of Samboja Lestari. Water from an area which was still a desert in 2001. This is what I call nature protection which also benefits human beings.

*Willie Smits*

*Success. At nearly the same speed at which trees shoot out of the ground, new refuges for orangutans, gibbons, sun bears, and hornbills are created (above left). Thick forest surrounds the BOS headquarters. Even the endangered proboscis monkey has returned.*

*The return of the reptiles. Amongst the animals who have found a refuge are crocodiles, snakes, monitor lizards, tortoises, and chameleons. One of the color-changing lizards is eating a cicada—also a new resident.*

*The forest is back—and the humans benefit from it. With the return of the trees a new life has begun for the poverty-stricken population around the BOS area. They again have work, are healthier and are starting families. The BOS band plays at weddings.*

*There is much to be done still. Children with an ecological education are the hope for the future. The 'modest' affluence of the inhabitants of Samboja Lestari—a motorbike is a status symbol—ensures that many residents want to take part in the project.*

*A refuge for humans. The 'eco-lodge', made purely from natural materials, is a haven in the middle of the new jungle. Willie Smits: "Whoever thinks that this is too good to be true should come to see with their own eyes that a dream became reality here."*

# Index

Aesthetic (with orangutans) 126, 128, 129, 139

Alang-alang grass 167, 178, 182, 302, 304, 306, 311

Altruism (with orangutans) 265, 267, 275, 281, 282, 284, 285, 299

Ammann, Karl 188, 189, 190, 192, 196, 198

Ape 24, 26, 32, 38, 98, 104, 124, 129, 188, 196, 201, 256, 262, 271

Bimaturity 76

Biodiesel 237

Borneo, diversity of species 146, 198

Birth rate 74, 76, 250, 254

Carbon dioxide (CO$_2$) 182, 236

Cheek-pads 34, 76, 79, 82, 86, 244, 247, 250, 254, 272, 282, 284

Corruption 152, 160

Culture (with apes) 5, 24, 47, 56, 120, 128, 129, 244

Daidai 63, 66

Darwin, Charles 28

Dayak 6, 12, 21, 29, 30, 58, 66, 69, 140, 169, 180, 182, 183, 212, 214, 228, 238, 242, 267, 278, 299

de Waal, Frans 114, 130

Debt-for-nature swap 234

Dipterocarpacea 146, 254

Dröscher-Nielsen, Lone 18, 20, 22, 86, 94, 106, 108, 178, 206, 208, 210, 292

Elaeis guineensis 160

Empathy 114

Environmental Investigation Agency (EIA) 32, 152, 190

Evolution 120, 123

Fish-catch (by orangutans) 104, 128

Fruits (on the menu) 38, 44, 47, 54, 64, 74, 114, 214, 225, 254, 285, 305, 306

Galdikas, Biruté 28, 181, 188, 189, 190, 199, 204, 206, 208, 256

Gestation 66

Gold hunters 6, 106, 108, 192

Goodall, Jane 199

GrASP 196, 198

Greenhouse gas 149, 160, 162, 198, 236, 241

Grzimek, Bernhard 26, 30, 38, 58, 60, 63, 74, 82, 140

Halfway House 214, 216

Hepatitis 79, 130, 183, 206, 208, 210, 211, 267, 272

IBI (inter-birth interval) 74, 76, 250, 254

Imitation 100, 109, 265

Intelligence 24, 28, 96, 98, 104, 106, 120, 122, 124, 129

Ketambe 79, 206, 284

Kindergarten (in the rehabilitation center) 106, 210, 214, 216, 225

Knott, Cheryl 86

"Language" of orangutans 98, 120, 265, 272, 273

Licuala palm 110, 114

Logging 122, 142, 152, 191, 198, 255

Long call 34, 76, 82, 254, 296

MacKinnon, John 24, 26, 28, 201

MacKinnon, Kathy 26, 60, 140

Mantangai 148, 182, 183

Mating 63, 86

Mawas 128, 234, 235, 236, 238, 241, 254

Medicine (by orangutans) 22, 56, 66, 113, 180

Meratus Mountains 51, 66, 184, 204, 244, 289, 312

Mother's milk 74, 80

Navigation 34, 40

Neesia 44, 120

Nutrition (by orangutans) 44, 60, 74, 86, 96, 122, 176, 250, 267, 288

Nyaru Menteng (BOS center) 16, 17, 18, 20, 21, 40, 44, 51, 94, 106, 128, 152, 178, 206, 207, 208, 210, 211, 214, 216, 219, 226, 230, 262, 265, 288, 297

Oil palm plantation 86, 142, 162, 164, 167, 178, 196, 198, 217, 236, 282

Orangutan butcher 142, 184, 198

Orientation in the rainforest 40, 44, 66, 84, 208

Palm oil 142, 152, 160, 162, 164, 171, 172, 173, 175, 176, 237

Pasha 11, 60, 76, 79, 86, 176, 244, 250

Peat (as source of $CO_2$) 182, 236, 240

PHVA study 30, 76, 147, 190, 192, 198, 201, 254, 255, 305

Physical power (by orangutans) 34

*Pongo abelii* 32, 198, 201, 244, 247, 250

*Pongo pygmaeus* 32, 198, 201, 244, 250

*Pongo pygmaeus morio* 32, 58, 244, 254

*Pongo pygmaeus pygmaeus* 32, 244, 252, 254, 255, 256

*Pongo pygmaeus wurmbii* 32, 250, 251, 254

Pramuka bird market 176, 291

Puberty 66, 74

Quarantine 113, 208, 211, 262, 267

Rainforest, destruction of the 147, 164, 171, 175, 181, 199, 210, 254, 289

Rehabilitation 203, 204, 208, 214, 286, 288

Release into the wild 6, 40, 66, 98, 114, 192, 203, 216

Reproduction 34, 66, 204, 244

Rijksen, Herman 28, 32, 198, 206, 208

RSPO (Round Table on Sustainable Palm Oil) 175

Russon, Anne 44, 58, 66, 96, 98, 100, 102, 128, 129, 130, 198, 200, 244, 250, 254, 255

Samboja Lestari 130, 142, 164, 255, 262, 300, 304, 306, 307, 309, 310, 311, 315, 317

Skull 22, 56, 140, 199, 244, 254

Slash-and-burn 142, 160, 162

Sleeping nest 27, 30, 36, 58, 60, 128, 214, 216, 287

Smuggling (animals) 63, 79, 148, 152, 158, 183, 184

Smuggling (timber) 152

Suaq Balimbing 63, 202

Subspecies 32, 196, 244, 253, 254, 255

Sungai Wain 24, 56, 63, 114, 258, 285, 312

Swampy rainforests 30, 122, 149, 243, 258

Swimming 102

Swinging climbers, four-footed 38, 129

Swartz, Karyl 96

Tanjung Puting national park 36, 40, 58, 100, 114, 124, 128, 152, 181, 189, 190, 192, 204, 254, 256

Territory 11, 40, 60, 76, 82, 86

Throat-pouches 34, 60, 76, 82

Tools, use of 47, 98, 106, 110, 114, 120, 122, 128

Ullal, Jay 24, 102, 128, 142, 181, 220, 256, 258, 260, 298, 299, 320

Uce 24, 106, 110, 114, 183, 204, 208, 211, 256, 257, 258, 259, 260, 267

UNEP 188, 196, 202

Unyil 106, 108, 113, 114, 128, 299

Utami, Suci 86, 284

van Schaik, Carel 24, 29, 38, 47, 63, 76, 104, 120, 122, 124, 128, 198, 200, 202, 250

Wanariset (BOS center) 36, 44, 63, 66, 79, 102, 108, 120, 183, 197, 204, 208, 210, 211, 213, 216, 253, 262, 288, 304, 307

Waste-emissions certificate, trade with 315

Winged-fruit trees 146, 254

WWF 30, 144, 146, 147, 152, 160, 162, 164, 188, 198, 201, 254

# Acknowledgements

The authors would like to thank *Stern* magazine most cordially for its generous support. We would also like to thank the staff of BOS, who have allowed us to use photographs, often taken under difficult conditions, about their work in the field. Finally our thanks go to Tim B. Frank for his design ideas and the good collaboration.

© 2007 Tandem Verlag GmbH
h.f.ullmann is an imprint of Tandem Verlag GmbH

Photographs © Jay Ullal, except: © Jay Ullal/*Stern*: pages 7, 56 right, 134 top right, 142 all, 160, 161, 165, 178, 179, 181 left, 190, 234, 235, 256–261, 271 top; © Willie Smits: pages 6, 16–23, 26–28, 29 right, 30, 31, 36, 39, 48, 56 left, 66 left, 104 right, 106 right, 108 left and center, 111, 123, 126–130, 134 left, 140 right, 146 center, 147, 148 right, 152–156, 158, 159, 162–164, 166–177, 181 right, 182–189, 191, 194–196, 198–203, 204 right, 211 center top and right, 212, 221, 236, 237, 238 left below and right, 240–243, 252, 255 left, 262 left, 271 below, 272, 278, 279, 286, 291, 296, 300–302, 304 left, 307 right, 308, 309 left below and right, 310–315, 316 right, 317 right; © Harald Schmitt/*Stern*: dust-cover portrait Jay Ullal

Text: Gerd Schuster, Willie Smits
Layout: Joachim Frank (responsible), Susanne Bremer
Infographics: Harald Blanck

© 2008 for this English edition: Tandem Verlag GmbH
h.f.ullmann is an imprint of Tandem Verlag GmbH

Translation into English: Marrie Powell (main text), Michael Scuffil (captions)
Typesetting: Oliver Hessmann

ISBN 978-3-8331-4623-7

Printed in China

10 9 8 7 6 5 4 3 2
X IX VIII VII VI V IV III II I

www.ullmann-publishing.com